THE
SOCIAL & POLITICAL IDEAS OF SOME REPRESENTATIVE THINKERS OF THE AGE OF REACTION & RECONSTRUCTION

Uniform with this Volume

MEDIÆVAL CONTRIBUTIONS
TO MODERN CIVILISATION
Edited by F. J. C. HEARNSHAW, M.A.,
LL.D. 268 pages.

THE SOCIAL AND POLITICAL
IDEAS OF SOME GREAT
MEDIÆVAL THINKERS
Edited by F. J. C. HEARNSHAW, M.A.,
LL.D. 224 pages.

THE SOCIAL AND POLITICAL
IDEAS OF SOME GREAT
THINKERS OF THE RENAIS-
SANCE & THE REFORMATION
Edited by F. J. C. HEARNSHAW, M.A.,
LL.D. 216 pages.

THE SOCIAL AND POLITICAL
IDEAS OF SOME GREAT
THINKERS OF THE SIXTEENTH
& SEVENTEENTH CENTURIES
Edited by F. J. C. HEARNSHAW, M.A.,
LL.D. 220 pages.

THE SOCIAL AND POLITICAL
IDEAS OF SOME ENGLISH
THINKERS OF THE AUGUSTAN
AGE
Edited by F. J. C. HEARNSHAW, M.A.,
LL.D. 248 pages.

THE SOCIAL AND POLITICAL
IDEAS OF SOME GREAT
FRENCH THINKERS OF THE
AGE OF REASON
Edited by F. J. C. HEARNSHAW, M.A.,
LL.D. 252 pages.

THE SOCIAL AND POLITICAL
IDEAS OF SOME REPRESEN-
TATIVE THINKERS OF THE
REVOLUTIONARY ERA
Edited by F. J. C. HEARNSHAW, M.A.,
LL.D. 252 pages.

THE
SOCIAL & POLITICAL IDEAS OF SOME REPRESENTATIVE THINKERS *of the* AGE OF REACTION & RECONSTRUCTION
1815–65

A SERIES OF LECTURES DELIVERED AT KING'S COLLEGE UNIVERSITY OF LONDON DURING THE SESSION 1930-31

EDITED BY

F. J. C. HEARNSHAW M.A. LL.D.
FELLOW OF KING'S COLLEGE AND PROFESSOR OF MEDIÆVAL HISTORY IN THE UNIVERSITY OF LONDON

BARNES & NOBLE, INC., NEW YORK

PUBLISHERS • BOOKSELLERS • SINCE 1873

First published 1932
by GEORGE G. HARRAP & CO. LTD.
Facsimile reprint 1967
BARNES & NOBLE, INC.
New York, N.Y., 10003

PRINTED IN GREAT BRITAIN
BY PHOTOLITHOGRAPHY
UNWIN BROTHERS LIMITED
WOKING AND LONDON

PREFACE

THIS set of lectures—the seventh and the last but one of the King's College series of discourses on social and political ideas—covers broadly the half-century which extended from the Peace of Vienna to the close of the American Civil War. The first part of this fifty years was a period of marked reaction throughout the Western world : it was dominated by horrid memories of the nightmare of revolution and by shuddering dread of the bogies of democracy and nationality whereby the Revolutionary era had been haunted. This period of reaction, however, was followed by a period of reconstruction, when it was discovered that the new spirits of democracy and nationality not only were potent to terrify tyrants and to scare away effete aristocracies, but were also capable of inspiring the creators of a new and better organisation of society.

The period of reaction lasted longer in some countries than in others. England got it over sooner than any other land; for England had suffered less from the Revolution than had any Continental state. The reconstitution of Liverpool's Ministry in 1822 marks the end of mere repression and the inauguration of constructive reform. On the Continent, however, another quarter of a century was required to bring the *régime* of reaction to a close. Not until the great upheaval of 1848 drove Metternich, Guizot, and scores of their coadjutors into panic-stricken exile did the spirits of democracy and nationality find themselves free to carry through such great tasks as the unification of Italy and Germany and the establishment of representative government among the European peoples.

A half-century so varied and so contentious as that which lay between 1815 and 1865 naturally saw the expression of many social and political ideas. The exposition of the principles of all the notable publicists of the time would have

5

THINKERS OF THE AGE OF REACTION

demanded a series of volumes and not a modest set of lectures. It is hoped, however, that the thinkers selected for consideration represent most of the great distinctive schools of thought. Chateaubriand, Hegel, and Coleridge —respectively French, German, and English—stand for ideas that were essentially conservative and authoritarian. Owen, Mill, and Hodgskin, however widely differing from one another, stand as exponents of progressive principles. Between the two groups Comte and Austin must be placed, each looking backward and striving to retain what was good in the old order, but each propounding a scheme of sociology that seemed to promise secure advance for the future.

F. J. C. HEARNSHAW

KING'S COLLEGE
UNIVERSITY OF LONDON
December 1931

CONTENTS

THE SOCIAL & POLITICAL IDEAS OF SOME REPRESENTATIVE THINKERS OF THE AGE OF REACTION AND RECONSTRUCTION

I

THE AGE OF REACTION AND RECONSTRUCTION, 1815–65

THE men of the first generation of nineteenth-century Europe grew to maturity under the shadow of a great disillusionment. The fathers had eaten sour grapes, and the children's teeth were set on edge. Nor was their *malaise* improved by the circumstance that the eighteenth-century philosophers, who had taken of the forbidden fruit of knowledge, had promised to inaugurate an era of liberty, equality, and fraternity among the nations of the world. Instead the belief in the natural perfectibility of man had brought great trial and misery upon their generation. It was natural, therefore, that the statesmen whose lives had been passed in building up the painful coalitions of resistance to France should resolve to eradicate all traces of the false ideas upon which the edifice of tyranny had been reared, as well as to obliterate from the map of the continent all political symbols of the Napoleonic empire. The restoration of European order involved as a necessary corollary the suppression of centres of liberal and revolutionary thought. The proud age of enlightenment having ended in scenes of oppression and excess, an age of reaction was its natural successor. It was thus that the new century became the battle-ground of the two irreconcilable principles of authority and liberalism, born alike of the struggles of the revolutionary era. The conflict between these opposing forces underlay the political and social changes which marked the

9

Age of Reaction and Reconstruction, and gave its peculiar character to the half-century which followed the overthrow of the first French Empire.

That the period should open with the attempt of the Congress of Vienna to refashion the map of Europe after its recent strange changes was as natural as that this reconstruction should follow conservative lines. The principles of its statesmen were prescribed by the circumstances of their assembly. Of the result of their deliberations much criticism has been offered. Later historians have striven to establish their reputation as seers by frequent assertion that the Powers at Vienna ignored the rising sentiment of nationality, restored the *status quo ante bellum* and with it the reactionary government of Metternich in Central Europe and Italy, and provoked the nemesis which waits upon attempts to suppress the forces of progress in the supposed interests of stability. This dogmatic verdict has been somewhat modified of late; in part by the researches of scholars, and in part by the chastening memory of the Peace of Versailles. Indeed, the conservatism of a century ago seems more sober than the jaunty experiments of yesterday; nor is it easy to dismiss Metternich and Castlereagh as prejudiced by their intimate knowledge of European countries and diplomacy, for ignorance may be the parent of error no less than of happy improvisation. At least Sir A. W. Ward has observed of the Congress of Vienna that,

> though not a few arbitrary arrangements had taken place, and though there are strange instances in the story of the appropriations made, offered, or sought, the charge of reckless bargaining with soil or souls is one which cannot, in fairness, be sustained. Meanwhile a great territorial system had been established which, with all its imperfections, had this advantage over all previous attempts in the same direction: that not only was the compact on which it rested signed by the principal European states, but that it could not be violated except at the risk of international outlawry, while it might be renewed or amended by the same authority as that which had established it.[1]

[1] Sir A. W. Ward, *The Period of Congresses*, p. 50 (1919).

Even from the more practical standpoint the settlement did not lack justification.

> Few great peace settlements are acclaimed by what is called public opinion, and that of 1815 was certainly no exception. But posterity should not withhold a grateful acknowledgment from pacifications followed, as the Second Treaty of Paris was, by a long era of peace, instead of by a brief and restless interval breathing thoughts of revenge and reconquest.[1]

If it be admitted that details of the treaty were open to objection it might be replied that their modification would be the proper concern of the Congress of Powers established by the settlement itself. The four chief Powers, Russia, Austria, Prussia, and Great Britain, had formed themselves into an international court for the maintenance of the peace treaties against revolutionary threats. Nor did their first efforts belie their profession of good intention. The withdrawal of the army of occupation from France and the admission of that country into the Moral Pentarchy were achieved with almost incredible swiftness—at least, so it must appear to the slower tradition of this present century —and the European outlook which dominated Castlereagh no less sincerely than Metternich seemed to promise a benign and pacific surveillance by the Powers.

The perversion of this hope into the policy of intervention and reaction championed by the Austrian statesman and seconded by the Tsar of Russia was a tragedy, lamentable though easily explicable from the standpoint of the Eastern monarchies. The Holy Alliance was from its inception what Metternich called it, a piece of sublime mysticism and nonsense ; but the Congress system, which was made of more substantial fabric, embodied more effectively that identification of stability with the support of existing institutions which was the cardinal principle of Metternich's philosophy. This philosophy was essentially pessimistic and provisional, fashioned to withhold as long as possible the inevitable catastrophe. " My most secret conviction," wrote Metternich, " is that the old Europe is nearing its end. I have

---

[1] Sir A. W. Ward, *op. cit.*, p. 72.

determined to fall with it, and I shall know how to do my duty. On the other side the new Europe is not near to its beginning; between the end and the beginning there must be a chaos." From this convinced diagnosis of the ills of the time there followed naturally the policy of hopeless propping of the decaying order. " My life has coincided with a most abominable time," said the same statesman,

> I have come into the world too soon or too late; I know that in these years I can accomplish nothing. Earlier I should have had my share in the happiness of the time, later, I should have taken part in the work of reconstruction; as things are, I am spending my life in underpinning buildings which are mouldering into decay.[1]

To such an outlook there could be no appreciation of the English dislike, voiced clearly and emphatically by Castlereagh, of armed intervention in the affairs of European countries.

> The Peace of Paris had brought material, not moral, tranquillity. A generation of repose was needed in which the young might learn the true laws governing the life of man in society. The transition from a period of movement to a period of repose was always difficult. During these years of moral education the incurable revolutionaries of an older time must be held down by force. For this work the co-operation of all the states of Europe was essential. Co-operation implied intervention.[2]

Between the dissimilar points of view represented by England and Austria there could be no concord; and upon this rock the Congress system split.

Accordingly the European stage between 1816 and 1830 presented the alternate spectacles of oppression and revolt. In France the restored Bourbons strove to obliterate both memories and results of the great interregnum. In Germany the enforcement of the Karlsbad Decrees marked the capitulation of Prussia to the Austrian demand for suppression of all liberal and constitutional movements. In England the Six Acts constituted a signal testimony of the fear of revolutionary outbreak, forming the high-water

[1] E. L. Woodward, *Three Studies in European Conservatism*, p. 30 (1929).
[2] *Ibid.*, p. 40.

mark of reaction after the period of international anarchy. But repression was countered by rebellion; in countries so far distant as Spain, South Italy, and Greece the forces of discontent found fugitive expression; and though the superior arms of the reactionary nations gained some temporary successes, the worst period of monarchical tyranny was passing away.

Great Britain was the country to feel the first and full effects of the changing tide; for though the policy of Canning is no longer believed to have been an entire reversal of that of Castlereagh, yet the process of emancipation from panic repression both at home and abroad was accelerated, if not inaugurated, by his *régime*. In a word the era of liberal Toryism had dawned, albeit the element of liberalism was carefully regulated to avoid shock to the debilitated constitution of European and English society. At home the reforms included the revision of the criminal code and the institution of a civic police force by Peel, the repeal of the Combination Laws, and the economic and administrative measures of Huskisson in the direction of Free Trade. Abroad the influence of the "baleful meteor," as Canning seemed to Metternich, signalised the final divorce of Great Britain from the series of congresses dominated by Austria, and helped the cause of liberal movements by a new interpretation of the principle of non-intervention, which led to virtual intervention in defence of threatened constitutional causes. The effect of his action in regard to the Spanish-American colonies justified his boast that he had "called the New World into existence to redress the balance of the Old"; and what he had achieved in a geographical sense in this relation he secured in the moral sphere by his action in the Greek rebellion and the untoward incident of Navarino Bay.

Such events indicated clearly that England was embarking upon a course dictated rather by its commercial and colonial interests than by adherence to the European code laid down by Metternich equally in the self-interest of the Austrian scheme of things. Not even the death of Canning and the assumption of control by the Duke of Wellington could

13

wholly stay the progress of liberal measures. For though
the Duke wished heartily to remain in the year of Waterloo,
and straitly *stare super vias antiquas*, he succeeded first in
completing the schism of Canningite Tories, and then in
passing, under the *ægis* of strict Toryism, Bills for the repeal
of the Test and Corporation Acts and for the granting
of Catholic Emancipation. The accident which darkened
the opening of the Liverpool and Manchester Railway, by
sweeping away Huskisson and leaving Wellington, was an
event of tragic indiscrimination; for the Duke was as ill-
adapted to guide the political destinies of his country in an
era of change as to appreciate the significance of the new
method of steam locomotion. The chief result of his efforts
was the negative, though not negligible, one of clearing the
ground for the revival of Whig fortunes and for the passage
of a series of reforms far beyond the dreams of liberal Tories.

Meanwhile the centre of attention had been changed to
the Continent, where the year 1830 saw the first serious
breaches in the old order which had been re-established by
the Congress of Vienna. The end of the Bourbons was a
predictable event from the moment when Charles X succeeded Louis XVIII on the throne of France. The new
monarch indeed observed in jest that there were only two
persons in France who had not changed since the Revolution—*Il n'y a que M. de la Fayette et moi qui n'ayons pas
changé depuis 1789*—but he failed entirely to relate this
circumstance to the realm of politics. Consequently the
hiatus between a country which could not forget the heritage
of the Revolution and a king who desired to ignore its occur-
rence could not long remain. A trivial incident in July
1830 overthrew the dynasty without any real resistance,
and the security not only of France but of Europe seemed
threatened. The unexpected caution of the leading Parisian
politicians and their resolve to render the necessary change
as conservative as possible reassured their neighbours, when
it was seen that the Orleanist Louis Philippe had succeeded
to a monarchy no longer *divino jure*, but constitutional and
anti-revolutionary. The fear of a general resurgence of
republicanism was disproved by the little strength which it

14

had shown in its native country. Notwithstanding, the reverberation of the July Revolution which occurred across the frontier in the Belgian capital occasioned far more difficulty and apprehension to the Powers.

The record of the separation of Holland and Belgium is a thrice-told tale, adorned often by moralising concerning the iniquity of the Vienna Congress which had violated so many canons of national feeling in its attempt to erect a strong barrier state on the frontier towards which French statesmen had cast ever-longing glances. But the success of the Belgian rebellion was by no means perceived to be inevitable at the time of its outbreak. More serious were the diplomatic difficulties created by the situation. For apart from the natural reluctance of Holland to forfeit so profitable an acquisition, there was the additional problem of the discovery of a suitable king for the independent Belgium. The proposal of Louis Philippe to plant a scion of the Orleanist house in so delectable a territory did not command such approval of the Powers as might have been expected from this convincing proof that the new France was bent on pursuing the continuity of Bourbon foreign policy; but the solution was sought eventually in the invitation of Leopold of Saxe-Coburg, though not without some suspicion between France and England. The persuasion of all parties concerned to acknowledge the separation and the new royal line was not achieved for many years; and even then there remained one disquieting feature of the episode which might not be forgotten. The sacrosanct settlement made and guaranteed at Vienna only fifteen years before had been broken in one of its vital parts, not at the instigation of the contracting powers, but in response to an uprising of popular feeling on the part of the Belgians. Such a precedent was certainly disconcerting, and is perhaps not without moral to a generation which, in celebrating the centenary of Belgian independence, may not be unmindful of similar problems awaiting its own resolution. For the moment, however, Europe contented itself with thanksgiving that the virus of revolt had not gained further victories. The outbreaks in Poland and Italy had been satisfactorily suppressed, a result of more importance in the eyes of Metternich and Russia than the triumph of rebellion in France and the Netherlands. Despite an uneasy shock, the fundamentals of European society remained standing.

In England, however, they were being removed by an extensive process of Whig reconstruction. The English people had awakened at last to the need for extensive reform in many branches of national life. To a student of the twentieth century the Extraordinary Black Book of 1831 presents a mine of curious and anachronistic information. Its perusal evokes a sentiment of amazed incredulity, instead of the impassioned indignation which moved its authors barely a century ago. Then it afforded abundant evidence for the apostles of reform, and constituted a formidable indictment of contemporary official life. Its publication synchronised with the rising tide of discontent among the people, of which the causes were manifold and diverse. But a sound political instinct inspired the concentration of all grievances, political, administrative, and economic, upon the single issue of Parliamentary reform. There lay the gateway to success in other spheres ; for not until the control of the borough-mongers was removed could the voice of the people be heard within Parliamentary walls. With the extension of the franchise and the redistribution of seats the interest of the townsmen could find its advocates.

Into this atmosphere the news of the July Revolution in Paris brought the assurance that anarchy was no necessary accompaniment of reform, and the spectacle of a *bourgeoisie* victory in France to stimulate the middle class of England. Accordingly the agitation for reform secured an accession of strength. Associations of diverse classes and divergent aims united in their demand for the first step along the road of redress. The attitude of quiet disdain which the Duke of Wellington assumed towards all agitation ensured the triumph of the agitators' cause ; and the Whig administration of Lord Grey had no option but to grasp the nettle. The story of the Parliamentary fortunes of the first Reform Bill and of the extra-Parliamentary campaigns to save its clauses belongs to other places than an introductory article.

After the lapse of a century the terms of the famous Act of 1832 seem singularly meagre; in general, it effected a wide redistribution of seats, together with the grant of a £10 rating franchise in boroughs and the extension of the county franchise to tenant farmers. The predominant influence in the reformed Commons rested still with the landlords, though the fence of their exclusiveness had been broken down to admit the wealthier middle class to share their privilege. Yet fundamentally the victory was portentous, though certainly not complete. *C'est le premier pas qui coûte* is an approved maxim of political no less than of other forms of strategy; and the Act, which to its Whig champions and to Finality Jack seemed the consummation of change, proved but a modest prelude to a succession of franchise laws of ever-widening scope.

Nor was the outburst of reforming legislation which ensued other than creditable to the intentions of the zealous Whigs. A series of royal commissions prepared the way for a series of reforming Acts: the Municipal Corporations Act of 1835, the Factory Act of 1833, the Poor Law Act of 1834, and the Act for the abolition of slavery of 1833: the cumulative effect of which was to abolish a host of obsolete and unseemly conditions which had survived in the various departments of national and civic life. Not even the Established Church escaped the itch for purgation. Profane radical hands were laid upon the Ark of the Covenant, and venerable abuses which the tolerant and cautious Tudors had suffered to remain were swept away ruthlessly in a second reformation which caused conservatives to shudder. The revenues of the Church were redistributed, the Ecclesiastical Commission was established as a legal corporation to administer the riches garnered from the plunder of such wealthy bishoprics as Durham and Winchester, and a beginning was made of the endless process of creating new parishes and smaller dioceses. Against such sacrilegious action on the part of a Whig administration the protest of Keble was apparently vain; but the determination to set the national state in order was an earnest of the spirit aroused by the Reform Act. The firstfruits of that measure had been considerable both in quantity and character; and the times of reaction were gone beyond recall.

During the years of comparative tranquillity between the revolutions of 1830 and 1848 both England and France set their faces along the path of liberal constitutionalism. In both countries, however, a new phenomenon was appearing ; for the establishment of political stability produced the realisation that the control of Parliamentary machinery was but the means and not the end for which the populace had striven. The most striking feature of these intervening years was the emergence and prominence of the social question. In France the pressure of economic problems upon the statesmen of the Orleanist *régime* was the most serious burden of the day. The achievement of Louis Philippe was judged in terms of it, and the fall of his dynasty in 1848 was due far more to the inability of Guizot and his master to grasp the necessity for legislation upon such matters than to the failure of foreign policy in the affair of the Spanish marriages. " Owing to his inability to read the economic and social needs of the time Guizot was deserted by the young and the generous. For this reason the monarchy which he had served with magnificence and devotion fell without a regret." [1]

In Great Britain circumstances and leaders combined to emphasise the fact that, " although the traditional way of expressing grievances was political, the real grievances were economic." The indefatigable Bentham, though his *Nunc dimittis* was said in the very year of the passing of the first Reform Act, had sowed seeds which fructified long after that event. The barest mention of the growth of the social movement must include a passing reference to the names of persons whose work will be discussed fully later in this course ; to Robert Owen, " the father of the Factory Laws and of the co-operative movement," through whose efforts Sir Robert Peel, famous father of a more famous son, projected the first Factory Bill in 1815 ; to William Cobbett, who revealed the sufferings and wrongs of the poor, and laboured to overtake unchecked economic change by

[1] E. L. Woodward, *op. cit.*, p. 144.

accelerating Parliamentary reform; and to Francis Place, an individualist radical, who was the real author of the repeal of the Combination Acts, by which the way was laid open for the establishment of trade unions, as well as of friendly and co-operative societies. Owen, in particular, diverted the nascent trade-union movement into a scheme of a National Grand Trade Union, designed as an impressive symbol of the strength of the people and provoking a bitter opposition, which found expression in the famous transportation of the Dorchester labourers in 1834. At the same time in the political sphere agitation centred round the enthusiasm for the People's Charter, which suffered a first collapse in 1839 owing to the activities of the physical force party, and a final disaster in the year of revolutions, 1848.

These tendencies were symptomatic of the serious economic condition of the unenfranchised labouring classes in the years following the Reform Act. When Peel secured office and power in 1841 the "condition of the people problem" had been rendered acute by the refusal of the Whigs to face boldly the real question around which discontent centred, the repeal of the Corn Laws. Ameliorative steps were measured by Peel's Budgets from 1842 to 1845, important in themselves, but particularly significant as a prelude to the great conflict between agricultural and industrial interests on the Corn Laws question, which was being brought nearer by the vigorous polemic of the Anti-Corn Law League, led by Cobden and Bright. This popular and convincing propaganda swept Chartism into insignificance, and, when reinforced by the Irish potato famine, finally relegated the Corn Laws to limbo and the Tory Party to political exile for the succeeding twenty years. Contemporaneous with the famous Ministry of Peel, the worst evils which had lent reality to the Chartist agitation were in process of decline. In 1844 had come the establishment by the Rochdale Pioneers of the Toad Lane Co-operative Store; two years earlier another enclave of *laissez-faire* had been broken in with the passage of Lord Shaftesbury's Mines Act; and in 1848 Chadwick succeeded in carrying

19

the Public Health Act. Partly in consequence of these measures and partly by reason of a revival of national prosperity, the sense of injustice and oppression had been lifted from the mass of the people, whose waning interest in the demand for further Parliamentary reform was reflected in the languid expiry of the Chartist campaign. This change was doubly fortunate for the British Government, for the year 1848 was famous in other directions than the interest of Chadwick in problems of sanitary reform. It witnessed the belated resurgence of the spirit of liberalism in a series of attempts to overthrow the despotic administrations of Europe and to cleanse the Augean stables of not a few reactionary states.

Into the details of the several revolutions of that year it is foreign to the scope of this article to enter. The conflagration began in its native home in France; but the demand of Paris for an extended franchise, which was the occasion of revolt, served but as a veil for the real cause, the necessity for remedial social measures. The urgency of the economic question found expression in the establishment of National Workshops by Louis Blanc, the failure of which led in turn to the sanguinary days of the barricades and the emergence of Louis Napoleon as the saviour of society and stability. His election as President of the second French Republic was an assurance that the extremists had been defeated temporarily; and the attention of Europe was diverted to follow the fortunes of insurrection in other kingdoms.

In Germany the revolts were inspired by the twin desires for national unity and its realisation through constitutional and Parliamentary institutions. In the Hungarian and non-German parts of the Austrian Empire the uprising was more definitely national, with the Czechs and Magyars fighting to throw off the yoke of an alien oppressor, though the zeal of the Magyars for independence was combined with a determination to refuse that boon to other subject races. In the Italian peninsula a series of sporadic rebellions had but one thing in common, the aim of expelling the hated Austrian rulers, though community of plan was lacking to give effect to the single purpose; and little was achieved

20

beyond the spectacular episode of the expulsion of Pius IX from his pontifical city and the establishment of a republic under the direction of Mazzini and Garibaldi. Despite the promise of initial successes, all these movements ended in disaster. Fundamentally their fortunes depended upon the issue of the conflict between Austria and its nearest rebels in Hungary; and the defeat of Kossuth and his followers presaged the failure of the revolutionary stirrings elsewhere. In Germany the refusal of Frederick William of Prussia to accept the crown of an imperial Germany, from which non-Germanic races were to be excluded, offered by the National Assembly at Frankfurt spelled the defeat of the hopes of the Liberal Constitutional party; while the victory of Austria was emphasised further by the subjugation of its rival in the humiliation of Olmütz. With the restoration of reaction in Vienna the hopes of the Italian insurgents evaporated. The old order was reinstated in the Lombard plain, in Naples and Sicily, and in Rome; with this new and ominous circumstance, that the foreign bayonets which protected Pio Nono against future indiscretions on the part of his subjects were those of a French force dispatched by Louis Napoleon to forestall the Austrians and to ensure the maintenance of French interest in the affairs of the peninsula. In the latter purpose they succeeded well, though with doubtful profit to Napoleon or his client. For the moment, however, revolution had been everywhere defeated. Even in France the fortunes of the day seemed to have deserted its cause, for by the *coup d'état* of December 1851 Napoleon secured his re-election as President for a further period of ten years, and on the anniversary of his victory converted the republic into the Second French Empire and himself into its Emperor with the title of Napoleon III. The year 1852 was a year of destiny for Europe. On October 22 the resignation of D'Azeglio made way for the succession of Cavour to the control of Piedmontese, and thence of Italian, affairs; and on December 2 the dynasty of Napoleon III began in France. For the next decade the main interest of European politics was to centre around the activities of these two men; and when Cavour was removed by untimely death in June

1861 the stage was cleared for the arrival of Bismarck on September 23, 1862, as Minister President of Prussia to consummate the unification of Italy and Germany and the downfall of France.

During these years of turmoil in Europe England might well congratulate itself upon the feeble flicker of Chartism which was all the effect of revolutionary tremors upon its peaceful course. But the age of Palmerston which succeeded the break-up of Toryism by Peel was more conservative in domestic policy than the *soi-disant* Tories. It was an age of stagnation and tranquillity, with Gladstone forcing through his Budgets by threats of resignation, and the radical members of the Cabinet compelled to hold over their reforming projects until the indomitable Pam had gone. The neglect of domestic problems was in some degree both pardonable and explicable by the increasing commercial prosperity of the country, of which the symbol and stimulus was the Great Exhibition of 1851, whereto less fortunate foreigners were invited to wonder and applaud. Their acquaintance with Great Britain and evidence of its resurgence were not to depend, however, upon occasional visits to its shores, for if Palmerston ruled England with a benign inactivity he sought to govern Europe with a masterful intervention. Neither interest nor excitement was lacking in the foreign relations of the nation during the last great period of his long ministerial career. The exuberance of his diplomacy was not universally admired, particularly by the Queen and the more nervous of his political colleagues. Notwithstanding, his self-confidence protected him against withdrawal from a position once taken up ; and his policy caused Great Britain to exercise an unwonted influence upon foreign affairs until the rise of the master-mind of Bismarck exploded the Palmerstonian legend. At the outset the Crimean War testified to the new situation and the aggressiveness of British foreign policy, no less than to the nascent ambitions of Piedmont under the prudent guidance of Cavour. Other incidents gave occasion to much searching of heart in the administration, such as the *Don Pacifico* and the lorcha *Arrow* episodes ; while in the serious blunders of the *Trent* and *Alabama* the neutrality of England in the American Civil War was grievously jeopardised. It has been said of Palmerston's adventures in foreign affairs that " only the Italian policy of 1859–60 was based on a real understanding of the people and the facts "; and even in this case the cession of Nice and Savoy to France was so obnoxious to him that only the pacific and restraining influence of other members of his Cabinet prevented a splenetic explosion against Napoleon III.

Meanwhile events in Italy followed the course which led to the unification of the peninsula save for Venice and Rome; and in September 1864 there was signed the famous convention by which the French Emperor sought an escape from the equivocal situation of the maintenance of his troops in Rome, and Victor Emmanuel undertook the delicate task of defending the Papal city against the zealots of his own allegiance. In the previous year the Polish rebellion had brought discredit to Napoleon and a welcome initial diplomatic success to Bismarck, which was followed shortly by a public demonstration before the eyes of Europe of the futility of Palmerston's methods in the unhappy Schleswig-Holstein controversy. To Denmark Palmerston had spoken brave words; but when Bismarck replied by decisive deeds the counsel of Great Britain was revealed as *vox et præterea nihil*. With this incident the meaning of the new Prussian policy was manifest; and with it also was realised the end of the age of Palmerston. Europe awoke to the masterful genius of Bismarck, and remembered that during the years of Metternich's pessimistic *régime* Prussia had begun its upward climb by the organisation of the Zollverein, the basis upon which was reared the imposing edifice of national unity wedded to autocratic government. Nor could Europe hope for a peer to Bismarck. France was absorbed in the misfortunes of the melancholy Mexican adventure to which Napoleon had committed his army, while in England the death of Palmerston himself in 1865 marked the beginning of a new era. The demand for further electoral and franchise reform, which had been proclaimed by the influential pen of John Stuart Mill, a philosopher who championed the emancipation of women no less than the enfranchisement of men, could be no longer ignored. Politically the reins were given into the hands of Gladstone, an indefatigable reformer, who was preparing to concentrate his powerful energies upon the task of domestic administration, in compensation for a resolute withdrawal from Continental affairs, which was the inevitable reaction from Palmerston's policy. England was therefore content to play the part of spectator in the drama which completed the unification of Germany and Italy at the cost of the downfall of the second Napoleonic Empire in France.

But in the year before Palmerston's death rang down the curtain upon his age there occurred an event in the realm of thought of more far-reaching influence than the rise and fall of political empires. In 1864 Pius IX had issued the encyclical *Quanta Cura*, accompanied by the famous Syllabus of Errors, in which were stated, with the sharpest antagonism, the issues of the conflict between the principles of freedom and authority, upon which turned the significance of many of the events of the century. The history of the Papacy, indeed, affords an index to the wider struggles of the age. At the outset of the century conditions seemed peculiarly favourable for a revival of Catholic zeal. The rationalistic philosophy of the eighteenth century had been discredited by the excesses of revolutionary France, from which men turned with a new sympathy for the axioms of authority and absolutism. In literature the reaction found expression in the Romantic Revival, driving Wordsworth to seek in the inspiration of nature

> that blessed mood
> In which the burden of the mystery,
> In which the heavy and the weary weight
> Of all this unintelligible world
> Is lightened;

or moving Scott to a sympathetic rediscovery of the Middle Ages, the *bête noire* of eighteenth-century historians; or rehabilitating the sense of the mysterious and supernatural in the poems of Samuel Taylor Coleridge. Such a movement away from the tenets of the age of reason found

24

natural affinities with the tendency towards the restoration of authority in religion. Deism and its belief in the virtues of the natural man gave place to a sense of the corruption of human nature and of the need of some authoritarian government of its conduct. In France the writings of Chateaubriand proclaimed the re-interpretation of Catholicism as a divinely constituted system of authority, in which society could find the school of political and private virtue and safeguard itself against the destructive outbursts of egalitarian doctrines. In England also there was an insular reflection of this tendency, when Keble asserted the divine commission and supernatural apostolic character of the Established Church against the interference of radical politicians with its administration and revenues. For the moment the situation of most European countries created an atmosphere favourable almost beyond precedent for a revival of Catholicism. Whether the Papal Church could profit by this advantage and seize the occasion for recovering the lost allegiance of the intellectuals of Europe would depend chiefly upon the ability of its apologists to reconcile the new ideals of liberty with the old tradition of authority. For a brief period this reconciliation became the dream and the inspiration of a new school of liberal Catholicism. Mr E. L. Woodward, in a recent study, has emphasised the importance in this connection of Görres in Germany and Lamennais in France.

> The career of Lamennais is the counterpart of the career of Görres; both reflect the movements of their time; but the order of their development was curiously contrasted. The one began with revolution and ended in belief in Catholic theocracy; the other began with theocracy and ended as a revolutionary.[1]

In truth, the enthusiastic adventure of the liberal Gallican party, led by the brilliant triumvirate Lamennais, Lacordaire, and Montalembert, was foredoomed to failure. Its condemnation by the Bull *Mirari vos* of Gregory XVI, in which liberty of conscience was denounced as *absurda illa . . . ac erronea sententia, seu potius deliramentum*, and the

---

[1] E. L. Woodward, *op. cit.*, p. 248.

freedom of the Press as *deterrima illa ac nunquam satis execranda et detestabilis libertas*, proclaimed the impossibility of the desired reconciliation.

Nor were the leaders of liberal thought in Europe anxious to lose the fruits of victory by concessions to ecclesiastical authority. Gregory XVI could hardly be censured for his unwillingness to thrust the ancient barque of Peter into the stormy seas of contemporary discovery and criticism, which were threatening on all sides to demolish rather than reconstruct traditional opinions. In the first generation of the nineteenth century the studies of Niebuhr in Roman history marked the dawn of the movement of historical criticism which has rewritten the story of European development. Nor could the standards thus applied to ancient Greece and Rome be refused admission to the records of the Hebrew people. During the first half of the century such scholars as De Wette, Gesenius, and Ewald were the pioneers of the application of methods of critical study to the narratives of the Old Testament. The modesty of historical students leads too often to forgetfulness or depreciation of the importance of the results achieved by the leaders of historical criticism before the more spectacular discoveries of science had enriched men with the concept of evolution as applied to the development of living organisms. This application was, indeed, part of the same process as that begun already by historians, though its influence secured a wider recognition and popularity. In England the publication by Darwin in 1859 of his *Origin of Species* marked the commencement of the revolution, and popular attention was attracted to its meaning in the following year by the debate at the British Association meeting in Oxford when Huxley crossed swords with Bishop Samuel Wilberforce. In the same year the appearance of *Essays and Reviews* indicated the ready acceptance of the new canons of critical investigation by a group of liberal English churchmen, and the controversies which followed the publication ensured the domestication of the principle of unfettered study in matters historical and theological within the Established Church. Such events were symptomatic of the intellectual atmosphere of the age ;

and amidst this ferment of discussion the deeper issues of the conflict between authority and freedom were in process of determination.

Into this *milieu* Pius IX had elected in 1854 to intrude the definition of the Immaculate Conception as a dogma of faith, and ten years later had launched his Syllabus of Errors. Pio Nono indeed had been innocent throughout his pontificate of any sympathy with intellectual liberalism, and his momentary patronage of Italian aspirations for political liberty had ceased after the incidents of 1848–49. His pontifical pronouncements extinguished the last hopes of the Gallican and German liberal Catholics of a reconciliation between the forces of progress and of tradition. In the Syllabus the Papacy pronounced against such characteristic features of contemporary constitutional Governments as secular education, the freedom of the Press, the separation of Church and State, religious toleration; and concluded with the comprehensive anathema against those who maintained that *Romanus pontifex potest ac debet cum progressu, cum liberalismo, et cum recenti civilitate sese reconciliare et componere.* It must be admitted that the recent signature of the September Convention, which left the Papacy to the uncertain protection of the Italian sovereign by providing for the withdrawal of the French garrison from Rome, was not without influence upon the acerbity of the Syllabus of the following December. Nevertheless its publication wrought acute distress amongst the liberal Catholics, who, in their attempts to minimise the severity of its censures, revealed the disquiet of their mind at such a defiance of the dominant political and intellectual movements. The reply of Pio Nono to the efforts towards a conciliation between authority and freedom was the simple distinction : *quæ pars fideli cum infideli?* But on all sides the victory lay with the infidel.

The difficulty of marking off periods of history by the intrusion of arbitrary dates to indicate the beginning or end of an epoch is illustrated clearly by the denomination of the years from 1815 to 1865 as the Age of Reaction and Reconstruction. It is impossible to believe that the year 1865 marked any division in the affairs of Europe. The fortunes of Italy, Prussia, and France were not yet brought to the logical conclusion dictated by the policies of Cavour, Bismarck, and Napoleon III respectively. Not even the *annus mirabilis* of 1870 can be regarded as marking the definite end of the age, although it witnessed the fall of the temporal power of the Papacy and the proclamation of Papal Infallibility, the resuscitation of the German Empire under the sway of Prussia, the completion of Italian unification by the capture of Rome, and the fall of the second French Empire. Two ensuing generations must think very differently from contemporaries of the events of that portentous year. Nor is it possible to forecast the verdict of future historians on the events of the Age of Reaction and Reconstruction. Perhaps to the eyes of posterity neither political nor social changes will seem of the greatest importance; but rather the contribution of the first half of the nineteenth century to the achievement of humanity will be judged to consist in the development of the scientific method of study, alike in history and natural science, and in the quest of students

> to find firm scientific ground
> whereon to found their creed in true history
> of social virtue and of its progress hitherto.

NORMAN SYKES

BOOK LIST

Cambridge Modern History, vols. x–xii. 1907–10.
CLAPHAM, J. H.: *Economic History of Modern Britain.* 1926.
FUETER, E.: *Weltgeschichte der letzten hundert Jahre.* 1921.
HALÉVY, E.: *Histoire du peuple anglais.* 1912 *et seq.*
HAZEN, C. D.: *Europe since 1815.* 1910.
MARTINEAU, HARRIET: *History of England, 1801–54.* 4 vols. 1864.
MOLESWORTH, W. N.: *History of England, 1830–74.* 3 vols. 1874.
TREVELYAN, G. M.: *British History in the Nineteenth Century.* 1922.
WALPOLE, SPENCER: *History of England, 1815–65.* 5 vols. 1878–86.
WOODWARD, E. L.: *Three Studies in European Conservatism.* 1929.

II

CHATEAUBRIAND AND THE FRENCH
ROMANTICS

IN the year 1788 Arthur Young was making the second
of his celebrated journeys in France. On August 31 he
entered Brittany, and the next day rode to Combourg.
He writes in his *Travels in France* :

> The country has a savage aspect, the people almost as wild as their
> country, and the town of Combourg one of the most brutal, filthy
> places that can be seen. Yet here is a *château* and inhabited.
> Who is this Monsieur de Chateaubriand, the owner, that has nerves
> strung for a residence amidst such filth and poverty ?

The Chateaubriands were one of the oldest families in
Brittany. They had also been one of the most illustrious.
They claimed descent from the dukes of the province, and
a member of the house had fought with St Louis in Palestine.
Chateaubriand affected later to think little of pedigree,
but he notes with pointed brevity in his *Mémoires* that he
belonged to the *noblesse*. On the eve of the Revolution
there was no place in France where feudal tradition was
stronger than in Brittany, or where the provincial noble,
tenacious of his privileges, was more loyal to the Crown.
George Sand in one of her letters attributes Chateaubriand's
hostile attitude towards the Revolution to the fact that he
was a *gentilhomme breton*; this certainly provides a clue to
those notions of *honneur* that lent dignity to some of his
actions and quixotic absurdity to others.

Those who have tried to master his mental anatomy
attach great importance to a study of his origins and youth.
The fact that he was for the most part neglected and solitary
deepened his sensibility and fed his genius ; it also led to a
weakening of mental fibre and to much that was morbid in
his life and writings. He says himself that his education

endowed him with ideas different from those of other men, and impressed upon his sentiments a character of melancholy. This celebrated melancholy is variously explained, but by no one better than Chateaubriand himself when he says that his youthful mind and heart were as two empty temples without altars or sacrifices. His exaggerated vanity and egotism were also developed in his early surroundings—the qualities that divided him from reality and were to raise up a host of enemies, the "valets" and "pygmies" of his letters. Those scenes in the *Mémoires d'outre-tombe* which provide the *décor* of his childhood and youth in Brittany, whether at St Malo or the melancholy Combourg, once read can never be forgotten. Equally striking are the portraits of his mother, the vivacious woman who consoled herself for an unhappy marriage with piety, and of his father, the sinister old man who was the terror of his servants. Towards the end of his life, when he is described by his son, he had become a hypochondriac dominated by family pride. In early life, however, he had broken with noble tradition, and revived the fortunes of his house by engaging in commerce. In his old age he had retained something of his early energy, for he was a critic of Court policy and an admirer of the notorious Abbé Raynal. If Chateaubriand's leanings towards piety can be traced to his mother, he owed his independence of judgment to his father, of whom he remarks that if he had lived until the Revolution he would have played a great part.

At the time when Young wrote his contemptuous description of Combourg the elder Chateaubriand was dead, and his son was in Paris. One of his earliest contacts with the world was a presentation at Court, where he was no more at home than the *Ingénu* of Voltaire. In any case it was not Versailles, but Paris, that drew him, and he lived here till 1791. In Paris he became acquainted with most of the men of letters, but the individual who made the deepest impression upon him was Malesherbes, the friend of Turgot, and the enemy of tyranny. The influence of this old man of ancient virtues and modern opinions, together with that of the *philosophes* with whose writings Chateaubriand had

30

made himself familiar, inclined him to liberalism, and he might have been won over by the Revolution but for the excesses of the mob. " The Revolution would have carried me away," he wrote, " had it not started in crime. I saw the first head carried on the end of a pike, and I drew back." As chaos increased it became clear that aristocrats would be persecuted, and Chateaubriand decided to leave the uncongenial scene and visit America. " I go in search of something new. There is nothing to be done here," he remarked to the Chevalier de Panat. " The King is lost, and there will be no counter-revolution."

We know now that he only accomplished a small part of the itinerary of which he boasted, but there is no reason to doubt his account of the intoxication of independence which seized him as he ran through the primeval forests of the New World, shouting his joy at the absence of roads and cities, monarchies, republics, and men. After five months of freedom, however, he began to see the advantage of closer contact with events, and when he heard of the arrest of Louis XVI at Varennes he decided, as he says later, to sacrifice himself to *honneur* and to join the army of the princes. He returned to France at the beginning of 1792, and soon after left Paris for the frontier. He was wounded at Thionville, but managed to make his way to Jersey, and thence to London, where he remained, except for a period spent in Suffolk, for seven years. Although he referred afterwards to the " happy days of garrets," his life in England was a time of misery. He was constantly hearing of the imprisonment or execution of his friends; his lack of money forced him to gain a scanty living by teaching; for part of the time he was on the brink of starvation; and for some months he was in danger of death.

It may be possible to study the works of some authors apart from their lives, but in the case of Chateaubriand, who was peculiarly open to the suggestion of events, life and works are inevitably linked. The biographical details of which the reader has been reminded are the prelude to the *Essai sur les révolutions* written during his exile, and published in 1797. The *Essai* is a work of pessimism and revolt. The

Revolution had thwarted the career of this young man of twenty-six ; it was still in progress, and none could tell when it would end. Chateaubriand hoped by a study of antiquity to provide a chart for new and perilous seas. His chart is only a jumble of youthful learning, far-fetched historical parallels, and ill-digested philosophy, and deserves to be forgotten, but for the evidence it provides of the religious feelings of the author, and of his attitude towards events in France.

Chateaubriand inclines to a defence of the monarchy, but, though he condemns the Revolution, he admits it to have been inevitable. Louis XVI is described as one of the best kings that ever reigned in France, yet we read of the monarch lulled to repose in the lap of pleasure, of weak or wicked Ministers, of ignorant or vicious nobles, of clergy who were a disgrace to their order. But if he judged the Revolution to have been a necessity he has nothing but blame for Robespierre, whom he calls a scoundrel, or for the Jacobins, who had imprisoned the men of property and deluged the streets with blood. It had to be admitted, however, that these monsters when they escaped from hell brought with them all the talents of demons, for it was they who had given to France a disciplined army, and had succeeded in bringing order out of anarchy. It might be, since no revolution could be entirely bad, that some of their principles would remain. Yet Chateaubriand rejects the ideas of the *philosophes*, for he disliked all eighteenth-century writers, except Montesquieu, his political prophet, and Rousseau, whose disciple (within limits) he was. The *philosophes* by their writings had undermined religion and the State. They had destroyed everything, and they had given nothing. It was the duty of their followers to repair the ruins, and to raise up a mansion fit for the French to live in. He was not prepared, however, to act as architect of State, for, if he disapproved of the Royalists who wished to remain men of the fourteenth century, and refused to be enlightened, he was equally unable to share the illusions of the Republicans, rushing madly as they were towards imaginary perfections. He explains that he is indifferent to all constitutions abstractly

32

considered, for it was waste of time to try to discover a perfect government, both because we ourselves are vicious, and
because civil liberty is a dream. All government is an evil
and a yoke, but it does not necessarily follow that it must be
abolished. Since we are born to be slaves let us support the
burden, whether it be monarchical or republican, but in any
case it is better to submit to an enlightened ruler than be led
by the ignorant multitude, who will overwhelm all with woe.
The argument is confused, but the general meaning is plain.
He saw nothing to satisfy him in the history of his country
past or present, or indeed in the history of the world, for he
concludes that man is so feeble in his means and genius as
to be capable only of repetition ; he moves round in a con-
tinuous circle of misery from which there is no escape.
Thus Chateaubriand denied the eighteenth-century religion
of progress, and condemned political optimism as the result
of ignorance.

After the publication of *Le Génie du christianisme* he was
reproached for having shown in the *Essai* as great a scepticism
in religion as in politics. It is true that he had reproduced
the objections of the *philosophes* to Christianity, and voiced
his own dislike of the priests, but although he had no
religious principles, he had shown some feeling for religion,
and had declared that if Christianity was an illusion it was a
social necessity. This was an idea which found an echo in
the new school of thought that was arising as a counterblast
to the Revolution, the school of the Catholic and political
reaction. In 1796 de Bonald had published his *Théorie du
pouvoir* and de Maistre his *Considérations sur la France*.
Both writers were profoundly hostile to the ideas of the
eighteenth century, and made a return to mediæval theory.
They denied the importance of individual rights in society,
and proclaimed the rights of the State. Society was not the
work of man's hands, but an emanation of the divine will.
It did not rest upon popular sovereignty, or any other
rationalistic conception, but upon authority which comes
from God. Man must adhere to a belief in divine revelation,
and return to tradition, the only guarantee of order.

Although points of similarity are to be found between the

33

political and social ideas of these thinkers and those of Chateaubriand, his *rôle* in the history of the reaction is entirely different. He never had enough conviction to be of value as a theorist. His part was rather to recruit the forces of sentiment, and this he did through the medium of art. He tells us that *Le Génie du christianisme* was the outcome of his conversion, and his conversion the result of the news of his mother's death and of her grief over his relapse from orthodoxy. " I wept," he says, " and I believed." This event doubtless intensified his pious sentiments, but he seems in any case to have been looking, like Rivarol, for a religious principle, which would save him from the anarchy of his ideas, and he found his mode of expression under the stimulus of the religious revival that was going on around him. The educated classes in England were in full reaction against all forms of irreligion and free-thought, which they naturally associated with Jacobinism, while a strong belief had grown up among the French *émigrés*, over whom the clergy had resumed their influence, that the restoration of religion was a fundamental basis of public morality. In France itself, where an orderly world was springing up again, the nostalgia for the past, which had been so ruthlessly destroyed, had led to the decline of atheism, and by the beginning of the new century, when Chateaubriand returned to Paris, the reviving interest in religion had been indicated not only by the newspapers and popular prints, but by a number of works written in defence of Christianity.

No one realised better than Napoleon that religious tradition was a valuable instrument in the hands of a ruler, and he took advantage of the religious revival to stabilise his government by reconciling France with the Church. On April 18, 1802, the Concordat was proclaimed by drum and trumpet in all quarters of Paris, and a solemn *Te Deum* was sung in Notre-Dame. This was the moment towards which Chateaubriand had directed his energies, for the literary decoration of the great *fête* which reconciled society to religion was provided by *Le Génie du christianisme*. The book is a defence of Christianity from the judgment of the eighteenth century that it was no better than a barbarous

34

system which retarded the progress of the understanding. Chateaubriand sets out to prove, *per contra*, that of all the religions which have ever existed it has been the most favourable to civilisation, and that the modern world is indebted to it for every improvement from agriculture to the abstract sciences. His work did not owe its immense popularity, however, to those pages which describe the services of religion and the Church, nor yet to his absurd arguments as to the existence of God and the truth of the Scriptures. Its brilliant success must rather be attributed to the appeal which it made to sentiment, and to its conquest of the imagination. The truth of Christianity was demonstrated by its beauty, and those who had been starved of religious emotion under the empire of Voltaire accepted the poet instead of the philosopher.

Chateaubriand's book had been dedicated to Napoleon, the " powerful man who has drawn us from the abyss," and if the latter did not read it through, as he confessed to Sismondi, for it was not his *genre*, he certainly ran his eye over the concluding passages which recommend morality as a cure for turbulence. He determined to make trial of the man who had gilded his policy, and Chateaubriand was appointed secretary to the embassy at Rome. This subordinate position failed to satisfy the ambition of the author of *Le Génie du christianisme*, and when a still humbler post in Switzerland was found for him as an alternative he decided to break with Napoleon, and regain his liberty. An excellent opportunity was provided by the execution of the Duc d'Enghien, which revived his feeling for monarchy. He sent in his resignation, and retired into private life. His colossal vanity prevented him from serving a master to whom he does not hesitate to compare himself as an equal, but he was genuinely disgusted by the act of tyranny which ended the hopes of the Royalists.

Although Chateaubriand admired the genius of Napoleon, to which he does full justice in his *Mémoires*, he abhorred his despotism, and made several courageous attacks upon it in the ten years following his retirement. A celebrated article in the *Mercure* contained allusions to the tyranny of Nero, which caused the journal to be suppressed, while the address to the Academy, which he was forbidden to deliver, but which was widely circulated, was a spirited defence of liberty. In the *Itinéraire* describing his eastern travels the evils of Turkish despotism are particularly emphasised, while Napoleon could scarcely fail to recognise himself and his *entourage* in the various portraits drawn in *Les Martyrs*. By the end of the Empire Chateaubriand had acquired considerable prestige in Royalist circles as the man who had resisted the tyrant, and as the sun of the Emperor sank his own ambition mounted, and he began to regard himself as the prophet of the future.

On March 31, 1814, six days before the abdication of Napoleon, the allies entered Paris, and Chateaubriand, who invariably staged his works with the hand of the artist, produced his first political writing, *De Buonaparte et des Bourbons*. " It was in these critical days," he wrote later, " that I threw down my pamphlet to turn the scale." He had detested the Empire which had cramped his talent, and had nothing to fear from its fall. He attacked it now with all the force of his genius, in one of the most passionate and vindictive pieces in literature. He speaks of Napoleon as the great culprit of the age who had done more to injure humanity than all the tyrants of Rome. It was he who had destroyed 5,000,000 Frenchmen, and had exhausted the resources of France. Chateaubriand pours contempt upon his administrative abilities and even his military genius, and concludes that, far from having any claim to greatness, he was nothing better than a comedian who had employed the mask of a Cæsar to hide a shallow intellect. As an alternative to Bonaparte, whose reign of glory was over, he offered another ruler who would be the saviour of France. " Let us re-establish the monarchy of Clovis," he cries, " the patrimony of St Louis and Henry IV. The Bourbons are the governors best suited to our unhappy situation, their charitable hands alone can heal our wounds." As in *Le Génie du christianisme*, of which *De Buonaparte et des Bourbons* is the political counterpart, the springs of sentiment were stirred by memories of the past. The glorious services

36

of the monarchy are recalled and the dry bones of kingship made to live.

The book was enthusiastically welcomed by a public that was tired of political experiment, and the author was justified in thinking that he would have his reward. But Louis XVIII, although he declared that the pamphlet had been of more use to him than an army, distrusted the influence of poets in politics, and Chateaubriand was ignored. He did not despair of gaining a place in the Government, however, and towards the end of 1814 published his *Réflexions politiques*, the most serious contribution that he had yet made to politics. In the interval that had occurred since he had written *De Buonaparte et des Bourbons* the constitution had been proclaimed, which had made an attempt to secure political liberty for France, and it was to the Charter, unacceptable as it was to theorists like de Bonald, who demanded a return to absolutism, and to the fanatics of the emigration, who wished for a restoration of privilege, that Chateaubriand pinned his faith. Although he was loyal to tradition and had supported the Legitimacy, he saw that it was impossible to ignore the results of the Revolution and to restore the old *régime*. His pamphlet, therefore, is a plea for the spirit of compromise as embodied in the Charter, which provided a link between past and present, and held out a hope of peace. Chateaubriand describes the Charter as a truce between Republicans and Royalists which combined all opinions, realised all hopes, and satisfied all wants, and he asks the nation to rally round the Government and to accept it loyally. He reminded critics that the constitution of England was the result of long ages of experiment, and that it was absurd for Frenchmen to demand immediate perfection. To those who complained that the King had insisted on receiving the crown as his inheritance, and not as the gift of the people, he replied that it would have been impossible to accept the principle of popular sovereignty, since France was no longer a republic. To those who wished for a complete return to the past he suggested that if the monarchy were an ancient tree whose trunk should be respected, it might be expedient to graft its branches with new fruits, for nations, like rivers, cannot return to their source, and men must move with the times. All had suffered from the misfortunes of the past, but all could take their lesson. They had seen the disadvantages both of a republic and of an excess of absolute power; it remained for them to accept the form of government best fitted to national dignity and most conducive to happiness —namely, a limited monarchy.

The *Réflexions* were condemned by the matadors of the emigration, who saw in the Charter the death of their hopes, but they were welcomed by Royer-Collard and other moderate Royalists, including the King himself. During the Hundred Days Chateaubriand followed the Court to Ghent, and was appointed Minister of the Interior, but he failed to conciliate Talleyrand and Fouché, the men of the moment, to whom he makes spiteful reference in his *Mémoires*, and after the return of the King to Paris the only substantial reward he received for his services was his entry into the House of Peers. He had hoped for a Royalist administration, but Louis XVIII, who realised the difficulties of his position and wished to keep the balance between the parties, chose a Government of Moderates. Disgusted at seeing the men of the Empire and Revolution in power, and disappointed at not having himself received office, the author of the *Réflexions*, in whom the passions of the *émigré* were now uppermost, abandoned his *rôle* of liberal monarchist and went over to the extreme Royalists.

The Ultras, representing the old feudal element, were naturally loyal to the King, through whom they hoped to recover their privileges, but they were determined to resist the new *bourgeoisie* and keep them from power. As a result of the reactionary feelings roused by the sufferings of the Hundred Days they had secured a majority in the House, and, although they disliked the Charter, which embodied revolutionary principles, decided to support the Parliamentary system it had established and to exploit it for their own ends. The men of the Revolution and Empire were equally determined to keep the advantages they had won, and, although they had accepted the Restoration without enthusiasm, were forced by the hostility of the Ultras to rely on the Crown. They looked to the monarchy to safeguard them against their enemies, and to the claims made by the latter on behalf of the Chamber they opposed the prerogatives of the Throne. The Ministry, alarmed by the extreme measures of the Royalists, which they feared would imperil the monarchy, turned more and more to the Left, and when a political crisis arose which gave birth to the hope that the elections would be in their favour advised the King to dissolve the Chamber. The royal ordinance by which this was effected on September 5, 1816, was at once a disavowal of the Ultras and an attack on Parliamentary power, and Chateaubriand, who had found little scope for his talent in the Chamber of Peers, decided to champion both.

The Charter, while nominally establishing constitutional monarchy, had left two questions in doubt, the extent and nature of the King's prerogative and the responsibility of his Ministers. Chateaubriand's main aim in writing *De la Monarchie selon la charte*, the most important of his political works, was to establish the principle of Ministerial responsibility, by which he hoped at once to destroy the power of the Government and to strengthen his own party. The King, he explains, can do nothing by himself; he can only act through his Ministers, and these must accept responsibility for the Crown. Although the Ministry should be controlled by the King, it should identify itself with the majority in the Chamber, and bow to the force of public opinion. Although he limits the royal prerogative by condemning the exercise of royal authority by ordinance, and denying the Crown the sole power of initiative in legislation, both of which rights had been conceded by the Charter, he holds, like a true Royalist, that all institutions must rest on traditional principles. He allows the dogma, formulated in the preamble to the Charter, that all authority resides in the King's person, and in a passage which modifies his previous pronouncements declares with the theorists of the reaction that the King is answerable to none save God and his conscience. He wanted to show the Royalists whose prejudices he did not really share how, without abandoning their

39

principles, they might accept and interpret the Charter. At the same time he hoped to strangle the democratic hopes of his enemies, whom he rightly suspected of wishing to dilute the monarchical principle with popular theory. He knew that the Charter was ultimately founded on the will of the King rather than on that of the people, and if he did not at this period actually foresee the Revolution of 1830 he must have regarded it as a possibility. Some of his pro-posals—for example, that for the appointment of Royalists to the highest posts as a safeguard against reaction—as well as his extraordinary claims on behalf of absolutism, confuse his general argument on behalf of representative government, but despite these characteristic lapses from logic the chapters he devotes to an exposition of the Parliamentary system are clear and sound, and in writing these he performed a real service. He set forth the doctrines of that system in a more practical fashion than they had been set forth before, and if it is hardly true, as he claims in his *Mémoires*, that if he had not been there to make himself the schoolmaster of constitutionalism all parties would have put the Charter in their pockets, he certainly demonstrated the importance of the theory that " the King reigns, but does not govern," which, although never acceptable to the Bourbons, was the formula of the July Monarchy.

As a result of his attack upon the Government Chateau-briand's name was struck off the list of Ministers of State, the pension involved in this honorific position was discon-tinued, and his pamphlet was seized. Infuriated by this blow, and by the fact that the Moderates had succeeded at the elections, he turned more fiercely to the Ultras, and founded the *Conservateur*, in which periodical he used his brilliant journalistic abilities to undermine the Ministry. After the fall of the Liberals in 1820, which was largely his work, his own party was returned to power, and the door of politics was at last open. He was sent as ambassador to Berlin and thence to London, and was subsequently chosen to represent France at the Congress of Verona. As Foreign Minister he produced the war with Spain, " the crusade on behalf of absolutism," which he looked upon as his greatest achievement. But his grandiose schemes of foreign policy were unacceptable to Villèle, who was more concerned with financial reform than with dreams of glory. An excuse was found to get rid of him, and he was abruptly dismissed. Chateaubriand, whose continual boast was that he was the restorer of religion, confesses in his *Mémoires*, with reference to his fall, that it would have been better to have borne the blow with Christian fortitude, but that he was unfortunately not the man to turn the other cheek. He abandoned the Ultras, and, although always a *solitaire*, may be said to have joined the Liberals, becoming the violent enemy of the Government to which he owed his disgrace. As he had attacked Decazes and the Moderates in the *Conservateur*, so he now used the *Journal des Débats* as a weapon against Villèle and the Royalists. In his speeches and newspaper articles he posed as the champion of the " public liberties," and, although the Restoration was inevitably doomed through its policy of reaction, there was no single individual who did more to secure its fall. After the Revolution of 1830, however, he refused to take the oath of allegiance to Louis Philippe, and resigned his seat in the House of Peers. Despite his attacks on the Government he clung to the last to the idea of the Legitimacy, and thus felt justified in declaring that he had been faithful to his principles, for he had betrayed neither liberty nor the King.

Chateaubriand has been accused of remaining throughout the political atheist that he had declared himself to be in the *Essai*, and he says himself on many subsequent occasions that he was a sceptic in politics. Towards the end of his life he wrote that, always a man of the past, he had never believed in his times, and that he had no faith in either kings or peoples. He was fundamentally an egotist, and perhaps an anarchist, yet he had the intelligence to see both the value of idealism and the necessity of discipline. He seems to have found his scepticism a burden, and he was always looking for some means to escape from it. He had not the patience, or perhaps the ability, however, to follow systematically any line of thought, and he disliked and distrusted all abstract reasoning. In *Le Génie* he condemns the works of the *philosophes* in that they contained nothing to satisfy or fill, while it was to "visionary speculations," which had neglected to take account of the lessons of experience, that he constantly ascribes the horrors of the Revolution. In *De la Restauration et de la monarchie élective*, written in 1831, he says that he was a Royalist by reason and conviction, and a Republican by taste and character. Inclined by temperament and the influence of his early surroundings to individualism, the Revolution had established his belief in authority, but he had acquired a profound distaste for despotism under Napoleon, and by the conclusion of the Empire the pupil of Malesherbes had arrived at a definite appreciation of Liberalism. At the Restoration he was certainly facing both ways, for he makes it clear in his writings that, while he still clung to the past and had not lost his faith in authority, he did not believe in political stagnation, and was prepared to accept the future.

His subsequent career is the history of his attempt to reconcile his sentiments. He was a sincere admirer of what he calls the "solidity of the English monarchy, kept in balance by an even swing of liberty and power," and once he had rejected his faith in absolutism he held firmly to his idea of constitutional kingship. In *De la Monarchie selon la charte* he shows that he understood the principles of the Parliamentary system, and after his defection from the Royalists he was a constant critic of arbitrary power. Yet, although he opposed the more violently reactionary measures of the Government, when he took up the *rôle* of the championship of Liberalism we are bound to suspect his sincerity, for he made it clear that he had no faith in popular government, and demonstrated on several occasions that benevolent despotism was nearer his heart. There was one liberty, however, which he always defended with sincerity and warmth, and that was the liberty of the Press. He had never forgotten the silence imposed upon public opinion by Napoleon, and as a journalist desired free play for his own most important weapon—namely, his pen. He declared that, the Press being the great instrument of public opinion, it was upon its unfettered action that representative government must ultimately depend. He realised that the power of the Press was tending to become a new tyranny, but it was useless to try to suppress it, for, as with the steam-engine, the more one aimed at compression the more violently it was likely to explode. He pointed out that it was the suppression of public opinion under the old monarchy to which Louis XVI owed his fate, and that by leaving the tongue of the people free grievances expressed might be remedied, and thus a sure support would be found for the Throne.

Chateaubriand boasts in his *Mémoires* that the Bourbons had flourished as long as they listened to him, and in *De la Restauration et de la monarchie élective* he implies that if he had held office he could have prevented their fall. But the foundations of the monarchy had been radically undermined by the Revolution, and the democratic forces which always threatened the Restoration would certainly have been beyond his control. He was, moreover, too often ruled by passion or sentiment to have kept the balance between the parties, and there is no indication that he would have made an effective statesman. Yet he was not merely the erratic phrase-maker or morbid *dilettante* that some would have us believe, for he showed sound sense in his plea for moderation in Church questions and other matters, and he had an excellent grasp of the political meaning of his times. Once the Revolution of 1830 was accomplished, for instance, he had no illusions as to the future. He had no belief in the July Monarchy, the half-way house between the Legitimacy and democracy, and he prophesied that it would not last. It would be destroyed by that public opinion which had already condemned the monarchy, and could only be satisfied with its natural expression—a republic. He viewed the world of the future as he imagined it with alarm, for he realised that the political revolution of 1830 would produce a social revolution, and he had no faith in democracy. In the *Essai* he had protested against the excessive philanthropy of the Age of Reason, which had failed to take account of the fact that the poor of every state are more dangerous than the rich, and often less valuable members of society; while his instinctive dislike of the crowd is evident from the description which he gives of the dangers of ancient democracy in the *Itinéraire*, and from a variety of passages in the *Mémoires*. Influenced doubtless by what he knew of the Terror, he considered that democracy in its thirst for equality was prepared to go to any lengths to procure it, and was only too apt to submerge liberty in despotism. He preferred an aristocratic system based on property and fortified by religion, as more likely to secure that order which is a guarantee of freedom, but in any case, as he said in a speech on conscription, he did not believe in what he calls a " metaphysical equality," which had no real existence in property, education, or manners.

He saw that society was about to enter an industrial stage, and, although he wrote an appreciative account of the marvellous progress made by science and industry since his childhood, he hated the age of the steam-engine. In *Le Génie* he had condemned the " vanity " of science, and poured contempt on those who imagined that the whole of human wisdom is comprised in the circle of the mechanical inventions, and, writing much later, when industrial development was more advanced, he expresses the fear that material improvement had brought no advance in morality. He seems to have had no sympathy with the miserable condition of the workers produced by the Industrial Revolution, nor to have shared the views of Saint-Simon and others who hoped to transform society. His only concern for a community in which, as he says, some were the possessors of millions while others were dying of hunger was that when the lower classes were unable, through loss of religious belief, to find consolation for their privations a convulsion would occur which would unbalance society. He continually repeats the idea of the *Essai* that the soundest basis of society is the moral law. The idea of duty involved in religion must be the controller and regulator of the democratic instinct; this alone could secure true liberty and

44

equality, and would destroy a formidable new idolatry, the love of man for himself.

In the *Essai* Chateaubriand had speculated as to what would follow the decay of Christianity. A general state of enlightenment might produce a new metaphysical religion, or even a universal state of happiness and friendship among nations who had learned to dispense with doctrine, but it seemed more likely that, torn by revolutions, wars, and anarchy, humanity would gradually revert to barbarism. But in the preface to *Les Études historiques*, written thirty-four years later, he declares that Christianity will not perish, for it has its roots in the sky, and only needs some man of genius to endow it with fresh life. In the *Essai*, in common with de Maistre and other thinkers of the reaction, he had denied the idea of progress as set forth, for example, by Condorcet, but he shows that he has now repented of his scepticism, and declares himself the apostle of evolution. In the interesting exposition of his new faith contained in *Les Études* he steers a middle course between the ideas expressed in the *Discours sur l'histoire universelle* and the *Essai sur les mœurs*. He acknowledges with Bossuet that Christianity had been the dominating force in history, but he also proclaims with Voltaire a belief in the powers of the intellect as a guiding force in human destiny. Christianity, or Catholicism—for with Chateaubriand the terms are synonymous—in order to obtain a desirable universality must avoid rigidity and expand with the needs of the times. If stable in doctrine it must be mobile in intelligence, and instead of hampering knowledge must accept it as an ally.

The belief in progress was again coming into fashion owing to the advance of science, which was opening up indefinite vistas of improvement. It was being implied in the new philosophy of history set forth by Cousin and Guizot. It was being proclaimed by some of the Romantic writers and by the more practical disciples of Saint-Simon. There is no doubt that Chateaubriand at this period was influenced by the views of his contemporaries, and particularly by those of Lamennais, the brilliant author of the *Essai sur l'indifférence*, who was then writing in the journal known as *L'Avenir* under the motto " God and Liberty." Lamennais at this stage of his career had abandoned his strictly theocratic attitude, and was trying to reconcile the principles of Catholicism and democracy. Chateaubriand in developing his argument on behalf of an intelligent and universal Catholicism considered that the Church should take into account the general progress of the peoples towards liberty, and conciliate political as well as religious interests. Unlike the formidable champion of Ultramontanism, however, who had not yet broken with the Papacy, influenced doubtless by his general dislike of despotism, he declared that the Pope, while remaining the symbol of Christian unity, should renounce his " mediæval pretensions "—that is, his temporal and dictatorial functions, for the political age of Christianity was over, its philosophical age had begun.

Of the fifty volumes of Chateaubriand's writings which stand on library shelves, with the exception of *Atala* and *René*, his literary masterpieces, only the twelve volumes of the *Mémoires* are likely to attract readers to-day. The political writings, although they include some valuable reflections and many brilliant aphorisms, contain no systematic political doctrine, and are often marred by contradictions and confusion of thought. They were nearly all written in the heat of passion to meet the needs of a particular occasion, and were apt to be merely a reflection of the mood of the hour. Of his social ideas that dealing with religion as a safeguard of democracy is of most interest and value. But his views on democracy were obviously coloured by prejudice, while he attempted no system of ethics. Chateaubriand was strongly attracted to all the great ideals involved in the terms tradition, liberty, and religion, but, despite his valiant efforts, he was never able to square them with reality or to explain them satisfactorily even to himself. In his youth he had seen the old order destroyed by the volcanic forces of the Revolution, and his career covers that period in which France was endeavouring to recover her equilibrium. If he shows a lamentable want of balance he is merely a reflection of his times. Yet if he was of his age he was also not of it. For, passionately desiring to play a part, he was not able to sustain any that he selected, and, wishing to be a leader of thought, his imagination unhinged his philosophy. " A man of action and a man of thought, I have placed my hand in the century, my mind in the desert." Such is the melancholy confession at the conclusion of the *Mémoires*. The *rôle* of this poet was to live like a giant among pygmies. He was never completely a citizen of the world.

The remarks on the Romantics which the title of my article will lead the reader to expect must necessarily be very brief. The Restoration, as is well known, gave an immense impetus to literary activity, owing to the removal of the intellectual restrictions imposed by Napoleon. In his *Histoire de la Restauration* Lamartine describes, in one of his most glowing passages, how the arts forgotten or enslaved under the police of the Empire seemed to spring from the soil under the feet of the Bourbons ; and Edmond Scherer, who also wrote with personal experience of these times, recalls in *Les Études critiques* how the young men, confronted with everything that was new from politics to literature, were filled with a glorious optimism. Side by side with the spirit of exaltation, however, there was the feeling of lassitude and fatigue described in *La Confession d'un enfant du siècle*, for the trials and excitements of the Revolution and Empire produced their reactions, and there were many who longed only for peace. It is a commonplace that after Rousseau and Bernardin de Saint-Pierre the Romantic school owed more to Chateaubriand than to any other writer. To those in revolt against the dryness and realism of the eighteenth century he opened up a new kingdom of feeling and imagination ; to those who were disheartened by the iconoclasm of the Revolution he offered an idealised past. The leading ideas that animated the early Romantics, and more especially Hugo and Lamartine, were naturally similar to his own—belief in the restored monarchy and adherence to the new Catholicism.

As a young man Hugo had declared that he wished to be Chateaubriand or nothing, and the influence of the

47

master is seen in all his early work. With Chateaubriand he condemned the eighteenth century for having destroyed in the pride of its knowledge the dogmas which are the support of tradition; with him also he attacked the Revolution, and poured contempt on Napoleon. His youthful imagination was fired by the themes that had been glorified in *Le Génie* and in *Les Martyrs*. The inspiration of *Les Odes* derives from Christian sources, the spirit of *Les Ballades* is that of ancient France. In a preface to both published in 1824 Hugo declares his enthusiastic approval of the new monarchical and religious society that was arising from the ruins, and, by his definition of the poet's function, proclaims his faith in the future. It was the duty of the poet to repair the evil done by a pagan and democratic literature. He must stir all hearts by singing the double glories of his country and religion. He must march before the peoples like a beacon, and show them the way to the great principles of order and morality.

Lamartine records that, having been born of a Royalist family who bitterly regretted the fall of the Throne and the crimes of anarchy, he was, as a young man, a passionate adorer of everything connected with the past. This youthful poet of the Throne and Altar, although later one of his severest critics, was during the early years of the Restoration also a great admirer of Chateaubriand. He speaks of him in one of the prefaces to *Les Méditations* as one of the two geniuses who had consoled him at his entry into life (Mme de Staël being the other one), and relates that he was a fanatical reader of *Atala* and *Le Génie du christianisme*. His early poetry shows the same reaction against the French Revolution as that of Hugo; it is inspired with the same religious outlook, it breathes the same ardent Royalism.

Although, according to a writer in the *Gazette de France*, Chateaubriand had lost the respect of all the political parties towards the end of the Restoration, it would be difficult to overestimate his influence in the realm of art. He was the prophet of nearly all the early Romantic poets, and the idol of the Paris *salons*. After 1830, however,

CHATEAUBRIAND

there was a marked difference. The revolt against classicism in literature, which was associated from the beginning with the Romantic movement, and for which Chateaubriand himself was largely responsible, had sowed the seeds of revolt against all forms of authority, and once the failure of the Restoration was assured there was a general movement in favour of Liberalism. The increasing importance of social questions led some of the Romantics farther in the direction of reform; there was a tendency to move from the literary camp to the political, and to engage in revolutionary activities.

The religion of the Romantics, in common with that of the author of *Le Génie du christianisme,* was æsthetic in quality, and founded chiefly on sentiment. It is not surprising, therefore, that when once a breach was made in the defences of tradition a relapse into scepticism should take place. After 1830 both Hugo and Lamartine, who threw themselves into politics, rejected practically all the Christian dogmas, and lost their feeling of loyalty to the Throne. The author of *Les Odes et ballades* produced *Notre-Dame de Paris*; the poet of *Les premières Méditations* wrote *La Chute d'un ange.*

Chateaubriand himself in his last speech in the House of Peers declared that the idolatry of a name had perished, for monarchy was no longer a religion; and soon afterwards paid homage to the god of ideas by proclaiming his theory of progress. Had he been a younger man he might have joined the forces of victory, but he was too old and discouraged for fresh enthusiasms, and he did nothing to help the heirs of the Revolution to build up a new world. He kept to the last to his *rôle* of the Bayard of the ancient monarchy, and shrank more and more from reality into a world of dreams. When he heard of the Revolution of 1848, which he just lived to see, he is said to have wept, for there was no more to hope for, and he had no love for the people whose hour had come. At the end of his life he was nothing but a ruin, a monument of the old society, a mournful relic of the past.

CONSTANTIA MAXWELL

49

BOOK LIST

A. Primary Authorities

CHATEAUBRIAND, F. DE: *Œuvres complètes.* 36 vols. 1836–39.
—— *Mémoires d'outre-tombe.* 12 vols. 1849; Edited Biré (6 vols., 1898–1901).
THOMAS, L.: *Correspondance générale de Chateaubriand.* 5 vols. 1912, etc.

For the doctrines of the Catholic and political reaction see the works of Ballanche, de Bonald, de Maistre, and Lamennais; for the political ideas of the Romantics, those of Mme de Staël, Hugo, Lamartine, de Vigny, etc.

B. Secondary Authorities

BALDENSPERGER, F.: *Chateaubriand et l'émigration française à Londres* (in the *Revue d'histoire littéraire de la France*). 1907.
BERTRIN, G.: *La Sincérité religieuse de Chateaubriand.* 1900.
BRANDES, G.: *Main Currents in Nineteenth-century Literature,* vols. iii and v. 6 vols. 1901–5.
BRUNETIÈRE, F.: *Histoire de la littérature française,* vol. iv. 1917.
CASSAGNE, A.: *La Vie politique de Chateaubriand.* 1911.
DEMPSEY, M.: *The Sources of the "Génie du christianisme."* 1928.
FAGUET, E.: *Études littéraires sur le XIXe siècle.* 1909.
—— *Politiques et moralistes du XIXe siècle,* vols. i and ii. 1891–1900.
FERRAZ, M.: *Histoire de la philosophie en France au XIXe siècle,* vol. ii. 1880.
GIRAUD, V.: *Chateaubriand: études littéraires.* 1904.
—— *Nouvelles études sur Chateaubriand.* 1912.
—— *Le Christianisme de Chateaubriand.* 2 vols. 1925–28.
LASKI, H.: *Studies in the Problem of Sovereignty,* essay on de Maistre. 1912.
—— *Authority in the Modern State,* essay on Lamennais. 1919.
LAVISSE, E.: *Histoire de France contemporaine,* vol. iv. 1920–22.
LEMAITRE, J.: *Chateaubriand.* 1912.
LESCURE, M. DE: *Chateaubriand.* 1892.
LOMÉNIE, E. BEAU DE: *La Carrière politique de Chateaubriand.* 2 vols. 1929.
MAURRAS, C.: *Trois idées politiques.* 1912.
MICHEL, E.: *Chateaubriand: interprétation médico-psychologique de son caractère.* 1911.
MICHEL, H.: *L'Idée de l'état.* 1896.
MOREAU, P.: *Chateaubriand.* 1927.
ROUFF, M.: *Chateaubriand.* 1930.
SAINTE-BEUVE, C. A.: *Chateaubriand et son groupe littéraire.* 3 vols. 1861.
—— *Portraits contemporains,* vols. i and ii. 1870–71.

CHATEAUBRIAND

SAINTE-BEUVE, C. A. : *Causeries du Lundi*, vols. i, ii, and ix. 1851–62.

—— *Nouveaux Lundis*, vol. iii. 1863–72.

—— *Premiers Lundis*, vol. iii. 1874–75.

SÉE, H.: *Les Idées et tendances politiques de Chateaubriand* (in the *Revue d'histoire littéraire de la France*). 1925.

—— *La Vie économique de la France sous la monarchie censitaire* (1815–48). 1927.

VIATTE, A.: *La Catholicisme chez les romantiques.* 1922.

VILLEMAIN, A.: *La Tribune moderne.* 1858.

VINET, A.: *Études sur la littérature française au XIXᵉ siècle.* 2 vols. 1849.

WEILL, G.: *La France sous la monarchie constitutionnelle* (1815–48). 1912.

NOTE. For a list of books on the French Romantic movement see Maurice Souriau's *Histoire du romantisme en France* (2 vols., 1927).

III

HEGEL THE GERMAN IDEALIST

HEGEL and the German Idealists is a subject that would suitably be included in a series of articles such as the present, but I propose to confine myself to Hegel, and that for two reasons. First, the space at my disposal is scarcely adequate even for the consideration of the philosophy of a political thinker so fundamental as Hegel. Secondly, the German idealists before Hegel, however true it be that they laid the foundation of much in Hegel's thought, are not in the least representative of the Age of Reaction and Reconstruction. In the history of thought a man's foes are often those of his own household, and it is against Kant and one school of Kantians that Hegel is in reaction. Kant had rejoiced in both the American War of Independence and the French Revolution. Hegel mostly refers to the French Revolution as a terrible warning, or an evident proof of the shallowness and dangerous character of the ideas upon which it is based. And Hegel himself seems to me entirely typical of the age we are considering. Opinions vary as to whether he is nearer reaction or reconstruction. There are reactionary things in him. When he talks about the sort of people who are often called doctrinaire Radicals a certain petulance and temper is apparent in his gibes. Yet he is no mere defender of the existing state of affairs. He gives a penetrating analysis of something which in his time was only coming into existence—the nineteenth-century modern State. He seems to me to be even more than Burke the great representative of modern Conservatism. He has all the Conservative's characteristic dislike of mere abstract principles; his respect for history and the accomplished fact; his wise insistence on the rationality of the existing institution; his appreciation of the different

52

parts to be played by different classes in the community; his reverence alike for the family and for the State; his national patriotism; and his distaste for cosmopolitan ideals.

Hegel was born in Stuttgart in 1770, in the same year as Wordsworth. Like Wordsworth, he shared in the hopes and enthusiasms of the early days of the French Revolution. While at the University of Tübingen he helped in forming a political club in which the ideas of the Revolution were discussed and was distinguished among its members as the enthusiastic champion of liberty and fraternity. Like Wordsworth again, he was disappointed and disillusioned by the development of the Revolution. In the six years after he left the university, from 1793 to 1799, he was a tutor in a private family, first in Berne and then in Frankfurt. In these years he thought out for himself his new position— a restatement of the principle of liberty. Rousseau and Kant had drawn some of their inspiration from classical Rome. Hegel brings into political philosophy an enthusiastic admiration for the theory and practice of the Greek city state. He found in an idealised picture of the Greek πόλις the conception of a state where ethical ideals had been wrought into the texture of social life, and he never ceased to contrast such a realised or objective ideal of " ethical observance" with what he considered to be the abstract and Utopian demands of the individualists of his time.

From 1800 to 1807 Hegel was at Jena. His house was plundered by French soldiers in the occupation of Jena just before the battle, and he escaped with the last pages of the *Phänomenologie* in his pocket. The war destroyed university life at Jena, and Hegel had to find other occupation. He got a position as rector of the gymnasium at Nürnberg, which he held till 1816, when he was made professor of philosophy at Heidelberg. In 1818 he was called to Berlin to occupy the chair vacated by Fichte's death. He was professor of philosophy at Berlin, occupying the most important philosophical post in Germany, and high in favour with the Prussian Government, till his death in 1831.

Hegel wrote several treatises on political subjects besides the *Grundlinien der Philosophie des Rechts* : an early treatise on the constitution of Germany in 1802, a pamphlet on the Würtemberg Estates in 1816, and one on the English Reform Bill in 1831. He also wrote in 1802 a work on the scientific treatment of Natural Law, and the *Encyklopädie* published in 1817 gives a sketch of his general political theory. But by far his most important work on politics is the *Philosophy of Right* published in 1821. There is so much to be said about this great and fundamental book that I shall confine myself to it in this article.

Hegel's political philosophy is with us still rather under a cloud. His extravagant remarks in glorification of the State were taken to be responsible in some degree for the War. He may be thought, with some justice, to represent the spirit of nineteenth-century Prussia, and that is something to which we still find it difficult to do justice. But, even apart from the lingering of war prejudice, it is true that Hegel is most defective in regard to the questions in which we are now most interested. He has little understanding of international relations. He is too much preoccupied with the independent nation State. We find more sustenance in Kant's tractate on perpetual peace, which Hegel despised, than in all Hegel's account of international relations. Further, he was too much concerned with emphasising the importance of the State against theories which wrongly depreciated it to have the time or the patience to discuss at all thoroughly the problems which we hear so much of—which concern the relation between the State and other associations.

Apart from these reasons the book is very difficult—for this political theory is part of, or, if you like, is essentially the application of Hegel's philosophical system, and to those who have not immersed themselves in that system and are concerned primarily with the political theory the book is full of dark sayings and mysterious technical terms and phrases. "The good is, in general, the essence of the will in its substantive and universal character—the will in its truth. It exists solely in and by means of thought." There is hardly a page which has not some dark saying of that kind.

54

Nevertheless this neglect into which the *Philosophy of Right* has fallen is undeserved, and I want to try not to expound Hegel's whole philosophy of right or law—that would have to begin with some account of the Hegelian system which would more than absorb the space available—but to set before the reader some of the things in the *Philosophy of Right* which both explain the great influence it has had on the subsequent history of political thought from Karl Marx to our own Green and Bosanquet and make it a profoundly inspiring and illuminating work.

The first point I want to consider is Hegel's conviction that the understanding of the nature of the State is not easy and is a task for philosophy. " We must learn that if it is difficult to conceive of nature, it is infinitely harder to apprehend the state." There are those who criticise the whole conception of political philosophy and wish to regard political theory as a science in the ordinary sense of the term. Hegel's answer is that the State " is the world the spirit has made for itself." What he means by that is this at least : that the State exists in the sphere of will, that it exists and is maintained by man willing, and that we can have no understanding or comprehension of it if we think of it as an ordinary thing unless we take the trouble to understand the nature of willing. Now to understand what will is we must have recourse to reflection, to making clear to ourselves what we are doing, to making explicit what we do implicitly. This act of reflection, of coming to comprehend what in a certain implicit sense we know already, is the peculiar business of philosophy. Such philosophical reflection is not an easy matter ; we have to be taught to philosophise. We have got to rise above our ordinary categories. Much political theory goes wrong because it will not take this original trouble of reflection, and philosophical theory of the State cannot be appreciated by those who will not make the necessary intellectual effort to understand it. The effort is worth while. Much of the remarkable and far-reaching influence which this *Philosophy of Right* has had on political thinkers of all schools is entirely due to the fact that it did achieve an apprehension of the State: there are many discussions which have not even begun to do that.

When we come to consider the nature of willing we find in it two characteristics which make the basis of Hegel's consideration of the State. It is the nature of will, as contrasted with desire, to be universal. In Hegel's words, " the individual is, according to the pure will, a universal being." This central position he derived, as he explains, from Rousseau and Kant. He added to it an insistence that will is not really will until it objectifies itself, expresses itself in the outside world, and above all in society and the State. He treats the State and social institutions as " objective spirit "; they are willing—reason in action—realised. They are the great instances of his fundamental doctrine, asserted emphatically in the preface: " The rational is the real and the real is the rational." Whatever we may think of this as a general metaphysical doctrine it has peculiar relevance when applied to social institutions. They are only to be understood as embodiments of the rational will. For an institution can only endure and be an institution in virtue of the universal and therefore rational will which supports it, whose expression it is.

From this fundamental position there follows in the first place a new conception of the nature of political philosophy. It is not its business to say what the State ought to be, or to construct Utopias or ideal States. It is concerned to understand the State as it is. But it takes philosophy to do that. For to understand this State as it is, to grasp its real or rational nature, as distinct from the accidental characteristics of this or that State, and to apprehend the rational will embodied in it,

> This treatise, in so far as it contains a political science, is nothing more than an attempt to conceive of and present the State as in itself rational. As a philosophical writing it must be on its guard against constructing a State as it ought to be. Philosophy cannot teach the State what it should be, but only how it, the ethical Universe, is to be known. To apprehend what is is the task of philosophy, because what is is reason.

56

HEGEL THE GERMAN IDEALIST

Only one word more concerning the desire to teach the world what it ought to be. For such a desire philosophy at least always comes too late. Philosophy, as the thought of this world, does not appear until reality has completed its formative process, and made itself ready. History thus corroborates the teaching of the conception that only in the maturity of reality does the ideal appear as counterpart to the real, apprehends the real world in its substance, and shapes it into an intellectual kingdom. When philosophy paints its grey in grey, one form of life has become old, and by means of grey it cannot be rejuvenated but only known. The owl of Minerva takes its flight only when the shadows of evening are fallen.

There is in this conception of the task of political philosophy a certain ambiguity which Hegel perhaps did not always escape. It may be used, as it is in the preface, where Hegel is rebuking in a rather petulant fashion contemporary Liberalism, to assert the superiority of established institutions, which are embodied reason, against the necessarily abstract proposals of reformers. It may assume that the fact, just because it is a fact, is rational and therefore to be defended. Both those great philosophical Conservatives, Burke and Hegel, are guilty at times of this most annoying of all the devices of reaction. " What seek ye? is the cry of tyrants in all times."

But Hegel's true position is other than this. For that implies that there is a difference between the rational will which is embodied in an institution and its accidental and defective expressions. Further, the will which is rational is never anything finally embodied in external form. It is a becoming, a perpetual willing, and is something which always holds its own criticism within it. Though Hegel may contrast the actual with the merely ideal, the real which is rational has always its ideal side. It is always seeking to go beyond its actual achievement. If an institution does not embody an ideal, criticising, reforming will, it has outlived its usefulness. Political theory on this view is not studying any abstract ' what ought to be.' It is studying something immanent in institutions, but immanent as a living, constructive, critical force. Hegel,

57

for accidental reasons, is more obviously concerned to rebuke the abstractness of ideals than the inertness of institutions, but the rational will which he finds in the State must be both ideal and actual, embodied in fact, but reaching forward to a truer expression of itself.

We can see from the *Philosophy of Right* itself that this is Hegel's true position. For "the State as it is," which he describes, is no State which was in existence when he wrote. It is the constitutional and industrial nation State of the nineteenth century, which in Hegel's time was only just coming into being. He did perceive in a remarkable way the idea which was immanent in the States of his time, which, because it was immanent, was shaping history. If we are to say with Hegel that it is the business of political philosophy to understand the State as it is, we must remember then that philosophical understanding is grasping the conception or essence of the State, and that is the same as grasping the ideal operating in the State.

We may perhaps sum up this side of Hegel's work by reminding ourselves that it was he who really brought historical method into political philosophy. His belief in history is what, more than anything else, distinguishes him from his predecessors and above all from Kant. The rational which is real is for Hegel always an historical process. Reality is to be understood in becoming and therefore in history. For Hegel the dialectical process, in which truth came from the coming together of opposing views, was only the mirror of a dialectical process in reality. He was convinced that we could not understand anything—and certainly not institutions—by looking at a cross-section, where time, process, and development are omitted.

This insistence on historical process made him affirm that rationality exhibited itself more in the process of events than in anyone's conscious planning about them. He opposes "the cunning of reason" which shows itself in the actual process of events to the shortsighted, onesided plans and purposes of the actors in historical events. Though he regards institutions as existing in the sphere

58

of will, he repels all such theories as the social contract which would make the will which is the State coincident only with what men consciously and explicitly will about it. It is from this aspect in Hegel that Bosanquet gets his illuminating, though obscure, conception of the general will which is more than any one member of the State wills, or more, indeed, than is generally willed by all members of society. So the will, which for Hegel is objectified in the State, is always more than anyone has consciously willed. An institution is, for him, realised will, but it reveals to us that there is more in our will than we are conscious of. No social institution, least of all the State, is only the sum of the wills of those who compose it—or any compound of such wills. It is always more, and that more comes, at least to some extent, from its life in an historical process.

If this were all there were in Hegel his position would be little more than a philosophical edition of the reaction from the narrowness of the Revolution. But there is more in Hegel than that. For the *Philosophy of Right* is a determined attempt to do justice to the " modern principle of subjectivism," which Hegel thought to have been the basis of the ideas of the Revolution, although the Revolution had given it a onesided emphasis. I have noticed already the importance which Hegel attached to the ideal of " ethical observance " which he found expressed in Greek political theory. But he criticised that theory for failing to do justice to the rights of the individual. His own political philosophy is the result of a lifelong attempt to do justice to both these ideals.

" Law," he declares, " is the reality of the free will." Morality and right and the State rest on respect for personality as such. The ancient world failed to recognise this fundamental principle, and its acceptance of slavery is the mark of this failure. The end of the State is liberty: the test of its success is the reality it gives to personal liberty. No doubt Hegel is prepared to insist that liberty cannot be realised without law; but law has to submit to the criterion of whether it does make personal liberty real.

The end of ethical observance has to be understood with the qualification that free will is its essential basis.

We do not always realise what a profound difference there is between the assumptions of Greek political theory and the modern doctrine of liberty or of individual rights. It is one of Hegel's great services that he began by seeing how far-reaching the problem involved in that difference is. Both Plato and Aristotle take it for granted that politics is the application or realisation of ethics. There is a phrase in the *Republic* which sums up this position succinctly when Plato says that the guardians are to be the craftsmen of the virtue of the citizens. Greek political theory assumes authoritarian morals. The nature of the good life is to be discovered by the philosopher and then by means of political institutions realised among the relatively passive citizens.

The same position is involved when Aristotle in the *Ethics* says that in the perfect State justice, in the wider sense of the term, would coincide with the law. In a modern State we take for granted that it is not the business of the law to lay down or enforce a perfect moral code, but only to enforce such a minimum standard of behaviour as will ensure to all the citizens their rights—that is, their liberties. We may, indeed, put the difference between the Greek and the modern points of view by saying that for Plato and Aristotle the law exists to realise what is right, for the modern to realise rights. Rights are liberties, and, just because they are liberties, there must be a difference between what is morally right and what is legal. For the law which maintains rights is maintaining for the individual who enjoys rights a moral choice. A legal right is therefore in one aspect of it a right to do wrong.

Hegel's problem is how to combine the deepened sense of conduct which he thinks got its full expression in the Reformation with the Greek ideal of ethical observance. He is convinced that the combination is essential. He is almost too well aware of the dangers and defects of what he calls morality, and thinks the absolutism of conscience worse than the absolutism of the State. He would have

60

sympathised with Dr Johnson when he said, " The inward light, to which some Methodists pretend, is a principle utterly incompatible with social or civil security." Yet for all that he never lost his conviction of the vital import- ance of the subjective and infinite element in morality which he thought characteristically modern. He did not think that a society could be built on it alone, but he did not think either that the best kind of society could be built without it.

How then does Hegel manage to reconcile those two principles, or rather, as we must ask, now that we have understood what his philosophy is trying to do, how does he exhibit the modern State as, in its real nature, combining these two principles? Let us begin by quoting his state- ment that it does do so. It will be found in § 260.

The State is the embodiment of concrete freedom. But the nature of concrete freedom is that personal individuality and its special interests have their complete development and the recognition of their rights in themselves in the system of the family and of the economic community, that they also, partly of their own accord pass over into the interest of the Universal, partly by their own knowledge and will recognise the Universal as their substantial spirit, and work for it as their own end. The result is that neither has the Universal any validity or completion without particular interest, particular knowledge, particular will; nor do the individuals live only for that particular interest as though they were private persons, but they also will at the same time in and for the Universal, and are in all their activities conscious of this end. The principle of the modern State has this enormous strength and depth, that it lets the principle of subjectivity fulfil itself to the most inde- pendent extreme of personal particularity, and yet, at the same time, brings it back into its substantive unity, and thus preserves particularity in the principle of the State.

The idea of the modern State has this peculiarity; that the State is the embodiment of freedom not according to subjective liking, but according to the concept of will, that is in its Universal and divine character. Incomplete States are those in which the idea of the State is still hidden and where particular phases do not come to free independence. In the States of classical antiquity the Universal is indeed to be found, but particularity has not been

released and set free in order that it may be led back to Universality
—that is, to the Universal purpose of the whole. The essence
of the modern State is that the Universal is bound up with the
full freedom of particularity and the welfare of individuals, that
the interest of the family and of the Economic Community must
connect itself with the State, but also that the Universality of the
State's purpose cannot advance without the specific knowledge and
will of the particular, which must maintain its rights. The
Universal must be actively furthered, but on the other side subjectivity must be wholly and vitally developed. Only when both
elements are there in all their strength can the State be regarded
as articulated and truly organised.

Particularity and subjectivity—that is, the wills of individuals, their private judgments—the family, the Economic Community, associations, and corporations are to be
'let loose.' They are to have an independent life of their
own, and their own principle of development. But they are
also to be 'brought back again': they are to be reconciled
by learning to understand and will the good of the whole.
This may be called an ideal which is only imperfectly
realised; but it is the actual idea of the modern State, because it is what the modern State sets out to do. This
outcome of philosophical absolutism is surely very far from
political absolutism.

But the most interesting theory in the *Philosophy of Right*
is not this affirmation of the union of these two aspects of
the modern State, far-reaching and important though that
is. It is the manner in which this conception is elaborated
in the general plan of the work.

That plan is at first sight artificial and bizarre, but it will
be found on examination most illuminating. I shall give it
first in Hegel's own words in §33 at the end of the Introduction.

According to the stages in the development of the idea of the
absolutely free will:
A. The will is immediate: its conception is therefore abstract
—the personality—and its embodied reality is a direct external
thing. This is the sphere of abstract or formal right.
B. The will, passing out of external reality, turns back on

itself, as subjective individuality determined against the Universal. This Universal is partly something inward—the Good—partly something outward, a presented world, and these two sides of the idea involve one another. This is the idea in its division or particular existence, the right of the subjective will in relation to the right of the world and to the right of the idea—the sphere of morality.

C. The verity and truth of these two abstract moments, the thought-idea of the good, is realised, both in the will turned back upon itself, and in the outer world, so that freedom exists as the substance both of reality and necessity and as subjective will, the idea in its absolute Universal existence—ethical observance.

This ethical substance is again

(*a*) Natural spirit—the family.

(*b*) Spirit in its division and appearance—the Economic Community.

(*c*) The State as Universal and objective freedom in the free self-dependence of the particular will. This actual and organic spirit (*a*) is the spirit of a nation, (*β*) is found in the relation to one another of national spirits, and (*γ*) becomes actual and revealed in world history as the Universal world spirit, whose right is the highest.

A strange scheme at first sight—three dialectical ' threes,' one within the other like puzzle boxes. The State is the climax of the second ' three,' but only the first member of the last! That would in itself give room for a more elaborate development of the subject of international relations than Hegel cared to give us. His concern was rather with the first two ' threes,' and it is these which are the framework of his account of the State to which I shall confine myself. But we may learn from the last ' three ' that the climax of these dialectical 'threes' does not supersede the reality of the earlier members. The world spirit not only allows, but in Hegel's eyes demands, the independent existence and vitality of nations. We are not to be allowed by expressions like ' passes over into,' or ' becoming,' or ' superseded by' to think that for Hegel the State swallows up or makes unreal the family or the Economic Community, or that the sphere of ethical observance swallows up or makes unreal the sphere of abstract personality, or of what Hegel calls morality. Rather are we to think that the greatness of the State comes primarily from it giving unity and harmony to the independent worlds of the family and of economics, and the greatness of the sphere of ethical observance depends not on this supersession, but on the union of the still essential vital and active principles of abstract personality and of morality. Hegel's apostrophes on the State and his sneers at abstract morality often make us forget that. But that is only because his temper sometimes gets the better of his principles. We miss the whole spirit of what he has to say if we are so misled.

Bearing this in mind, let us look at the first ' three.' *A* is the sphere of abstract right. We have there Hegel's discussion of the legal principles of personality, of contract, and of crime and punishment. This part of the plan is often criticised. It is indeed strange to find a discussion of law here, separated from the discussion of constitutional and other law by the section on morality. Hegel's most recent editor, in his masterly introduction to the *Philosophy of Right*, points out that as there can be no law without the State, this division is mistaken and is only the remnant of the outworn doctrine of Natural Law. This is a mistake. Hegel has seen, and in this section makes clear, that the State is not the source of all law. We need not justify all the details of his discussion. It is enough to notice the importance he attaches to this independent spirit of law—working on general principles common to all peoples, and founded on the worth and indefeasible nature of human personality.

In the State it loses actually its entire independence, but that does not prevent its reality as a relatively independent activity maintaining certain universal principles of human relationship against any attempt of this or that State to deny or belittle them. That in modern States the working out of law is, as a matter of fact, so influenced cannot be denied; the principles of Natural Law or natural rights have been far too important a factor in history for that to be possible. The misfortune is that, because the supporters of Natural Law have given it a rigidity and entire independence, they have made claims for it which cannot be defended, and

Natural Law so defined has been abandoned altogether. Hegel's doctrine of Natural Law—for that is what this section really is—gives it a vitality and worth and activity of its own, but also asserts—as Hegel asserts of morality, of the family and of the Economic Community—that it must work within the State. It keeps its own essential nature as an assertion of the worth and implications of personality as such, and yet it is in the Community, a living principle working along with other living principles, affecting and being affected by them. If we try to make a State out of the principle of this abstract personality we shall fall into the fallacies of the social contract theory : we shall miss much of the richness and variety of corporate life : but equally if we try to make a State without this principle that State will lack true Universality and it will not realise, because it will not understand, the principles of liberty.

The next part deals with what Hegel calls morality, distinguishing it from ethical observance. It is the sphere of conscience, of the inward light. It is concerned with that in conduct which represents the infinity of the claims of goodness, which is therefore always dissatisfied with legal standards and also with the actual realised standard of ethical observance. It represents also the subjective element of conduct—the refusal to acknowledge any authority save that of the individual conscience.

Hegel thinks that the sphere of ethical observance is a higher stage than what he calls morality; but he does not mean that ethical observance can do without morality. He does not really reduce right conduct to " my station and its duties." He has no use for the moral demands which do not realise themselves or demand to be realised in ethical observance. Indeed, he resented the absolutism of conscience so much that he sometimes seems to do less than justice to its importance. But this, as I have said, is Hegel's temper, not his philosophy. He thinks it as important for the State that the infinite demands of morality should be actively and certainly alive within it as that those demands should be ready to realise themselves in the practical sphere of ethical observance.

65

It will not now be necessary to discuss at any length the second of Hegel's triads—the triad of ethical observance with its three spheres of the family, the Economic Community, and the State. For the same principle rules there which we have already examined in discussing the first triad. The most original contribution of Hegel's in this second triad is his account of the Economic Community. That again has its distinctive nature—not to be confounded either with the family or the State. It has its own laws and its own relative independence. Hegel is the first political philosopher to acknowledge the independent importance in the State of economic relations and of economic law and yet to show how, while remaining relatively independent, the Economic Community plays its part in the whole and is ' brought back' by the action of the State to serve the general good.

The important thing to notice about this triad is that when Hegel comes to describe the State he regards its constitution as the most important aspect of it. No political philosopher has given such an adequate account of the constitutional State. The purpose of a constitution is to demarcate power and function, to give relative liberty and freedom of action to departmental power, and yet preserve the unity of the whole. That is what Hegel's State does—not only for the various departments of political organisation, but for the different aspects of social life. Only in so far as it is throughout playing the part of a constitution does the State, as he describes it, leave room for the play of the various social forces which make up the life of a modern community—abstract law, ideal morality, the family, and all the personal and voluntary associations which count for so much in modern life and the whole network of economic relations. None of them are to be given entirely free play, or allowed to have absolute rights in themselves. The work of the State is to ensure that all contribute to the harmony of the whole. But the State does that, not by denying the relative right of the several elements, or by trying to do their business for them, but by a process of continual adjustment.

HEGEL THE GERMAN IDEALIST

I have been trying in this article to give an appreciation of the general teaching of Hegel's *Philosophy of Right*, and have said little in criticism. This does not mean that there is nothing to criticise. The common criticism, for example, of the inadequacy of Hegel's account of the relation of Church and State is, I think, justified. But I have thought it more important to show the truth and greatness of Hegel's apprehension of that great social phenomenon which was just coming into being when he wrote—the nineteenth-century constitutional nation State.

A. D. Lindsay

BOOK LIST

Hegel, G. W. F.: *Grundlinien der Philosophie des Rechts*, edited by Georg Lasson. 1930. Translation by S. W. Dyde, 1896.
Reyburn, H. A.: *The Ethical Theory of Hegel.* 1921.
Bosanquet, B.: *The Philosophical Theory of the State*, Chapter X. 1899.

IV

COLERIDGE AND THE ENGLISH CONSERVATIVES

FOR the comparative immunity of England from the Revolutions of 1789, 1830, and 1848 many reasons have been given, though the weight we assign to any one of them may be matter for argument. There is the conservative body of Dissent, on which M. Halévy lays such emphasis. There were powerful men, liberal in sympathy but aristocratic in substance, such as Canning, Palmerston, and Shaftesbury. There is the plain fact of a society till 1860 predominantly rural which impressed even on Radicals like Cobbett some purely conservative or even reactionary aspirations. There are economic truths, like a general rise in the level of real wages and the world-elements which allowed *laissez-faire* to represent itself at that date as in the interests of British farming. And there was, finally, the unaccountable agency of genius in Disraeli or Carlyle. But if England till the middle of the last century was clearly directed by an aristocracy of talent, the mental influences bearing upon that talent must qualify or shape the course of all the forces we have suggested, and among those influences—whether we take them as source or channel, as deep root or mere blossom—a place must be given to the Oxford Movement and the Lake Poets, who between them constructed a new philosophy of authority, and, both by affinity and repulsion, greatly affected the leaders of other schools.

Older than these schools, than Mill and Maurice, Carlyle and Maine, the Lake Poets survived their creative period into a new age, Coleridge till 1834, Southey till 1843, and Wordsworth till 1850. They lived, that is, to become eminent Victorians; two of them achieved the respectability of the Poet Laureateship, Browning's *Lost*

Leader passed his court suit literally to Tennyson, and their children became pillars of the Established Church. Yet the setting sun sometimes cast a curious, almost fierce, shadow over the Lakes; in that decorous landscape of reformed England the poets lay like ancient rocks, scarred by geological revolution, last survivors of an age older than the sudden heat and the long, binding frost.

The venerable and cheap charge of apostasy does at least bring out one important truth, that these conservative thinkers had been brothers in revolution, and before we look at each individually we can treat them on the ground of that common experience. We can say summarily that their attitude to it passed through three phases. The first begins in 1792 with the French war and ends about 1798; it was the period, short but extreme, when Coleridge and Southey planned, after devoting six months to spade husbandry and carpentering, to lead a " small but liberalised " party of emigrants to the Susquehanna to practise communism and poetry; when worried Government eavesdroppers pondered what Coleridge could mean by " Spy Nozy "; when Wordsworth walked in Revolutionary France; the period of Southey's attack upon private property in *Wat Tyler*, and of Wordsworth's letter to Bishop Watson of Llandaff. None of the three was a Jacobin, but all alike condemned England's attack on France as an iniquity, and conceived a hatred, never lost, of the Pitt system, both within England and without.

The Terror at Paris and the Directory's wars, in Italy and above all in Switzerland, began the disillusionment which Bonaparte was to complete, and from 1798 till 1812 we have a period of subsidence, as it were, in those volcanic fires. Wordsworth's preface to *Lyrical Ballads* and the composition of *The Prelude* show that he has reached, after much wandering, his ultimate principles in art and his philosophy of nature; all three found themselves able to give to Pitt's successors what they had refused to Pitt—was not Perceval, asked Coleridge, the best Minister of the century?—for French aggression in the Peninsula reconciled, in their eyes, the cause of England with freedom, of which reconciliation Wordsworth in his volunteer uniform at Grasmere may be taken as the symbol. Not that they passed without effort from one camp to the other; Southey, for instance, fiercely attacked our seizure of the Danish fleet and opposed the restoration of the Bourbons, while all three retained their old, intense, and significant worship for Milton, Marvell, Sidney, Hutchinson, and the other aristocratic idealists of the Commonwealth.

But against France, French politics, and French ideas they became set and determined, and announced their change to the world. In *The Friend*, published during 1809–10, Coleridge framed his anti-Jacobin teaching; from Wordsworth, in *The Convention of Cintra*, came the finest expression given to English patriotism since the seventeenth century; and the *Quarterly Review* provided Southey with a regular opening for his consolidating opinions. They were now in their prime: it is the period of the *Life of Nelson*, of *France : an Ode*, and *Kubla Khan*, of the *Ode to Duty*, *The Happy Warrior*, and the *Ode on Intimations of Immortality*.

Their third and last phase begins after 1815, in the post-war time when their contemporaries, even those who eschewed opium, aged rapidly and suddenly became old in heart. Wordsworth's *Ecclesiastical Sonnets*, Southey's *Book of the Church*, and Coleridge's *Lay Sermons* mark the path of the Westmorland magistrate, the Poet Laureate, and the mystic; in his brief career as a Unitarian minister Coleridge had once described his sermons as " preciously peppered with politics," but now their politics were precious like sermons. Their long monologues on the Reform Bill and the Catholics strike on us bleakly, and with little profit;

> Where are they now, those wanton Boys?
> For whose free range the dædal earth
> Was filled with animated toys?

You can get one answer in Byron's *Vision of Judgment*. But not until 1850 did this long twilight on the Lakes sink into night.

COLERIDGE

" Once a Jacobin, always a Jacobin," said the scornful Hazlitt, and those whom he denounced as renegades had, in fact, come out of lands to which Eldon and Croker had never penetrated, and carried with them to the end signs very unlike that conventional conservatism. Nearest to earth of the three, by many fathoms deep, was Southey, a good man who gave most of his life to others, but one whose egoism and little complacencies are more exasperating than wickedness. " Conservation and improvement " was his motto, but let us skirt rapidly the first part of it, as he would have had it practised—over his opposition to Catholic Emancipation and Parliamentary Reform, his specific of more missionaries for India, or of an aristocratic special constabulary for Great Britain. What there is of any permanent significance in his teaching lies, rather, in all that Macaulay criticised in his review of Southey's *Colloquies*, and in the Christian Socialism of his conservatism. For if his mentality was a melancholy one and his proposed remedies often panic-stricken, he had at heart, now, just as much as in his days of Pantisocracy, a "political system of Christianity," and consequently he loathed rapacity, derided social irresponsibility, and dreaded ignorance. He conceived that the ill done by Adam Smith and Malthus much outweighed the gain. Mankind were naturally good and perfectible, the shortcomings of civilisation were the fault of bad government, and competition was " awfully opposed to the spirit of Christianity." While, then, he exposed the ulcer of the old Poor Law and demanded the stopping of doles to the able-bodied, his own final remedy, urged perhaps with unnecessary optimism, was popular education. Lord Liverpool's long Ministry seemed to him " deficient in everything except good intentions," and to Liverpool's unbending party he set forth an immense programme of conservative reform ; to steepen the income tax, develop savings banks, check enclosure, assist emigration, reform the game laws, recreate the parish, and federalise the Empire. By incessant quotation from Tudor example he showed the same desire as did Cobbett to " get behind " the social effects of the

Reformation, a sympathy which led him to give a fair hearing to Robert Owen and the first co-operators.

In short, and in spite of much that is ridiculous about his pretensions and his commonplace books, Southey was a man of high character and learning, who had the merit of criticising contemporary conservatism in the eye of Christian practice and of the whole national history. But we can hardly call him more than the minor prophet of one generation, and his voice strikes no perpetual echo like that of Coleridge or Wordsworth.

To Coleridge, " the rapt one, of the godlike forehead," the greatest men of the next age paid repeated and memorable homage. But the system of thought to which Mill, Maurice, and Newman have admitted their debt is hard indeed to discern, and harder for one not philosophically expert; it was given out in ephemeral essays and conversation, is embedded in mystical theology, and reminds one of nothing so much as the scanty islets in the delta of an intraversable river system. Even his purest virtue makes it all the harder to tie his thinking down, in that no one ever more insisted on the good to be found even in the worst thought, or more consistently denounced " angry misrepresentations " of one's opponents.

He was, first and last, a religious teacher, bent upon finding an explanation which would cover the whole of things. He could not, therefore, rest content with any mixed mental equipment. Utilitarian ethics could not co-exist with idealist theology, and a generation in conflict with the Revolution of 1789 could not defend authority on the principles of 1688. The " mixed policy and *bonhomie* " of Locke and " the generalisation of experience " must, in his view, logically end in a sandy, mechanical materialism, while a philosophy which made the mind issue from the senses must rend the last raiment of the eighteenth-century Church.

Throughout his long mental voyages—from Hartley to Spinoza, from Berkeley to Kant—Coleridge was looking for a ruling principle, the idea of things, rooted in the will, and therefore for him in morals and religion, which

72

would explain the end of the whole. Without it history would become mere anecdotage, government only presumption or tyranny, and religion a mere police regulation. Only principle, the Revolution taught him, could rouse men to intense action, and it is the prerogative of principle to be reincarnate. Only a thin partition separates opinion without principle from unprincipled opinions, but "the lonely walks of uninterested theorists" may change the face of the world.

True, then, to the Greeks whom he worshipped and the Germans whom he was said to plagiarise, he begins with the human soul, looks not to outward experience but inward, and finds in freedom of the will and in conscience not only the original of intelligent life, but his whole political sanction. Almost a Wordsworth inverted, he finds that "the mind of man represents the laws of nature." "O lady," runs the saddest of his poems,

> O Lady, we receive but what we give,
> And in our life alone does Nature live.

He must therefore repudiate any morality drawn from external pressure, from an association of ideas, or a doctrine of consequences ; it was not in utility, with its ramified individual criteria of happiness, that he could find something common to every conscience, absolute, essential, and universal.

From this intuitionist philosophy flows the whole of Coleridge's thoughts, even to their detailed political application. The individual soul, lit with this original fire, is his real interest ; he must therefore champion the cause of education. He gloried in the national resistance to Bonaparte, because it was built (unlike that of Pitt's war) on a moral unanimity. He grounded his detestation of the new factory system on the sufficient ground that it treated men and women not as beings, but as things. He is sometimes, because they coincided in practical conclusion, compared with Burke, but it is vital to say that they set out from very different principles. For with the historical experience of this, or of any other generation, if designed as the basis of a philosophy, Coleridge had nothing to do—nor with the will of men, but of God.

73

There is another consequence of weight: he thought politics of only secondary importance. Even political liberty was not an end in itself, but rather a channel for moral welfare, and we shall see that he solves the dilemma of politics, the conflict of good man and good citizen, by a sort of political Manichæism: "let us become a better people, . . . sow beside still waters," says the *Lay Sermons*, and Acts of Parliament will sink into the background. He could never isolate an abstract question of reform from the character of its agents, suggesting, possibly with too little allowance for the dispassionate momentum of a people in revolt, that "a system of fundamental reform will scarcely be effected by massacres mechanised into Revolution."

It is, however, possible, though laborious, to construct out of his ceaseless digressions something like a theory of the State. Since men are made in God's image and are moral agents, it cannot rest upon force or fear; only consent gives it validity, and that was not a mirage of fictitious contract, but an " ever-originating," " a still-beginning, never-ceasing force of moral cohesion." What, then, is the relation of this thought to that of Rousseau and the democratico-metaphysical school? It is defined in Coleridge's charge that Rousseau confuses potentiality and substance, and transfers the law of the inner spiritual life to material experience. For reason, " the potential divinity in every man," cannot be susceptible of degree, which is the very cord and condition of human intercourse, circumstance, and expediency; and a power which is to determine the purity of inward motive cannot be the criterion of outward regulation, or become applicable to " our mixed and sensitive nature," which is something besides reason. Furthermore, reason, taken in itself, becomes " mere visionariness in intellect," and " hard-heartedness in morals "; as the science of all as the whole, " it must be interpenetrated by a power that represents the concentration of all in each, a power that acts by contraction of universal truths into individual duties "—that is, by religion. Apart, then, from its fearful consequences in practice, " the system " revolved on a falsifying of principle. Right, which was in fact a term

74

of law, did indeed include the idea of duty, but all nature is raw material for duty, and the actual or external expression of one's duty must be a matter of temper, experience, and prudence.

The State came into existence to protect property, which is justified as the manœuvring-ground of free moral agents, both Nature herself and the human mind determining that this property shall be unequal. But the talk of abstract right was as idle in those who would make one and the same constitution for China, Russia, and Great Britain, as in those who declared for an indefeasible right of property, regardless of degree ; nor for that matter did Rousseau's principles necessarily involve a democratic form of government. The State represents the ordering of nature, and thus must rest in an equilibrium between classes and interests, land and industry, " permanence and progression."

Yet this State is a developing being ; " look round you, and you behold everywhere an adaptation of means to ends." Its functions are not merely the negative *corvée* of defending limb, property, and personal freedom ; " a natural instinct is a natural right," and society must set before all its members an increase in substance, a nourishment of hope, and a rise in the scale.

Two strong merits seem to adhere to this uncomposed body of teaching. Coleridge would relate every institution to its final purpose, and put every society on trial before reality. " The spirit of trade," for instance, has invaded the whole national polity, has corrupted the original conception of property as a trust, and only a revived sentiment of honour can stop its course. Other examples may be found in the economic cheapness which is bought so dear, in the forced changes of employment which dehumanise society, in the tying of property in masses which destroy its social content, or the mockery of " equal rights " to those who laboured twelve hours in every day. Finally, what was the State save " a word of convenience," meaning a number of immortal souls?

Again, whatever the verdict on Coleridge's hopes for the

Church, let it not be forgotten that he made man, as he found himself, first and foremost a religious animal.

Ready, if need be, to appropriate Church funds for education, he extended his view of religion to everything that concerned the soul, and recalled every conservative instrument of England to remember the spiritual as the life of nations. It is in his work that is to be found the real, because the most selfless, condemnation of the *rôle* played by the British aristocracy during the Napoleonic war, whose sin it was to confound enthusiasm with sedition, and to endeavour the setting up of a monopoly in the love of England. The Coleridge of 1796 could have taught them better:

> There lives nor form nor feeling in my soul
> Unborrowed from my country. O divine
> And beauteous island ! thou hast been my sole
> And most magnificent temple, in the which
> I walk with awe, and sing my stately songs,
> Loving the God that made me !

But now, as in every generation since 1848, for one man who reads Southey's verse and ten who read Coleridge's prose, there are a hundred who know Wordsworth's poetry, and this alone perhaps should make it the most enduring monument of the Lake School.

Now Wordsworth was more deeply impressed by the Revolution than either of his brethren. He was, in fact, a more enduring man. He did not, like Southey, live the repetitive life of political correspondence—indeed, for long he took in no newspaper—nor had he the soft, yielding *moral* of Coleridge; that "rough grey face" (on which, said one, you would expect "lichens to grow"), his calm conviction of a mission, and a view of the individual as designed for great causes, seem to set him apart from men who lived with books and dreams. Does any poet sound more directly an admiration for deeds, not words, or an envy, almost, of men of action? The *Character of the Happy Warrior* is echoed by the supreme poem of his later life, entitled *To Enterprise*—enterprise which

> a prostrate Nation can restore,
> When but a single Mind resolves to crouch no more.

76

If he long wandered it was as a man at arms ; a little more, and he had taken service in the army of France, and pacifism is the last ingredient in this disciple of the Gironde ; " specious sensibility" is what he called it, or " the hoarding up of life for its own sake."

Like Dante's, the progress of his soul came out of great tribulation. He has told us himself, at sufficient length, of the golden hours in France, when fraternity seemed to be realised and joy to be its own security, welcoming what to the son of Cumberland statesmen appeared only a normal and long-postponed victory for social justice. From that dream he was torn by England declaring war upon the France of his ideal, and he passed through a phase of rejoicing at English defeat, and of detesting "the clamourous friends of ancient institutions." He turned in disillusionment, for he had brought everything to the bar of reason, and reason seemed to fail him ; in her name he saw crimes committed, "the life in the soul has been directly and ruthlessly warred against," and

> Warfare waged with desperate mind
> Against the life of virtue in mankind

—in turn against the independence of Switzerland, of Germany, of Spain, and of England, and, worst thing of all, a Pope brought in to crown an Emperor of the French.

For nearly ten years Wordsworth wandered between his lost world and another which seemed " powerless to be born," finding nothing left to venerate but the noble living and the noble dead, stranded between the lost soul of France and the stagnant fen of Eldonian England. *The Prelude* and the flood of great sonnets tell us the process of his recovery, brought about by a very different " return to nature," to which her faithful priestess, Dorothy Words-worth, led him ; and *The Convention of Cintra*, written in 1808, records that it was satisfactory and final. If, then, we can find the strands of thought and of feeling which brought him to this resting-place, we shall at the same time discover the lessons that he wished to leave us, for he never changed again.

First, and by repeated asseveration, being a moralist, he
finds that " by the soul only " a nation is great and free.

> The power of Armies is a visible thing,
> Formal, and circumscribed in time and space.

Reflecting on the enormous energy of organised evil (which
he saw in Bonaparte), his mind, filled with the peasants
of Tyrol and Saragossa, returned, as it always did, to
Milton, Vane, and all who called Milton friend, and found
in them a will to be free.

When he thus deliberately makes national independence
prior to civil liberty we feel that it comes in great part from
the instrument he used, that his conception is a visual one,
drawn in through the eye. Through the eye he relates
his spiritual interpretation to political fact, with the eye he
sees the English Channel covered with a thousand ships,
the solitary pine, the mighty heart of great cities asleep,
and, as it were, stamps his strong foot and swears all this
shall be free.

Again, if life comes by the soul, that is not bare reason.
For what have science and art, " those barren leaves,"
done for enslaved Germany? Better the ignorant Spanish
peasant, with his gaze on the Mother of God, than " the
laboratory of unfeeling philanthropists " in Paris. Their sen-
sualist philosophy has banished conscience, " the supreme
embracer of consequences," and has replaced sensibility
by " a shadow calling itself good sense." The mind, bend-
ing under its own weight, either makes of itself a little
god of complacency,[1] a poor blind creature of egoism and
delusion, or, " lost in a gloom of uninspired research,"
sweeps the soul, " the heart within the heart," till it is
empty, finding no peace.

The Cintra tract leads, then, directly to *The Prelude* and
The Excursion. They teach that the affections, which " are

---

[1] "Magnificent desires, when least under the bias of personal feeling, dispose
the mind, more than itself is conscious of, to regard commotion with complacency,
and to watch the aggravations of distress with welcoming ; from an immoderate
confidence that, when the appointed day shall come, it will be in the power of
intellect to relieve. There is danger in being a zealot in any cause, not excepting
that of humanity."

their own justification," hold the key to the riddle; pleasure is "the grand elementary principle"; "we have no thought . . . but as far as we have love and admiration"; a people comprises "a solemn fraternity"; and biography is "philosophy enlightened by the affections." In this acceptance of love he was strengthened by his desire to found things upon a rock, lasting longer than this world of getting and spending, which ebbed and fluctuated with the tides; from the spheres, say lines of 1814,

> The stars of human glory are cast down;
> Perish the roses and the flowers of kings.

If anywhere lay a "central peace subsisting at the heart of endless agitation" it must be built in "a few strong instincts and a few strong thoughts," in "the primary laws of our nature," wherein all could share. It is in this steady search at the base of society for lasting truths and in this perpetual illustration from the life of the poor that Wordsworth, as something like the St Francis of English conservatism, gives his teaching of social liberty. In spite of all his premature despair and jeremiads over the "feudal" frame destroyed by the Reform Bill, to the end he insisted that man was not "a tool or an implement," but born to obey "the law of life and hope and action," so that the moral judgment, which "alone is genuine liberty," carried with it a right to be educated and to be master of the soul. On such a people, he predicts, will rise a new empire, a change "wide and deep and silently prepared."

He would, therefore, refer reason back to nature, "the image of right reason" and the "original of human art"; he would heal the inward discontent by looking outward, and blend nature with reason as "reciprocally teacher and taught." Among their permanencies he reckoned duty, or the "rich bounties of constraint," taught alike by the invincible law of moral retribution, by the waters at their priestlike task, or by the stars, that "vision of endurance and repose." The good life, in short, must be practised before we can hope to enjoy it; it could not be ensured by merely rational effort, it was "no mechanic structure built by

79

rule," but partook of the part-prediction, part-experience, of religious faith.

If we are, in Bacon's language, to rise to a great place Wordsworth insists that morally it must be by a winding stair, and the process of history was not like a Roman road. Like his yew-trees, which made " sounding bows at Azincour," a great country was

> a living thing
> Produced too slowly ever to decay;
> Of form and aspect too magnificent
> To be destroyed.

The structure of nature was eternal, but in itself composed of never-ceasing exchange, decay, and vicissitude, of functions transmitted and powers transferred. Into this world came man, with only a fleck of glory on his mind to remind him whence he came, but compelled, if he would survive, to view himself as part of a plan, and to draw from nature the material for that second and better will of the willing bondman which must replace selfish instinct and consolidate a purified reason.

It was Wordsworth's power at his highest—and we need not judge any man by less—to universalise a corner of English earth and make it for ever eloquent—to dedicate the actual country of Milton and Nelson to the powers which move all created things, law and duty, nature and affection. He seems to carry England with him, like the benefactor in mediæval art offering his church in his arms, and to be able to carry her very high, without losing sight of his native village and its spire, " whose silent finger points to heaven."

KEITH FEILING

BOOK LIST

A. PRIMARY SOURCES

COLERIDGE, S. T.: *Complete Works.* 7 vols. 1884.
SOUTHEY, R.: *Essays Moral and Political.* 1832.
—— *The Book of the Church,* fifth edition. 1841.
WORDSWORTH, W.: *Complete Poetical Works,* edited by W. Knight. 8 vols. 1882–86.

COLERIDGE

Wordsworth, W.: *Complete Poetical Works*, edited by J. Morley. 1888.
—— *Complete Poetical Works*, edited by E. Dowden. 7 vols. 1892–93.

B. Secondary Sources

Brinton, C.: *Political Ideas of the English Romanticists.* 1926.
Cobban, A.: *Edmund Burke and the Revolt against the Eighteenth Century.* 1929.
Dicey, A. V.: *The Statesmanship of Wordsworth.* 1917.
Muirhead, J. H.: *Coleridge as Philosopher.* 1902.
Stephen, L.: *Hours in a Library*, new edition. 3 vols. 1892.

ROBERT OWEN AND THE EARLY SOCIALISTS

THE transition from the eighteenth to the nineteenth century was an epoch of fundamental importance in the history of England. At the end of the eighteenth century the political, religious, and social system of the country was an intolerant oligarchy; by the middle of the following century this system had been challenged and shaken by the inception of new principles—principles of a new order of democracy and tolerance. The life of Robert Owen (1771–1858) coincides with this period of transition. It began at the height of the aristocratic *régime*; it saw the revolutionary era with its promise of change, and the disappointment of that hope in a period of violent reaction; it saw finally the emergence of new ideals of reconstruction. The time of Owen was the bridge between old and new, past and present—a structure which was the work of men's hands, the labour of human lives and brains. Among the builders Robert Owen may claim a place, not as the steady worker who put stone on stone, but as helping to provide the guiding principle of their construction—the principle of human worth and human possibility.

Robert Owen, the son of an ironmonger, was born at Newtown, Montgomeryshire. Educated in the meagre trilogy of reading, writing, arithmetic, then considered adequate for the lower classes, he became at the age of seven an usher in the school of his former master; "thus," he says in his autobiography, "I early acquired the art of teaching others what I know." [1] Equipped for the struggle of life with nothing more than this scanty education and a determined character, Owen made his own way from the age of ten. He first obtained the post of assistant to a

---

[1] *Autobiography*, p. 3.

Stamford linendraper; thence he went to London to a haberdasher's establishment; and eventually became assistant to another linendraper, this time at Manchester, in the year 1787.

Fate seemed to have marked out for him no opportunities for wider fame, for a place in national politics, and for an influence in determining national thought at a critical time in history. For the aristocratic *régime* had no official knowledge of the lower classes. All power was still in the hands to which it had been entrusted at the Restoration settlement, the landed and commercial oligarchy and the Established Anglican Church. It was secured by an effete franchise system, by numerous pocket-boroughs in the gift of the governing caste, by a widespread bribery and corruption in the elections of both borough and shire. It was protected by a savage penal code; and by the Mercantile system of protective tariffs which kept prices high for the benefit of interested classes. Though the Toleration Act of 1689 had removed the restrictions upon the exercise of religious worship, the Act imposing tests for office was unrepealed, and Dissent, coinciding mainly with the lower classes, was outside the pale of official life. The political ascendancy of the upper class was thus completely identified with the religious and educational autocracy of the Anglican Church. Into this system came, in the later eighteenth century, the Industrial Revolution, involving stupendous but for long unrecognised transformations in the existing order. The mechanical inventions, dependent first upon water- and then upon steam-power, shifted the centres of industry from the south-east and south-west to the north, where the rapid hill-streams gave the water-power and the coalfields the genesis of steam. Population followed industry, new factory-centres grew up altogether outside the operation of the already effete representative system. The application of science to industry inevitably involved the supersession of man-power by machine-power, and, however much the fact might be disguised by the greater possibilities of output, the future unemployment problem was foreshadowed from the first in the distress of the handloom weavers. In the field of agriculture too the scientific movement gave tremendous impetus to enclosure, and the years 1760 to 1801 were the age of the Private Act which turned men from their small holdings and the common land. Deprived also, by the concentration of industrial activity into factories, of their profitable by-industries, these went flocking to the towns, where at first they found ready employment.

Then, just at the time when the real effects of the industrial changes would normally have been felt, England entered the Revolutionary wars against France, which continued without cessation for twenty-three years. The war created artificial conditions which blinded the manufacturers and the country to the normal implications of the supersession of man- by machine-power. Foreign competition ceased, while the demand went up by leaps and bounds; and instead of there being an unemployment problem, it was necessary to use to the full all the existing resources, manual and mechanical. All types of labour were pressed into the service, for women and children could tend the machines, working in the textile mills for fourteen or sixteen hours a day, often in an atmosphere full of fluff and refuse, and a temperature raised to 75° damp heat. Child mortality was considerable, and the span of adult life shortened. But humanity was cheap, for there was an endless supply of recruits, who would work for wages scarcely above subsistence level. The Poor Law of Elizabeth, imposing a workhouse test for relief, was abrogated in favour of the Speenhamland system of outdoor doles, given proportionally to the size of the family. This, together with the prevalence of child labour in factories, was a direct encouragement to large families among the lower classes, and gangs of pauper children were regularly sent by the J.P.s to work in the mills.

Such were the special conditions heading for over-production and the inevitable slump in the immediate future, and the not far distant menace of over-population; together with appalling effects on national physique, character, and morale resulting from this wanton exploitation of the entire working-class population. It might well seem to be, as

84

Owen afterwards saw it, a society founded on falsehood, fraud, and fear, for the maintenance of the vested interests of the Anglican aristocracy. "The rich wallow in an excess of luxuries injurious to themselves, solely by the labour of men who are debarred from acquiring for their own use a sufficiency even of the indispensable articles of life."[1] It was indeed "two nations, the rich and the poor,"[2] and, as was frankly stated by a politician of the day, " we do not want the masses to become wealthy and independent of us, for how could we govern them if they were ? "[3]

The arrival of Owen at Manchester coincided with the great cotton boom which made it the pioneer town of Northern industrial development. The population doubled in the decade 1780–90, the imports of raw cotton rose from 6,000,000 to 31,000,000 lb., and the exports of worked cotton from 300,000 to 1,000,000 lb. Owen was engulfed in this maelstrom of industrial life, and his career illustrates the meteoric rise possible for any man with a good business head, and the resulting temptations to sacrifice all ideals for the certainty of rapid returns. In 1789 he abandoned the retail assistantship, and set up as a manufacturer of Crompton's mules for the making of fine cotton yarn. A year later, at the age of nineteen, he entered the arena himself as an independent manufacturer of yarn, employing three men, and making a profit of £6 a week. Wider opportunity was soon to offer ; Owen obtained the post of manager in Mr Drinkwater's cotton-mill—one of the first factories for cotton-spinning on a large scale—earning a salary of £300 a year, and with supervision of 500 workpeople. Here, at the centre of British commerce, Owen made his name as a successful contributor to the technique of industry. By the use of North American " sea-island " cotton, with its peculiar properties for fine spinning, he was able to increase the number of hanks in the pound of yarn from the 120 of his predecessor to an average of 250. For the raw cotton he gave 5s. a pound ; for the finished

[1] Letter to Lord Liverpool, 1818. *Autobiography*, Appendix M, p. 187.
[2] Disraeli's *Sybil*.
[3] F. von Gentz, secretary to the Congress of Aix-la-Chapelle.

yarn he received £9 18s. 6d. a pound—this being 50 per cent. above ' list price '; and the war gave an additional stimulus to the vast output and profits of his mill. Here, too, he had opportunity to observe the effects of mass-production upon the operatives. " I early noticed," he tells us, " a great attention given to the dead machinery, and the neglect and disregard of the living machinery "; [1] and it was now that he began to develop views upon the influence of environment on humanity—views afterwards to be trumpeted to an astonished England as a call to awake from the sleep of complacency and the lust of gain. Owen was gradually ceasing to be a *type* of the eighteenth-century industrial magnate, and was becoming an *individual* of opinions strongly opposed to those of the rest of his class.

At the end of four years Owen entered into partnership with Messrs Barton, of Manchester, and Borrodale and Atkinson, of London, in the Chorlton Twist Company. While in pursuit of his business, travelling as a managing director, buying raw cotton, and selling the produce of the Chorlton mills, Owen met, at Glasgow, Caroline Dale. Her father, David Dale, like Owen himself, typified in his career the rapid advance possible in this age of cataclysmic change. From a herd-boy at Stewarton he had risen to be owner of important cotton-mills at New Lanark, founded in conjunction with the inventor Arkwright; he was also a director of the Glasgow Bank, and as pastor to the Scottish Independents of Glasgow preached in forty churches of the surrounding district. His religious views were strict, and he applied to practical uses in his factory the humanitarian principles often singularly lacking, save in theory, in the devotees of the Established Church. It was the daughter of this man, to whom he was entirely unknown, that Owen soon aspired to marry, and the greatest step of his life, the purchase of the New Lanark mills, was but an incident in the pursuit of this ambition. Caroline Dale, from the moment of their first meeting, had apparently marked down Owen as her future husband, but in spite of this rapid decision her progress was but timid, as she required the

---

[1] *Autobiography*, p. 34.

good offices of a mutual friend to inform him of his fortune; while.Owen for his part was shy and diffident, feeling keenly his inferiority with regard to her father, without whose consent she refused to marry. At this juncture rumour arose in the manufacturing world that the New Lanark mills were for sale, and Owen seized this opportunity of making himself known to Dale, on pretext of investigating this report on behalf of the Chorlton Twist Company. The property eventually changed hands for £60,000, and in 1797 the New Lanark Twist Company was formed, Owen with his wife going to Lanark in 1800 to take charge of the mills.

Owen was twenty-eight when the transference of New Lanark set him upon the stage which he was to occupy for twenty-four years, and where he became a world-famous figure. It is probable that by this time his main social theories were fully formed. He states in his autobiography that on first viewing the New Lanark site he exclaimed to his companion, " Of all places I should prefer this in which to try an experiment I have long contemplated." From childhood, although we may disregard his later insistence upon the precocious formation of his opinions, he had possessed a thoughtful, if not analytical, mind, and had been an extraordinarily wide reader. At an early age he appears to have examined the dogmas and history of the sects and religions of the world, "claiming each for itself to be . . . the 'true religion' ; . . . and the study of these contending faiths and their deadly hatred of each other," he says, " began to create doubts in my mind respecting the truth of any one of these divisions."[1] Further thought produced a theory of the common underlying fallacy of these religions. All were based on the assumption that man was responsible for his good and bad qualities, and was answerable to God and to his fellow-men for their effects—" that greatest of all errors, the notion that individuals form their own characters." [2] Owen was convinced that his own character was not of his making, but was the product of two forces, nature and society; " nature gave the qualities,

---

[1] *Autobiography*, p. 3.
[2] *A New View of Society*, fourth essay, p. 65.

and society directed them." [1] From this theorem Owen derived the two great postulates of his entire system of thought, the twin foundation-stones of his life's work. In the first place that " character is formed for and not by the individual," [2] so that no man can be properly the subject of praise or blame. And in the second place that once this truth were realised a spirit of universal charity was bound to replace the hatreds of sect, party, and person, for there would be " no conceivable foundation for private displeasure or public enmity." [3] These fundamental hypotheses Owen reiterated in different ways, in a lifetime of voluminous writing and verbal propaganda, but the essence was the same. He has sometimes been called by his own generation and by posterity a monomaniac, for his views were impressed upon all and sundry with whom he came in contact, in places suitable and unsuitable, with relentless insistence and boring monotony. Yet his defence against the criticism of Hazlitt that he was " a man of one idea " must be accepted as valid : " Had he said that I was a man of one fundamental principle and its practical consequences, he would have been nearer the truth." [4] For it is certain that once his premises are accepted the system which he built up on them follows inevitably. From his first conception of these theories the way was prepared for their application to the evils of the times along certain definite lines—for their advance from a mere apology *for* mankind, to a system for the regeneration *of* mankind. His great exoneration of humanity would lead him to the championship of the under-classes, groaning under the exploitation of the self-satisfied and intolerant aristocracy. First, by attempting their emancipation from the tyranny of a State and a Church which created conditions conducive to misery and ignorance and to the inevitable increase of crimes which were afterwards illogically penalised ; " the working classes . . . are now trained to commit crimes, for the commission of which they are afterwards punished." [5] Secondly, by a

[1] *Autobiography*, p. 16. [2] *A New View of Society*, second essay, p. 23.
[3] *Ibid.* [4] *Autobiography*, p. 76.
[5] *A New View of Society*, first essay, p. 14.

denunciation of the religions and sects which had preached the false doctrine of individual responsibility for character, and which by their quarrels had added to the Great Uncharitableness. Thirdly, by a constructive effort to remould society upon new principles, to reform character by an altered environment. Exploitation and aristocratic autocracy must be replaced by socialism and co-operation.

It is probable that Owen's opinions were already known by 1800, though naturally to a limited public. He frequently took part in the discussions of Manchester College, afterwards the Unitarian College, with Dr Baines, John Dalton, Winstanley, and Coleridge. Coleridge, Owen tells us,

> was particularly anxious to meet me in discussion, as I was the one who opposed the religious prejudices of the sects: though always in a friendly and kind manner, having now imbibed the spirit of charity and kindness for my opponents which was forced on me by my knowledge of the true formation of character.[1]

He also read papers on social subjects to the Manchester Literary and Philosophical Society; and there is a suggestion that he regarded his religious views as a possible barrier in the eyes of David Dale to his marriage with his daughter. In his firm belief that he had made a new discovery of inestimable import to the world he must have always intended to be a propagandist. " I always endeavoured," he states, writing of the year 1802, " to enforce these subjects by plain and simple arguments and explanations." [2] He always thought that the truth about the formation of character had only to be made known for all classes to co-operate in the reconstruction of society in the light of its principles.

It is impossible and unfair to criticise Owen's theories in isolation, without considering them first in their concrete setting. Owen now found the material for a practical exposition of his views at New Lanark, where he remained, though in active partnership in three successive companies, until 1824. The village consisted of 1300 people, of whom from 400 to 500 were pauper children, and Owen

---

[1] *Autobiography*, p. 36.   [2] *Ibid.*, p. 76.

draws (in his " Second Essay on the Formation of Character ") a dark picture of their condition, despite the remedial measures attempted by David Dale. Immorality, drunkenness, and theft were common on his arrival, but these faults, true to his principles, Owen attributed to defective environment, and, without any artificial rewards or punishments, he set himself so to alter these conditions as to appeal to the best and not the worst motives in human nature. The housing problem was fundamental, and Owen meant to enlist the interest of the inhabitants in favour of clean, orderly dwellings and streets. A set of rules was drawn up enjoining periodical whitewashing of the houses, sweeping of the streets, and banishment of cattle and poultry from the living-rooms ; and these regulations were administered by visitors chosen from the villagers themselves. The doors were to be shut at ten o'clock each night in winter, and immorality was checked by a system of fines, which reduced the number of illegitimate births to twenty-eight over a period of ten years, and, in accord with Owen's ideal of charity, the offenders against convention were received back into society without backbiting or condescension. Special injunctions were issued to the villagers to observe the practice of religious toleration, and this ruling for the New Lanark community is interesting as showing Owen's earlier religious views. Rule 18 runs :

> As there are a very great variety of religious sects in the world (and which are probably adapted to different constitutions under different circumstances, seeing that there are many good and conscientious characters in each), it is particularly recommended as a means of uniting the inhabitants of the village that while each faithfully adheres to the principles which he most approves, at the same time all shall think charitably of their neighbours respecting their religious opinions, and not presumptuously suppose that theirs alone are right.[1]

A store was established, where goods, bought wholesale, were sold to the inhabitants at 25 per cent. below ordinary

---

[1] *The New Existence of Man upon the Earth,* appendix to Part V, Rule 18.

retail prices, a first attempt at the co-operative principle later to be developed upon a vast scale; and in this store spirit was wisely sold, in order to prevent recourse to the gin shops of New Lanark. A savings-bank was erected to receive the fruits of thrift and self-control; and the people were persuaded to safeguard themselves against sickness and old age by contributing one-sixtieth of their wages to a Benefit Society, and to make subscriptions towards ultimate admission to an old-age hospital, situated in the pleasantest part of the village. All this was not gained without opposition from the inhabitants. "Him and his English havers," grumbled the suspicious Scotch; but Owen gradually gained their confidence. During the United States' embargo on British cotton in 1806 he paid out £7000 in wages to his idle operatives while other employers were turning their surplus hands adrift; and after this there was no more trouble, the villagers willingly co-operating in his schemes for their betterment.

A local government committee, chosen from the workers, met the resident partner every month to report, to suggest improvements, and to adjudicate complaints. In the mills themselves no more pauper children were employed, and the age for employment was raised to ten; while the hours of work were ultimately reduced, in spite of opposition from Owen's partners, from Dale's $11\frac{3}{4}$ to $10\frac{3}{4}$ (exclusive of meals). Weekly wages remained the same in spite of this reduction of hours, but as most of the work at New Lanark was piece-work the operatives might therefore have lost by a decrease of time, were it not for the fact that production actually increased as the result of the lesser strain and the improved conditions. Good conduct and industry were assured, not, as under the old system, by the fear of punishment or dismissal, but by appealing to the self-respect and pride of the worker. A coloured block, indicative of the standard of his conduct, was hung publicly over each man's head, and by this means, without a word of praise or blame, but merely by a look, Owen produced a change in character which resulted from the development of man's inner qualities: " the pleasure of good conduct increased," and man was taught to realise his value in higher terms than mere money.

Novel as these experiments were, the most interesting exposition of Owen's views was in the sphere of education, a basic element in his environmental theory of the formation of character. " I know that society may be formed so as to exist without crime, without poverty, . . . and with intelligence increased a hundredfold," he said, " and no obstacle whatever intervenes at this moment except ignorance to prevent it."[1] He had always shown a practical interest in the existing educational system, then under the *régime* of Bell and Lancaster, but both these systems had grave defects in his eyes, though he supported both financially. Bell's education was strictly sectarian, and he refused, even with the bribe of an increased subscription from Owen, to open his schools to Dissent. Lancaster's scheme favoured the monitorial system. This, involving the rapid mass-education of the younger by the older children, merely crammed the child's mind with ill-digested facts, probably not understood by those who taught them, burdening the memory without developing the mental qualities. Owen, in his own system, put into practice at New Lanark, made three fundamental departures from the existing English system of education, and each, a permanent contribution to educational science, was the direct result of his principles concerning the formation of character. It was not until some years afterwards that he visited the Continental schools of Pestalozzi, Fellenberg, and Oberlin, conducted upon methods akin to those he himself had evolved; it is doubtful whether he had ever read Rousseau, and his views were almost certainly, in spite of their resemblance to those of other theorists, the independent product of his own mind. In the first place, his education was non-sectarian and universally compulsory. In the second place, it was to start at an earlier age; Owen held that the period of greatest malleability was in the first two years of life, and he was therefore the founder of the infant school in England. In the third place, he

---

[1] *A New View of Society*, " Address to the Inhabitants of New Lanark," p. 106.

made a development in the theory and technique of instruction:

> Reading and writing are merely instruments by which knowledge, either true or false, may be imparted, and when given to children are of little comparative value, unless they are also taught how to make a proper use of them.[1]

Acting upon this oft-obscured distinction between the way to knowledge and knowledge itself, Owen aimed at substituting for the mere cramming of the memory with facts a method which would give the mind a permanent equipment to use and interpret such facts. For, according to his view, the function of education was to form the brain into a reliable steering-gear in the situations and problems of after-life.

Owen's school was therefore described as the " Institute for the Formation of Character." It was divided into the infant school, where about 274 children up to ten years of age were taught, and the evening school, where some 485 workers from ten years upwards came for instruction when the day's work was over : the infant school was free, but in the evening school a charge of 3d. a week was made, " on account of the Scot's aversion to charity." There was also an area serving as a *crèche*, where children could be sent as soon as they could walk, while their parents were at the mills. Here they played under supervision and were taught the first rudiments of a correct formation of character—namely, that they should never injure their playfellows, but do all in their power to make them happy.[2] The methods of the infant school are worth brief notice. Much depended on the personality of the teachers, who were chosen for their personal qualities rather than for their learning. Molly Young was a seventeen-year-old mill-hand, and James Buchanan a middle-aged operative who had been " previously trained by his wife to perfect submission to her will." [3] Discipline obviously was to be maintained by personal influence rather than by reward

---

[1] *A New View of Society*, fourth essay, p. 74.
[2] *Ibid.*, third essay, p. 40.   [3] *Autobiography*, p. 139.

and punishment; the children being brought to see that their own interests lay in the maintenance of pleasantness and order. No lesson was to be more than three-quarters of an hour in length, to avoid weariness and consequent disgust with learning. Parrot-learning was strenuously avoided: the child was questioned on what he read in order to develop a faculty for analysis and penetration rather than the blind acceptance of facts as they stood. For the same reason copybooks were shunned, on account of the trite platitudes they impressed upon the memory. The teaching method was founded on the system of sense-impression practised on the Continent by Pestalozzi. All truths were illustrated in concrete and visible form, rather than learned from the symbols of the printed page. " With these infants everything was made to be amusement." [1] In arithmetic the effects of addition and subtraction were clearly shown by a table representing each unit by a line; similarly fractions were represented by divided squares. In geography maps, charts, and models were used, and the fundamental lesson of environment pushed home by explaining to the children, after showing them pictures of the inhabitants of other countries, that they would have been like them had they been born into the same circumstances. Even grammar was given pictorial life by personifying the parts of speech as soldiers, their relative importance in the sentence being shown by their position in the military hierarchy—as, for instance, General Noun, Colonel Verb, Corporal Adverb. Historical study gained concrete illustration by the use of a chart representing seven rivers, one for each of the main countries, with the events marked upon each stream and the whole divided by vertical lines to mark the centuries. In this way the child could see chronological relativity and general movements at a glance, and did not keep the history of his country in a watertight compartment, and learn a narrow, sectional patriotism. Owen laid great emphasis upon the true historical sense as an educative force for the child. " By these means," he wrote,

[1] *Autobiography*, p. 140.

he will early learn what he is in relation to past ages, to the period in which he lives, to the circumstances in which he is placed, to the individuals around him, and to future events; he will then only have any pretensions to the name of a rational being.[1]

This was the system at New Lanark, the concrete illustration of Owen's theories on the formation of character. The experiment showed the possibility of producing great wealth without injury to the human element; the happiness and intelligence of the children showed the formative effects of a careful training from infancy; the village showed the effect of a bettered environment even upon the hardened adult character. Thousands of visitors of all sects, religions, and parties came to New Lanark, and went away impressed by the success of this model establishment. The Duke of Kent, Dr Sutton, Archbishop of Canterbury, Richard Oastler, the factory reformer, and the Grand Duke Nicholas of Russia were among the converts. In 1813, however, Owen had propagated his views to an even wider public by the publication of his *New View of Society: Four Essays on the Formation of Character*. These were sent to the crowned heads of Europe and all leading statesmen, while copies were circulated in the United States, many being provided with plain leaves, inviting comment and criticism. The first three essays merely explained the theory of the New View, on the lines already indicated—that " man's character is formed for and not by him," and that there was therefore no rational excuse for enmity or blame. The fourth presents a constructive programme for carrying the theory into effect. All religious tests were to be abolished—that is, " declarations of belief in which all cannot conscientiously join," [2] and the Church, thus purged of its errors, put at the head of the reform movement. All obvious temptations to vice, such as pot-houses and state lotteries, were to be abolished, for, by these, tendencies which might develop into punishable crimes were illogically encouraged by the State itself. The existing

[1] *A New View of Society*, " Report to the County of Lanark," p. 284.
[2] *Ibid.*, fourth essay, p. 67.

Poor Law was to be repealed, as a similar source of crime and encouragement of pauperism. A bureau was to be established in each district to provide quarterly statistics of labour. Finally a national system of compulsory education was advocated, on the lines of that at New Lanark.

Opposition to Owen's views came not from the Government, but from his own partners, on grounds first of commercial greed, and later of religious prejudice. His first group of partners were of the class whom Owen describes as those "in whose estimation to forsake the path of immediate individual gain would be to show symptoms of a disordered imagination."[1] In 1809 they grumbled at the alleged financial loss resulting from the application of profits to improvements instead of to their own pockets. Owen admittedly regarded the undertaking as "an experiment for the benefit of the world, as much as for cotton-spinning." He therefore, in 1809, bought out the New Lanark Twist Company for £84,000 and formed the New Lanark Company with Messrs Campbell and Atkinson. They, in 1813, made the same complaints, and a fresh partnership was formed, the mills being bought this time for £114,000.[2] The new partners included Jeremy Bentham, the Utilitarian, whose views on the functions of government were akin to Owen's,[3] and several noted Quakers, William Allen, John Walker, Joseph Fox, and others. These, though not devoid of commercial motives, attacked primarily from the religious point of view. The basic principle of non-sectarianism was distasteful; the Highland dress of the children was considered indecent; the drilling was offensive to pacifist tendencies, and any type of secular song discouraged in favour of "psalmody." Owen was obliged to introduce modifications in accordance with these opinions in 1824; and James Buchanan was dismissed, going to teach at the infant school set up by Henry

[1] *A New View of Society*, third essay, p. 61.

[2] Note the increase in value.

[3] "That government then is the best which in practice produces the greatest happiness to the greatest number "—*A New View of Society*, fourth essay, p. 63.

96

Brougham at Westminster. The educational experiment then bore fruit elsewhere, and Samuel Wilderspin founded the London Infant School Society at Spitalfields in the same year.

New Lanark had made Owen a public figure not merely in the manufacturing, but in the political world; and he came prominently forward in the Government schemes for dealing with the crisis following upon the Treaty of Paris in 1815. In this year there was necessity for reconstruction in every branch of economic life. The coming of peace ended the artificial conditions which, for the past twenty-three years, had caused a false view of the effects of the Industrial Revolution. Owen's first sphere of governmental action was to voice the appeal of the Glasgow manufacturers for the abolition of the import duty on raw cotton, which, he pointed out, was simply a bounty for the foreign producer, now that foreign competition was released with the coming of a normal *régime*. This end was gained in the abrogation of all but a nominal tax by Vansittart. This was the first step towards the downfall of the Protective system. Owen attached to his demands, however, an appeal for general factory reform. So far the only national factory legislation was the Health and Morals of Apprentices Act, passed in 1802, applying only to a limited class, and left to the unpaid administration of the interested local J.P.s. Owen's suggestions formed the basis of the first general Factory Act, entrusted to the charge of Sir Robert Peel, to raise the age of employment to twelve, with an educational test before admission, to reduce the hours for "young persons" to $10\frac{1}{2}$ a day (exclusive of meals), to obviate night work, and to appoint paid inspectors for the administration of the Act. In its support Owen made his famous denunciation of the accepted aristocratic standards. "Perish the cotton trade, perish even the political superiority of our country (if it depends on the cotton trade) rather than they shall be upheld by the sacrifice of everything valuable in life by those who are the means of supporting them." [1] This speech implies what Owen unfortunately nowhere

[1] Observations on the cotton trade, *Autobiography*, Appendix F, p. 18.

directly stated, that the country was, in the wide view, eating up its capital blindly and disastrously at the very moment when it imagined the greatest profits were being made. For the industrialists were killing the next generations, exhausting their working power and destroying their brain-power, mortgaging the future for the sake of immediate returns. But the manufacturing world remained complacently and dangerously ignorant of this aspect of Owen's teaching. Opposition to the Bill from self-interested sources was acute, and Peel was all too sensitive to it. The inspectors were offensive as paid spies " upon a class necessary to the prosperity of the country "; it was stated that England's monopoly of foreign markets would be threatened by a reduction of hours, and that wages would decrease for the same cause and the Poor Law increase. Owen unfortunately provided nothing to support his contention that production would increase owing to improved conditions. To these arguments was added false statistical evidence to refute the facts upon which the Bill was based, and the Manchester manufacturers proved that the deaths in the then system were only two in a thousand; and that of 4938 employees only eighty were under the age of nine.[1] The attack was further supported by scandal-hunting at New Lanark, to diminish Owen's influence with the Government. Here the manufacturers found a ready tool in " the Rev. Mr Menzies " (offended by Owen's negligence of sectarian persons and principles), who " had preached in and presided over the town of Lanark for twenty years; and there was no perceptible change for the better among his parishioners."[2] When the Bill became law in 1819 it was shorn of most of its good points. It was to apply only to the cotton-mills, the age of employment was raised to nine, not twelve, and the " young persons " class ceased at the age of sixteen instead of eighteen. But though the result fell short of the hope, a principle was nevertheless established. A wedge was thrust into industrial *laissez-faire*. The foundations were laid upon which national control of economic con-

[1] Hansard, April 3, 1816.   [2] *Autobiography*, p. 117.

ditions was built up. The State had been induced to take official cognisance of its working classes, and aristocracy and exploitation were challenged.

In another sphere also Owen's governmental action had important results—namely, in the Poor Law problem. On the signing of peace came the slump, and the consequent unemployment made clear the real effects of the introduction of machinery. Driven from industry, driven from the land, or returning from the wars, there seemed no hope for humanity in the early years of the nineteenth century. The Corn Laws, restraining foreign import in the interests of the landed Tories, kept food-prices at an artificial height. Population, stimulated by the Poor Law, threatened to outrun the means of subsistence, and Malthus propounded his theories for the suppression of the redundant lower classes; while the abject poverty gave rise to Ricardo's Iron Law of Wages. Discontent and occasional rioting and machine-breaking was met by the suspension of Habeas Corpus, and finally by the Peterloo massacre of 1819. The reaction was at its height. In 1817 Owen put forward a plan for the consideration of the Commission on the Administration of the Poor Law. This programme was directly opposed to the hopeless view taken by the economists. Far from suppressing the poor, he argued that work, not dependent on the fluctuations of the market, could be found for all the unemployed. This was to be accomplished by their organisation in communities, consisting of from 500 to 1500 persons, with surrounding land, on the model of the New Lanark establishment. Here they would be enabled to work for their own subsistence, sell their surplus produce, and at the same time be educated towards a right formation of character. By his advocacy of a Labour Bureau, providing statistics of available work, he evidently intended the communities to be a temporary expedient to meet a particular crisis, and to drain off the members in process of time to ordinary work.[1] The plan was rejected on account of its expense, for the cost of a single community was estimated

---

[1] Owen's plan was almost identical with that for the unemployed community recently founded at Blackborough, Devon.

at £96,000. But it obtained wide support, in particular from Ricardo, Archbishop Sutton, Liverpool, and Peel.

At this time Owen was at the height of his power, both as a Scottish manufacturer and as a figure in national politics ; and he was well known internationally. Some analysis of his theories may now be attempted. Owen has been doubly unfortunate. On the one hand, political and sentimental bias has worshipped him as the founder of socialism and co-operation, and refused to see either the defects of his thinking or his incapacity in the sphere of practical politics. This has inevitably led to a reaction ; and on the other hand are those who condemn him as a visionary—a madman and advocate of a pernicious philosophy of fatalism. The truth, as usual, lies between the two. And in the attempt to present a fair analysis of Owen's essential social thought may be seen my previous insistence upon the examination of his theories in their concrete setting. For Owen " was not in any true sense of the word a student," his son writes.

> One who had made his own way in life, unaided by a single dollar from the age of ten, could not well be. I never found in his extensive library a book with a marginal note, or even a pencil mark of his. . . . Except for statistical works, . . . I never remember to have seen him occupied in taking notes from any book whatever.[1]

Owen's lack of early training affected considerably his power of exposition. He had no analytical faculty, and no power of scholarly presentment. Above all, he never defined his terms, that first essential of clear thinking ; and as a result an analysis of the theories as they were actually written is almost bound to be a misrepresentation of his real intentions. One is never certain what Owen really meant. His written work is a mass of sweeping, unqualified statements, and their logical implications he never saw. He generalised widely from particular instances, and he seldom backed up his statements with statistical or analytical proof for the satisfaction of his readers. His views were enforced more by sheer repetition than by the conviction of his public by scholarly explanation, and with

[1] *Threading my Way*, p. 67.

each repetition his opinions became more dogmatic, more of a mechanical formula or philosophy, more of a departure from his original empirical ideas and experiments. All these defects laid Owen open to misrepresentation and misinterpretation, and gave a loophole for the opposition of the self-interested classes to his practical schemes for social reform. The most common criticisms of Owen's doctrines are three. The first is that his basic hypothesis, that man's character is formed for and not by him, deprived man of free will, and was a creed of necessarianism offensive to God and humanity. The second arises naturally from this; if by his own showing man was deprived of the power of choice it was illogical for Owen himself to claim the possibility of exercising over the conditions of life a control which could only be illusory.

> Can Mr Owen show us how irrational circumstances have made himself a rational being? If it be true that Mr Owen is a rational being as the effect of the operation of irrational circumstances, it appears to me expressly to contradict his first principle.[1]
> Mr Owen cannot explain to us consistently with his scheme . . . how, . . . out of the rubbish of the old irrational world, he sprang up so beautifully rational.[2]

The third criticism is that Owen's theory of environmental influence was an incomplete determinism, an anticipation of Marxian doctrines; for he omitted, it is said, to give due weight to heredity and to spiritual influences in his estimate of the forces forming character.

Of these attacks the first two, based on the assumption that Owen's theories necessarily involved denial of free will, may, I think, be modified by an analysis of his writing in the light of his practice. Both statements appear reasonable inferences from Owen's insistence that man's character is formed for and not by him, and upon his consequent irresponsibility. But it seems evident that Owen in his vigorous manhood never intended to propound a doctrine of fatalism in the sense of an abstract philosophical system.

[1] *Public Discussion between R. Owen and the Rev. J. H. Roebuck*, p. 22.
[2] *Ibid.*, p. 57.

Owen was no philosopher ; he was simply stating an empirical theory of social and biological influence upon character,
and insisting upon its realisation as a root cause of the evils
of nineteenth-century society. When he inferred that man's
character was formed for him he at first meant it in no
abstract philosophical sense. In his " Second Memorial to
the Governments of Europe and America "[1] he defines the
" circumstances " which he considers to form character—
defines them as six concrete factors—religion, sect, country,
language, class, and parentage. These influences form the
" national or local character," " a six-fold barrier of error
and prejudice " impressed upon the helpless child, whom
Owen emphatically regarded as father of the man whose
character is formed for and not by him. This brings us
to another point. What did Owen really mean by " character "? For the most part in his earlier writings, before
in his old age he abandoned all the modifications of his
" doctrines," he seems to imply not the whole organised
self, including the will, but rather that " children are beings
whose dispositions, habits, and sentiments are to be formed
for them."[2] This narrowing down of the term ' character '
to mean feelings, convictions, and prejudices involves no
denial of free will, for the will is isolated. And the theory of
formation of character viewed in this way, as Owen seems
fundamentally to have intended it, leaves the individual free
to act or not to act in accordance with these feelings and
prejudices—it leaves room for a distinction between potential and actual. Notice how the system at New Lanark
expressly disproves the submergence of the individual in
its insistence upon the full development of mental capacities. Owen's description of Peel as a man " whose natural
talent with growing experience led him by degrees to overcome the many disadvantages of an Oxford formation of
character "[3] is scarcely the negation of free will. Notice
also that in many passages Owen insists upon the collective
application of his theory. "Children are . . . passive and

[1] *Autobiography*, Appendix O, p. 217.
[2] *A New View of Society*, "Report to the County of Lanark," p. 282.
[3] *Autobiography*, p. 214.

wonderfully contrived compounds, which . . . may be formed collectively to have any human character " ; [1] again, " the old, collectively, may train the young, collectively, to be ignorant and miserable, or to be intelligent and happy." [2] Any *general* character, in short, may be given to a community " by means which are to a great extent at the command and under the control of those who have influence in the affairs of men." [3] By providing the right environment and instruction a society could acquire, without moulding its individuals to one helpless pattern, certain general characteristics such as reason, charity, and intelligence. Thus far most thoughtful people would agree unhesitatingly with Owen. At times, however, and especially in his old age, he included the ' will ' among the individual attributes moulded by forces outside individual control. Upon this point he became increasingly dogmatic as the years went on, and by 1830 he is *stating* uncompromisingly, whatever may have been his analysed sentiments on the subject, that

> Man is compelled to receive his feelings and convictions independent of his will : his feelings or his convictions, or both of them united, create the motive to action called the will, which stimulates him to act and decides his actions ; and thus man's whole character, physical, mental, and moral, is formed independent of himself. [4]

How much influence, then, in this determinism did Owen allocate to forces other than environmental in the formation of character? The third criticism of Owen's thinking is that not sufficient emphasis was placed on heredity and religion as a controlling factor, and this criticism bears directly upon this point. Certainly Owen stressed the economic and external factors, for these were more easy of control ; but he was far from thinking with his contemporary Godwin that the child's mind could be regarded

---

[1] *A New View of Society*, second essay, p. 22.
[2] *Ibid.*, fourth essay, p. 64.
[3] *Ibid.*, first essay, p. 16.
[4] *Outline of the Rational System of Society*, Appendix to Report of the Proceedings of the Festival in Commemoration of the Centenary Birthday, p. 30.

as *tabula rasa*, for the reception of external impression.
" Nature gave the qualities," though " society directed
them." Though the evolutionary theories of Darwin and
Lamarck were not at this time generally public, Owen is
quite clear that heredity had immense force. " The child is
formed by a double creation," he wrote, " the one previous
to birth, the other a secondary or new creation, chiefly
through the agency of matured humanity ";[1] man is a
compound being, whose character is formed by hereditary
influences, and by external circumstances acting upon it;
and Owen regarded it as his special mission to bring home
the importance of this " second creation " made possible
through the agency of man by creating new surroundings.
But the influence of heredity is not unrecognised. Again,
" children are born with certain faculties or qualities . . .
differing in each individual in strength and combination;
whatever these powers may be in each child, he could not
create the smallest part of them."[2] It is perhaps not
generally realised that the *Lectures on the Marriages of the
Priesthood*, published in 1835, was dictated in part by this
realisation of the effect of pre-natal circumstances upon the
child. Besides being an attack on the hierarchy and the
sects, it was also an inseparable part of his scheme for
social reconstruction, and should be considered as such.
Owen recognised the obvious fact that the sex-relationship
is the basis of society, and that this basis could never be
sound as long as it remained under the irrational control
of the Church. The " ascetic ideal " distorted man's view
of the natural, inculcating the idea that nature's means of
creation was antagonistic to religion and to God, instead of
seeking in it a sacrament in itself. The existing marriage
system was also based on irrational and false values. The
Church attempted to impose an arbitrary and indissoluble
union regardless of the motives of the persons concerned.
Marriages entered into for money, for social position,
economic security, or mere convenience, were dignified
with the ' sacramental ' tie of the Church, together with the
anathema upon the breaking of it. Even if the one great

[1] *Autobiography*, Preface, p. xliii.   [2] *Ibid.*, Appendix O, p. 216.

motive for marriage were present, to demand a marriage vow was to enforce a kind of perjury: for one could only pledge the action and not the spirit of the future, and the marriage vow of the Church imposed not only the promise of a concrete tie, but also the spiritual obligation to love and to honour *in perpetuum*: feelings which were outside man's control. The union could perhaps be maintained in the letter, but not always in the spirit, which is the essence of faithfulness; and to force people to live together hypocritically adhering to the form of marriage for fear of the censure of Church and society was forcing them to sin. In such an atmosphere children were born and brought up. Even in the most ideally affectionate marriage no care was taken to enforce any system of eugenics. People were allowed to marry who, for reasons of health, should not, though efforts were made to improve the breed even of the lower animals. Owen summed up his arguments as follows: "The priesthood [like the State] first adopt the most effective measures to create vice, and then turn round and say that men are bad by nature." He was not, however, advocating the abandonment of marriage and a career of free love, as his opponents wilfully misrepresented; for regulation, rather than licence, was obviously the essence of his ideas. Actually he wanted an improvement in the marriage system. Three months' public notice before marriage was advocated; then, if the parties found themselves unsuited, they could give notice of intended separation after a year of marriage, but were to continue to live together for a further six months before separating, in order to ensure that the disagreement was not merely of a temporary nature. Family life was, however, eventually to disappear, for at best it taught a narrow sectional loyalty, and was to merge in his plans for including the family group in the larger unit, the socialist community.

It was this series of lectures which aroused opposition to Owen to a climax, and brought about the Holy War of 1840, conducted by the "fighting Bishop" of Exeter, Phillpotts. But it is from his denunciation of the religions of the world, made in the City of London Tavern in 1817, that his unpopularity with the governing class must date, though the full effects of this unfortunate speech, which merely put into concrete form Owen's implied and inherent hostility to the Church, were deferred for some years. *The Times* and *The Morning Post* withdrew their support at once, but dislike was far from general, and at the actual meeting the attack on the fallacies of "religion" seems to have been received with enthusiasm; the borough of Lanark was actually kept open for Owen as Parliamentary candidate in 1819, and his *New View of Society* made a great impression when put before the Congress of Aix-la-Chapelle in 1818. What exactly was involved in the attack on the religions of the world? The question is of more than academic interest, for its decision gives us the extent to which Owen recognised a spiritual influence in the formation of character, and affects our view of his gospel of determinism. Here again, as in discussing his environmental views, we are confronted by a lack of definition. What exactly did Owen mean by "religion"? It seems clear that when he denounced religions as causing most of the misery of the world he never intended to strike at "true religion," but only at the contemporary identification of it, and of love for the Godhead, with the Churches, as institutions, dogmas, and hierarchies, fettering private judgment and religious liberty.[1]

> I am not going to deprive you of religion, but only of its errors. For true religion can alone create and secure permanently the goodness, wisdom, . . . and everlasting happiness of man. . . . What is this true religion? It is the essence of all your religions freed from the garbage with which man . . . has more or less surrounded the modicum of truth in each, . . . the spirit of pure, undefiled, universal love and charity for man, . . . and of love for that energy and power which composes, decomposes, and re-composes perpetually the elements of the universe, and which is called God.[2]

Owen, therefore, might perhaps be considered an agnostic, but he was certainly no atheist; he acknowledged a principle

---

[1] *New View of Society*, "Address to the Inhabitants of New Lanark," p. 100.
[2] *Autobiography*, pp. 209–10.

behind the universe, but denied man's present power to plumb the depths of its nature in the complacent manner claimed by the Church. Worship of the unknown was irrational, and true religion in the rational system of society consisted in the service of truth, charity to one's fellow-men, and obedience to the laws of nature. There is no place for a personal God in his system. He seems to identify God with truth and nature. His religious system was ethical merely, and, though he gave to the world a better code of ethics than that inculcated by the Church, his theories left no room for the influence of a personal God in the formation of character. The denunciation came at an unfortunate moment, when, in the height of the reaction of 1815-19, the governing classes were insanely suspicious of anything subversive of the existing system. Nevertheless Owen's declining influence after 1817 is due as much to the visionary nature of his practical plans as to the denunciation. The courage required for the denunciation seems to have acted as a gradual solvent for all the unpractical, visionary, and prophetic elements in his character. It is thus to be regarded as important less in itself than as exemplifying a mental change. After 1817, though yet under fifty, Owen suddenly seems senile. He ceases to be the practical business man; he casts aside constitutional methods, and gradually loses root in reality. Impatient for the immediate realisation of the millennium, he lost sight of the slow and careful *means* in his high enthusiasm for the far-off *end*. Public opinion, even if not ultimately prejudiced by the propaganda of the self-interested classes, could not airily leap over the concrete obstacles in the way of the Kingdom of God; and from now onwards Owen as a practical proposition cannot be taken seriously, though his principles and his inspiration remained the guiding light for those pursuing the policy of reconstruction.

In the same year as the denunciation, in a letter to *The Times*, he asked for the immediate formation of socialist communities on the lines of those advocated for the unemployed; but this time to consist of all classes and conditions, rich and poor. It was the first step in the millennium; the communal education of the people in the right principles of governing society. These communities were to cultivate the soil by the spade, and not by the plough, on the model of the experiments of Mr Falla at Newcastle. There was to be no cash standard, but only a labour standard; each member receiving notes on the communal store to the extent of his week's labour. In 1821 Owen presented his report to the county of Lanark on these lines; it was rejected. From this time Owen ceased altogether to be the manufacturer, working for the betterment of working conditions, the solution of specific national problems, and became an eccentric social philanthropist, gradually deserted by the more practical-minded of his disciples. Communities were started at once, under the inspiration of *The Economist*, Owen's journal. Owing to the enthusiasm of Abram Combe, who started a communistic profit-sharing experiment in his own tanyard, a community was begun at Motherwell in 1822, and James Hamilton of Dalzell promoted the Orbiston community in 1825, while a third attempt was made at Queenwood, Hampshire, in 1839. Meantime Owen had gone to the United States to try the plan on new soil, away from the hampering conditions of the old country. New Harmony was founded in 1825, and another attempt was made in Texas, but the Mexican Government refused to pass the Act of Toleration necessary for its establishment.

These communities were founded on the ideas of John Bellers' *Colledge of Industry* (seventeenth century) and on the Shaker and Rappite communities and Spencean Clubs of Owen's own day; but the programme was subject to the gravest economic and psychological objections, of which Owen showed a childish disregard. It was impossible to allow, as he did, the unrestricted growth of population: any but a celibate community would inevitably outrun its means of subsistence. Then there was the expense of a self-sufficing society not subject to the influence of competition. It cost 7s. 1d. to support an adult community member who did not find his own roof, taxes, or support for wife and family; but Owen argued that the ordinary labourer who did all this was paid 8s. a week, and that community membership effected a saving of 11d.! The inhabitants obviously worked only enough for their own support, and supplied no surplus for public burdens, such as taxation, so that the communities were invariably in debt. The spade husbandry was the application of a system which worked under specific conditions to general purposes, where the soil, drainage, and climate were not the same. The labour standard involved the extreme difficulty of the reduction of all types of work involving different payments and different stages of exhaustion to a single unit; and the skilled workers naturally objected to the levelling of their labour to the same unit as the unskilled. Throughout, the communities founded on the Owen system failed owing to this opposition of the inhabitants themselves to any abrogation of their individual rights. And, as the socialists themselves acknowledged, " it would be a poor excuse for failure to urge that the subjects of our experiments were ignorant, poor, and vicious ; for we set out to overcome ignorance, poverty, and vice." [1] The later socialists used Owen's diagnosis of the evils of society, but were bound to apply different remedies, in particular organised political action through the party system; and infinitely more important than these schemes was the work of those Owenites who had already broken from the practical connection with their master, and were applying his principles under his inspiration, indeed, but away from the bad business effects of his unanalytical mind. Co-operative societies, born of the New Lanark store, sprang up all over England while Owen was in the States. The London Co-operative Society was founded in 1824, and by 1830 there were three hundred societies, holding the first Co-operative Congress in 1831. At first it was intended to apply the middleman's profits thus saved the members to the foundation of socialist communities. This idea is found in William Thompson's book *Directions for the Speedy and Economical Establishment of Communities.* Unpractical though the community scheme was proved, yet in this decision was involved a realisation of another of

[1] Alex. Cullen, *Adventures in Socialism.*

Owen's fundamental mistakes—namely, his upper-class paternalism. All his measures and experiments were patronised ideas, the capital provided from above. The Co-operators saw that the workers must not depend on patronage, but work out their own salvation; and this led to the inevitable application of economic societies to political ends. The repeal of the Combination Laws in 1824 led to the rapid development of trade unions under Francis Place and Cobbett; and in the general disappointment at the failure of the Reform Act of 1832 to enfranchise the lower classes these unions turned to political agitation. On his return from America in 1829 Owen, deserted by the upper classes, and denounced as an atheist and subverter of the social order, unexpectedly found himself hailed as leader of this working-class movement. He was, however, utterly incapable of grappling with the situation. His great venture was the Grand National Consolidated Trades Union, with its newspapers, *The Crisis* (edited by J. E. Smith) and *The Pioneer* (edited by J. Morrison). The attempt at general union ended with the transportation of the five Dorsetshire labourers in 1834, and trade unions and co-operative societies went down in the crash of the Grand National Consolidated Trades Union. Owen took no further part in governmental action, or in the association of socialists with the Chartist movement; though to the unfortunate agitation which he set on foot for an eight-hour day is certainly due the failure of Richard Oastler's ten-hour movement in 1834. Owen could never accept the millennium in instalments or work through the machinery of the existing system. It was no use, he argued, agitating for an extension of the franchise which, in the lack of good character under the present *régime*, would merely result in more uneducated and uncharitable voters. Similarly he had no interest in money and financial technique, since coinage as a medium of exchange would not be used in his New Society. The old methods must be abrogated, not used and perpetuated. After 1834 " Owenism " became the name for a sect of " Rational Religionists," who proclaimed in their journal, *The New*

ROBERT OWEN

Moral World, the immediate reconstruction of society by a moral revolution in humanity. Owen himself died, a convert to Spiritualism, in 1858.

What just estimate is possible of this amazing man? One thing is certain, that Owen was neither saint nor sinner. In his first years he did much good ; he laid the foundations of national factory legislation, national care of the poor, and national supervision of a new system of education. In his last years he undoubtedly did much mischief to the cause he had at heart, and it was at the price of a breach with Owen that his disciples saved his principles for the world by bringing them into the sphere of earthly accomplishment. For the co-operative and socialist movements as working propositions the credit belongs to others. Yet Owen is not to be judged by what he did, but for the abstract principles which he laid down. Not that he enunciated anything new. His gospel of benevolence and brotherhood, his insistence upon the equality of man, were as old as God Himself. But the truth needed re-emphasising, for the current thought of the eighteenth century had forgotten it. It is the work of many thinkers simply to adjust the contemporary emphasis on the fundamental truths of life, to restore the balance and perspective of contemporary thought by concentrating on one particular aspect of the ultimate ideal. If Owen in the end lost touch with the real, and at the end of his life was blinded and dazzled by his ideal, it does not detract from his true importance. He found the nightmare of a machine-run universe, a Juggernaut car crushing the poor beyond apparent hope of redemption. He ended that nightmare. For, from the welter of misery, exploitation, and stark despair, he held out to the world a new conception of human worth and human destiny.

FRANCES M. PAGE

THINKERS OF THE AGE OF REACTION

BOOK LIST

A. Primary Authorities

A New View of Society (Everyman edition), including (*a*) "Four Essays on the Formation of Character" (1813–14), (*b*) "Observations on the Effects of the Manufacturing System" (1815), (*c*) "Address to the Inhabitants of New Lanark" (1816), (*d*) "Report to the Committee of the Association for the Relief of the Manufacturing and Labouring Poor" (1817), (*e*) "A Catechism of the New View of Society and three Addresses" (1817), (*f*) "A Further Development of the Plan for the Relief of the Poor and the Emancipation of Mankind" (1817), (*g*) "On the Employment of Children in Manufactories" (1818), (*h*) "Address to the British Master Manufacturers" (1818), (*i*) "Address to the Working Classes" (1819), (*j*) "Report to the County of Lanark" (1821).

The Rational System of Society. 1830.
Lectures on the Marriages of the Priesthood. 1835.
The Book of the New Moral World, Part 1, 1836; Parts 2 and 3, 1844.
The New Existence of Man upon the Earth. 1854.
Autobiography. 1857.

B. Secondary Authorities

Public Discussion between Robert Owen and the Rev. J. H. Roebuck. 1837
Public Discussion between Robert Owen and John Brindley. 1841.
The Orbiston Register.
The New Harmony Gazette.
The Co-operative Magazine. The British Co-operator. The Co-operative Miscellany. The Economist.
Owen, Robert Dale: *Threading my Way.* 1874.
Podmore, F.: *Robert Owen.* 1906.
Cole, G. D. H.: *Robert Owen.* 1925.
Cullen, A.: *Adventures in Socialism.* 1910.

VI

JOHN STUART MILL AND THE
PHILOSOPHICAL RADICALS

IT is difficult for us to realise the dominating and wide-spread influence of Mill in the England of the middle of the nineteenth century. From the publication of his *Logic* in 1843 and his *Principles of Political Economy* in 1848, he held almost undisputed sway for some forty years. Lord Morley, writing in 1873, bears testimony to his influence in Oxford: " For twenty years no one at all open to serious intellectual impressions has left Oxford without having undergone the influence of Mill's teaching."[1] Lord Oxford says: " When I went to Oxford in 1870 his influence was still predominant, though it was being slowly undermined."[2] Lord Balfour, writing of Cambridge a little earlier, considers that " Mill possessed an authority in the English universities comparable to that exerted by Hegel in Germany forty years earlier, and in the Middle Ages by Aristotle."[3] Professor Marshall tells us that he was led to study economics by reading the *Political Economy* in 1867, " when Mill reigned supreme." As a systematic text-book Mill's *Political Economy* was not superseded till Marshall's own *Principles* appeared in 1890, and it was still necessary to know Mill in the nineties, when the writer read moral science at Cambridge. Fifty years is a long life for a text-book. Lord Morley suggests that the mid-nineteenth-century journalists took their ideas from Mill and their style from Macaulay. " Mill taught some to reason, Macaulay taught more to declaim." Yet Mill's influence on thought, great though it was at the time, is now considered to have been transitional and

[1] *Miscellanies*, vol. iii, p. 39.   [2] *Victorian Age*, p. 16.
[3] *Theism and Humanism*, p. 138.

temporary. He inherited the ideas of Jeremy Bentham, of his father, James Mill, of Ricardo and Malthus, and gave the final expression to them—an expression that completed one epoch and inaugurated another. As a child he was steeped in the ideas of the eighteenth century, as a young man he absorbed eagerly the ideas of the nineteenth, but he never really broke with his inherited faith— never entered into the promised land. It was his modest boast that he was always learning, but he did not co-ordinate the old and the new. The result was not fusion, but confusion. He added new floors to the structure, but weakened the foundations. This lack of unity and consistency destroyed his permanent influence.

II

John Stuart Mill was born on May 20, 1806, the eldest child of James Mill, the friend and disciple of Jeremy Bentham. Bentham (1748–1832) was the great formulator of what is called the Utilitarian philosophy. He taught that legislation and morals should aim at happiness, " the greatest happiness of the greatest number "—" each to count for one and not more than one." He begins his great book *Principles of Morals and Legislation*, published in 1789, with these words: " Nature has placed man under the governance of two sovereign masters, *pain* and *pleasure*. It is for them alone to point out what we ought to do, as well as to determine what we shall do." " Bentham," says Professor Dicey,

> was primarily neither a Utilitarian moralist nor a philanthropist; he was a legal philospher and a reformer of the law. The object of his lifelong labours was to remodel the law of England in accordance with Utilitarian principles. These labours were crowned by extraordinary success, though the success was most manifest after the end of his life—in 1832. He was in very truth the first and greatest of legal philosophers.[1]

His " principle of utility " dominated English legislation for half a century. He and James Mill applied this prin-

[1] *Law and Opinion in England*, pp. 126–133.

ciple to ethics, economics, and politics. They assumed that men desired pleasure only, and asserted that those actions were right which brought pleasure or happiness, and those wrong which brought pain. They overrated self-interest and reason, they underrated the emotional and æsthetic side of life. They were very clear, definite, and powerful thinkers, but they took a narrow and limited view of human nature, and overlooked the complexity of life. They recognised but one motive, self-interest, and considered that each man was the best judge of his own interest. Hence Governmental interference should be reduced to the minimum, and legislation should aim at the removal of all those restrictions on the free action of individuals which are not necessary for securing the like freedom of others. They contended that mind was merely a bundle of sensations, and character the result of circumstances. Hence they expected too much of education. In politics they had an almost unbounded confidence in the efficacy of two things—representative government and complete freedom of discussion. " So complete," says J. S. Mill in his *Autobiography*,

> was my father's reliance on the influence of reason over the minds of mankind, that he felt as if all would be gained if the whole population were taught to read, if all sorts of opinions were allowed to be addressed to them by word and in writing, and if, by means of the suffrage, they could nominate a legislature to give effect to the opinions they adopted.

Mill and Bentham entered into a compact to educate the infant John to be the apostle of their own teaching. It was the most astounding education on record. James Mill was a hard, austere, and imperious character, " with the temperament of the Scotch Covenanter of the seventeenth century, inspired with the philosophy of eighteenth-century France." [1] He set himself, with maximum labour but minimum patience (" He was one of the most impatient of men," says John), to save twenty-five years in John's education. He succeeded, but it was a dreadful

[1] Lord Morley, *Miscellanies*, vol. iii, p. 66.

experiment. John must have begun to read at two years of age. Greek was begun at three, and by the time he was eight he had read many Greek authors, including six of Plato's dialogues—which he could not possibly have understood. He pathetically remarks, " My father demanded of me not only the utmost that I could do, but much that I could by no possibility have done." Along with Greek he took arithmetic and history in an astonishing range (including Hume, Gibbon, Robertson, and Burnet), which he recounted to his father on their daily walks. At eight he began Latin, which he taught to the younger children. From eight to twelve, in addition to the classics, he took mathematics to the differential calculus, English literature, and chemistry. At twelve he attacked moral science, with logic and political economy. He had no holidays, no games, knew no other boys, and doubtless became a conceited prig. He later said to Miss Fox, " I never was a boy, never played cricket. It is better to let Nature have her way." Francis Place visited the family and said, " John is a prodigy, but I am afraid he will grow up morose and selfish." He did not do so, but it is a miracle that he escaped. The wonder is that he did not break under the strain of over-developed intellect, starved emotions, and repressed instincts. The strength and nobility of his character pulled him through. At fourteen his formal education was complete. It was not mere cram. He was taught to think, to analyse, to criticise. " My father," he says, " was often, and much beyond reason, provoked by my failures in cases where success could not have been expected, but in the main his method was right, and it succeeded." [1] " A pupil from whom nothing is demanded which he cannot do never does all he can." [2] In 1820 (when he was fourteen) he went to the South of France for a year on a visit to Sir Samuel Bentham, brother of Jeremy Bentham. There he studied French literature, enjoyed social life, enthusiastically cultivated botany, and was deeply impressed by the beauties of nature and the magnificent scenery of the Pyrenees. His education has been irreve-

[1] *Autobiography*, p. 17.   [2] *Ibid.*, p. 19.

rently described in some verses by my undergraduate son
and daughter, which I venture to quote :

> O woes innumerable that spring from over-education;
> Of this my subject would appear the aptest illustration.
> Son of a most inhuman Pa, he started Greek at three ;
> At eight he turned to Latin, which he taught the family,
> And occupied his leisure by reading Gibbon's *Rome*,
> On which his father questioned him, while wandering round
> their home.

> His father was agnostic, the son, of course, the same,
> So Logic was the goddess, and Psychology the flame.
> Political Economy at thirteen was begun,
> About which time the father gave a free hand to the son,
> Who forthwith took a holiday in France's sunny parts,
> Where he broadened his horizon with Botany and Arts.

On his return he resumed his studies. He read psychology and philosophy by himself and Roman law with
John Austin—an ardent Benthamite. He had imbibed
Bentham's principles from his father, Dumont, and from
Bentham himself, and he now found the " principle of
utility " the keystone of his beliefs. " I now had a creed,
a doctrine, a philosophy, a religion, the inculcation and
diffusion of which would be made the principal outward
purpose of my life." [1] At sixteen he began to write for
the Press, and to form friendships. He already knew
Bentham, Ricardo, and Hume, his father's friends. He
became intimate with George Grote, John and Charles
Austin, through whom he met Macaulay, Hyde, and
Charles Villiers, and other Cambridge men. In 1822
Mill visited Charles Austin at Cambridge, and had great
discussions with the Macaulay group of friends. A Trinity
don pressed him to join the college, but James Mill would
not hear of it. He did, however, attend Austin's lectures
on jurisprudence at University College in 1828–29.
There are some interesting comparisons between him
and Macaulay. Mill was six years younger. Both had
strict fathers of narrow creeds—Zachary Macaulay, the
Evangelical philanthropist, and James Mill, the Rationalist

[1] *Autobiography*, p. 38.

philosopher. Both were precocious; Macaulay was a voracious reader from three years of age, and never forgot anything he read. Both revolted from their inherited creeds. Macaulay attacked Utilitarianism, but was really a Benthamite Whig and never changed. Mill was a militant Utilitarian, but became more and more critical of it. Both were in Parliament for a time, but both preferred literature. Mill became the most popular philosopher and Macaulay the most popular historian of their time.

Mill formed a small society of young Benthamites in 1822, to which he gave the name of the Utilitarian Society, and so the name passed into the language. Among others, W. E. Tooke, William Ellis, and J. A. Roebuck were members of this society. It only lasted till 1826.

James Mill was an official of the East India Company, and John was appointed to a clerkship in the Company's house in 1823 at seventeen. He remained there, rising to the head of the office, till the Company was dissolved in 1858, when he retired with a pension. His enormous literary output was written in the leisure from his official duties, and it indicates his incessant industry and mental vigour.

In 1824 Bentham started the *Westminster Review*, and the youthful John became its most frequent contributor from 1824 to 1828—no mean achievement for a youth of eighteen to twenty-two. When he was nineteen he undertook to edit Bentham's *Rationale of Evidence*, and saw it, in five large volumes, through the press. This was done in one year, in addition to his official work at India House, his writing for the *Review*, his leadership of the Utilitarian Society, and his founding of the Speculative Debating Society, where he began public speaking. On the top of this he was learning German! It was no wonder that he broke down and had a severe depression in 1826. He calls it " a crisis in my mental history." " It occurred to me," he says,

> to put the question to myself: Suppose that all your objects in life were realised; that all the changes in institutions and opinions which you are looking forward to would be completely effected at

118

this very instant; would this be a great joy and happiness to you? An irrepressible self-consciousness answered, No! The end had ceased to charm. I seemed to have nothing left to live for.[1]

The education system of his father seemed to be a failure. Nature was taking her penalty for over-activity in depression and inertia. In this state he read Wordsworth, and felt his healing touch. He began to feel as well as to think. Beauty in nature, art, poetry, and music, hitherto neglected, made their appeal to his repressed emotional life. His inherited creed that pleasure is the only desirable thing and the only test of right conduct had broken down, and he realised that happiness was to be found only indirectly.

> Those only are happy who have their minds fixed on some object other than their own happiness; on the happiness of others, on the improvement of mankind, followed not as a means, but as itself an ideal end. Aiming thus at something else, they find happiness by the way.[2]

This "paradox of pleasure" was sound ethics, but certainly not Benthamite Utilitarianism. "It is, in fact," as R. H. Hutton remarked,

> a paradox which should suggest to Utilitarians the deepest suspicion of the truth of the fundamental idea of their philosophy. That the true end of life should be always in the position of the old gentleman's macaroons, which he hid amongst his papers and books, because he said he enjoyed them so much more when he came upon them unawares, is surely a very odd compliment to the true end of life.[3]

As Carlyle put it to Miss Fox,

> Ah, poor fellow! He has had to get himself out of Benthamism, and all the emotions and sufferings he has endured have helped him to thoughts that never entered Bentham's head.[4]

This crisis left Mill's health permanently impaired. Ten years later he was seized with an " obstinate derangement of the brain." One symptom was a " ceaseless spasmodic

[1] *Autobiography*, p. 77.   [2] *Ibid.*, p. 81.
[3] *Contemporary Thought and Thinkers*, vol. i, p. 185.
[4] *Journals of Caroline Fox*, vol. i, p. 109.

twitching over one eye," which never left him. An illness in 1854 caused the "partial destruction of one lung." In spite of these illnesses he continued his incessant work, and issued volume after volume. He formed new friendships with men of very different views from his own—idealists like John Sterling and F. D. Maurice; disciples of Coleridge. He read Coleridge and Goethe. Coleridge made a great impression on him, and in a later essay he said that Bentham and Coleridge were the two great seminal minds of the age. He thought that he reconciled the new truth to the old, but this he failed to do.

> If I am asked what system of political philosophy I substituted for that which I had abandoned I answer no system—only a conviction that the true system was something much more complex than I had previously had any idea of.[1]

There he witnessed against himself. He could not make a new system, and could not definitely renounce the old. He was not a creative thinker. In a letter to Carlyle he admitted, " I am fitted to be a logical expounder rather than an artist. Poetry is higher than logic, and the union of the two is philosophy." About the same time he read Comte and the works of the Saint-Simonian school of writers, and got from them his first reaction from classical political economy in the direction of socialism. The friendship with Carlyle began in 1831. Their letters were frequent and cordial for ten years, and then languished. The last was in 1869. Carlyle began by saying, "Here is a new mystic," but soon discovered his mistake. In 1834 he said to Mill, " You are yet consciously nothing of a mystic. Your mysticism (for there is enough of it in you) you have to translate into logic before you give it place." [2] One well-known incident in their friendship was the accidental burning of the manuscript of the first volume of Carlyle's *French Revolution* by Mill's servant. It had been lent to Mill, who was greatly distressed by its loss. He offered Carlyle £200 for the loss of time, but could not persuade him to take more than £100. Both men came

---

[1] *Autobiography*, p. 92.   [2] *Letters to Mill*, p. 94.

out of the ordeal well. Carlyle's letter to Mill is noble and unselfish. Mill greatly helped Carlyle with books and material for the history, and gave it an enthusiastic welcome in the *London Review*. In fact, it was Mill who suggested to Carlyle that he should write a history of the French Revolution. The last essay Mill wrote for the *Westminster Review* in 1828 was a review of Sir Walter Scott's *Life of Napoleon*. He read so much in preparing the essay that he intended to write a history of the French Revolution, and collected much material for it. A few years later he abandoned the idea, and proposed that Carlyle should do it, handing over to him his collection of books and papers.

His greatest friendship of all was with Mrs Taylor. They met in 1830, when he was twenty-four and she twenty-two. After a close and intimate friendship for twenty years, which he calls " the chief blessing of my existence, as well as the source of a great part of all I have attempted to do for human improvement," she became his wife in 1851, Mr Taylor having died in 1849. It was a platonic and intellectual friendship. He describes it as " one of strong affection and confidential intimacy only." He adds:

> For though we did not consider the ordinances of society binding on a subject so entirely personal, we did feel bound that our conduct should be such as in no degree to bring discredit on her husband, nor therefore on herself.[1]

Mr Taylor was an admirable husband, but not a worthy intellectual companion for her, and he accepted the situation. Mrs Taylor and John Mill dined together twice a week, when the husband considerately dined elsewhere. This unconventional arrangement offended Mill's family and friends, and led to an estrangement from them when he married. He retired from the social world altogether for some years. He thought that " men of mental superiority are almost without exception greatly deteriorated by society." During this period of seclusion he wrote his chief books.

[1] *Autobiography*, p. 132.

Mrs Taylor evidently was a remarkable woman. She touched the emotional depths of Mill's nature, as yet unplumbed, and provided the sympathy he needed. Mill's exaggerated tributes to her can only be regarded as his cry of anguish after her death in 1858. Her judgment, he declares, was " next to infallible," her qualities included Carlyle's and his own and " infinitely more." " The highest poetry, philosophy, oratory, and art seemed trivial by the side of her." The dedication of his essay *On Liberty* is well known. " Only John Mill's reputation," says Grote, " could survive such displays." George Mill, a younger brother, probably told the truth. " She was a clever and remarkable woman, but nothing like what John took her to be." Carlyle told Morley, " She was a woman of unwise intellect, always asking questions about all sorts of puzzles —why, how, what for, what makes the exact difference— and Mill was good at answers." [1] Her influence on Mill's work appears to have been smaller than he thought. She humanised his *Political Economy*, and suggested the chapter on " The Probable Futurity of the Labouring Classes." She helped him in writing *On Liberty*, published in 1859, the year after her death, and she certainly inspired the later book on *The Subjection of Women*. A recent Swedish critic thinks that Mill was a romantic and mystic at heart, and that Mrs Taylor's influence kept him a radical rationalist.[2] This is not the general view, and the evidence is rather against it.

III

Mill slowly recovered from his depression. He began to write again for newspapers and reviews, and in 1830 began to write on politics, logic, and political economy. He remarks that his writings from 1832 to 1834 would fill a large volume. In politics he was associated with his father and others in a group of Benthamite Radicals who became known as the " Philosophical Radicals." They inherited

[1] *Recollections*, vol. i, p. 63.
[2] K. Hagberg, *Personalities and Power*, p. 196.

the ideas and activities of the Radicals, Jeremy Bentham, Joseph Hume, and Francis Place—the men who worked for the repeal of the Combination Acts in 1824, and were associated with the *Westminster Review* (1824–28). In the first Reformed Parliament of 1832 they formed a small party consisting of George Grote, J. A. Roebuck, Charles Buller, Sir William Molesworth, Hobhouse, Burdett, and others. J. S. Mill was their representative in the Press. Sir William Molesworth started the *London Review* in 1835, and owned it till 1837, when John Mill took it over till 1840. After the death of James Mill in 1836 the leadership fell to John Mill, but they had no leader in Parliament. Grote would not lead. Francis Place said that there was not a man in the Radical Party with the exception of *Mrs* Grote. Mill had hopes of Lord Durham, but he died in 1840. Molesworth and Buller also died young. The group exercised an influence in the 1832 Parliament out of all proportion to its numbers. They were convinced Utilitarians, setting the general happiness —" the greatest happiness of the greatest number "—as the true end of legislation, believing intensely in liberty and individualism, and appealing entirely to reason. They stirred up the Whigs to undertake the removal of abuses and the abolition of restrictions. It was they who inspired electoral reform (1832), the first State grant for education (1833), the new Poor Law (1834), and the Municipal Corporations Act (1835). They co-operated with the Evangelicals in the abolition of slavery in 1833, because they loved freedom, but opposed the Factory Act of 1833, because they believed in *laissez-faire*. They were doomed, however, to extinction. They declined in 1837, and as a group disappeared in 1841. They were too academic and theoretical, a London group of intellectuals with no backing in the country. The new Poor Law of 1834, inspired by their principles, was unpopular with the working classes, who turned to Chartism. Cobden and Bright captured the middle classes for the anti-Corn Law movement. The Manchester School (who were business men, not philosophers) carried on the Bentham tradition. The

Philosophical Radicals dissolved as a party, but they deeply influenced public opinion, inspired the Liberal Party, and moulded legislation in favour of liberty and *laissez-faire* for fifty years. Professor Dicey shows this clearly in his *Law and Public Opinion in England during the Nineteenth Century*. He considers that Benthamite Individualism was dominant from 1832 until the rise of Collectivism in the last quarter of the nineteenth century.

One of the greatest things the Philosophical Radicals did was in the sphere of Colonial reform. They were virtually the authors of the new policy of self-government which saved the Empire. Lord Durham, Charles Buller, and Sir William Molesworth in Parliament, E. G. Wakefield and J. S. Mill outside, all laboured earnestly for the new policy, and they succeeded. Durham's report on Canada, written mainly by Buller and Wakefield, who had been to Canada with him, was warmly supported by Mill in the *London Review*, and this prompt action contributed materially to its success.

IV

From 1840 to the death of his wife Mill was writing his principal books. He became well known as a political philosopher, and in 1865 was invited to stand as Radical candidate for Westminster. He agreed on certain terms. He would find no money, would not canvass, would attend no meetings except in the week before the election. Would that we had a few Mills in these days! He was elected, and was in the House for three years—during the passing of the Reform Bill of 1867. In the debates on this Bill Mill advocated two of his pet doctrines—votes for women and the representation of minorities, on the lines of Mr Hare's plan (substantially the 'Proportional Representation' of to-day). His speeches carried no great weight, he was no orator or phrase-maker, though he dubbed the Conservatives the "stupid party." He explained that he did not mean that Conservatives are generally stupid, but that stupid people are generally Conservatives. He was

124

not at home in Parliament, but he impressed the House by his character and high-mindedness and independence. Gladstone called him the " saint of rationalism." Disraeli characteristically referred to him as the " political finishing governess." Bright disliked his opposition to vote by ballot, and said, " The worst of great thinkers is that they so often think wrong." He was defeated in 1868, and retired to his books and his garden at Avignon, where he died in 1873.

V

His first important book was the *System of Logic*, published in 1843. It is an empirical view of logic as the science of proof, based on his father's psychology. He restates and improves the old logic of deduction, and combines with it a new constructive logic of induction. This is the most valuable part of the book, but it is not unified with the earlier part, and it is inconsistent with the sensationalist and associationist psychology on which it rests. He inherited from his father and the English school of philosophers—Locke, Hume, and Hartley—the strictly empirical view of knowledge. It is entirely derived from experience : the sensations of the individual and their association together in the experience of the individual. ' Individuals ' and ' things ' are isolated units. Hence Mill's logic tends to be merely psychological and not philosophical in the strict sense. He never grapples with the central problems of reality and truth. He remained much more faithful to his inherited creed in psychology and logic than in ethics and politics, but he makes admissions in the *Logic* and in a later work, the *Examination of Sir William Hamilton's Philosophy* (1865), that are inconsistent with his empirical psychology. He came to recognise the synthesising activity of the conscious self; a mere series of sensations could not be " conscious of itself as a series." Human beings " look before and after, and pine for what is not." He admitted the reality of an external world, a " permanent possibility of sensation." He saw the importance of voluntary choice as a factor in the formation of character, but he never fully realised the effect of these admissions. As some one has aptly said, " He opened a trapdoor in the middle of his psychology." He never reached the freedom of the conscious self, though he was a great champion of liberty. The problem of free will and determinism weighed on him like an incubus. He wished to believe in freedom, but could not.

> I often said to myself, what a relief it would be if I could dis-believe the doctrine of the formation of character by circum-stances. I said that it would be a blessing if the doctrine of necessity could be believed by all in regard to the character of others, and disbelieved in regard to their own.[1]

His view of inductive logic is that it investigates the methods of the discovery and proof of new knowledge in the field of natural science, and he extends this to the mental and moral sciences. It is really a study in scientific methods, and as such it is spoilt by being pre-evolutionary. The new ideas of organic evolution came later—after 1859—and Mill never incorporated the new knowledge, as Spencer and others did. The *Logic* had great merits, and had a great influence. George Grote said it was the " best book in his library." Mill had a singularly lucid style, a great gift for clear arrangement, convincing exposition, and apt illustration. His style was sometimes clearer than his thought, but he had the rare quality of making philo-sophical subjects—usually written in technical jargon—intelligible and interesting to the general reader. These qualities were even more evident and popular in his next book, *Principles of Political Economy* (1848). It was the final expression of the old classical economics derived from Adam Smith, Malthus, and Ricardo, but it was also the beginning of a new treatment of what had been called the " dismal science." It enlarged the scope of the subject, and made it more concrete, human, and practical. Mill was influenced by Comte to regard economics as part of a larger science of sociology, and therefore hypothetical in its

[1] *Autobiography*, p. 97.

results, but rightly differed from Comte in considering economics a science in itself, capable of separate exposition. " No writer before Mill," says Bagehot,

> had ever surveyed the subject as a whole with anything like equal ability; no one had shown with the same fulness the relation which the different parts of the science bore to each other; still less had anyone so well explained the relation of this science to other sciences and to knowledge in general.[1]

He dealt with its social applications more and more in successive and revised editions. In these he showed increasing sympathy with the working classes, and moved further and further from his original individualism. In this he was influenced by Owen, the Saint-Simonians, and Louis Blanc. As Leslie Stephen says, " He had come to sympathise with the aims of the Owenites, but not with their theories."[2] Like Professor Marshall, he " sympathised with socialism in every way except intellectually."[3] It is difficult to say what his attitude to socialism was. He was brought up in the strictest school of individualism, but calls himself a socialist in his *Autobiography*, and his wife's influence evidently tended in this direction.

> Our idea of ultimate improvement went far beyond democracy, and would class us decidedly under the general designation of Socialists. . . . The social problem of the future we considered to be, how to unite the greatest individual liberty of action, with a common ownership in the raw material of the globe, and an equal participation of all in the benefits of combined labour. . . . We saw clearly that to render any such social transformation either possible or desirable an equivalent change of character must take place both in the uncultivated herd who now compose the labouring masses and in the immense majority of their employers.[4]

He knew nothing of modern State socialism or the doctrines of Marx, and would probably have disapproved of them. The socialism he approved was an ultimate ideal to be attained by voluntary co-operation, aided by State

[1] *Economic Studies*, p. 279.
[2] *English Utilitarians*, vol. iii, p. 159.
[3] J. M. Keynes, *Memorials of A. Marshall*, p. 50.
[4] *Autobiography*, p. 133.

action, universal mental and moral education, and prudential restriction of the population. The productive co-
operation from which he expected too much has been a
failure, while distributive co-operation has been a success.
He firmly believed in competition. " I utterly dissent
from the socialist declamations against competition. They
forget that wherever competition is not, monopoly is." [1]
He also distrusted State interference. " Letting alone in
short should be the general practice; every departure from
it, unless required by some great good, is a certain evil." [2]
To this general rule he made an increasing number of
exceptions. His individualism was deep-rooted, and all
the concessions he made seem to be based on private property and capital, contract and competition. His treatment
of international trade is exceptionally good, and still remains
a classical exposition. His theory of value was defective,
though he thought it final. Later writers, especially Marshall, have made it more scientific, especially by the addition
of the marginal theory. His economic theory was dominated by Ricardo's law of diminishing returns, which he
calls " the most important proposition in political economy,"
and Malthus' theory of population; the " niggardliness of
nature " and the multiplication of man were the two great
twin foes of economic progress. Yet he had optimistic
visions of the future and destiny of man, and an unlimited
belief in the effects of education. This optimism rests, as
Professor MacCunn points out, " not on faith in God or
institutions, but on faith in man; yet no optimist has ever
avowed so low an estimate of men as Mill." [3] When he
stood for Parliament he was asked if he had written that " of
the few points on which the English as a people are entitled
to the moral pre-eminence with which they are accustomed
to compliment themselves, the one of greatest importance is
that the higher classes do not lie, and the lower, though
mostly habitual liars, are ashamed of lying," he replied,
" I did," and his courage in making the frank admission
received tumults of applause. " His whole essay on *The*

[1] *Political Economy*, Book IV, chapter 7, § 7.
[2] *Ibid.*, Book V, chapter 11, § 7.   [3] *Six Radical Thinkers*, p. 42.

Subjection of Women," says Fitzjames Stephen, " goes to prove that men have all the vices of a tyrant, and women all the vices of a slave." [1] His vision of a future " stationary state of society " depends on a stationary population kept down by prudential restraint and emigration. These problems are with us still. The population question is menacing us now, and diminishing returns, though scotched, is not dead, and will sooner or later confront us. Since Mill's time we have made great progress in scientific and mechanical inventions, in control over nature, in material wealth, and in widespread education, but one feels that Mill would be disappointed with the results.

His *Utilitarianism* (1863) is one of the least convincing of his works. It was written as an exposition and defence of the pleasure philosophy applied to ethics, but he makes so many changes that there is little left of the original creed. We have already seen that he discovered that the direct pursuit of pleasure was futile, and that happiness was to be found only by not seeking it. He sees that human nature is not entirely moved by self-interest, as Bentham and his father had taught, but is capable of self-sacrifice.

> Though it is only in a very imperfect state of the world's arrangements that anyone can best serve the happiness of others by the absolute sacrifice of his own, yet so long as the world is in that imperfect state I fully acknowledge that the readiness to make such a sacrifice is the highest virtue that can be found in man. [2]

He also undermined Utilitarianism by admitting that pleasures differ in quality as well as quantity. Some are better than others. This introduces another standard of what is good. The end is no longer a pleasure or set of pleasures, but a kind of person, a state of character. " It is better to be a Socrates dissatisfied than a fool satisfied." Here is self-realisation of a personal moral ideal, something very like T. H. Green's idealism. Liberty is essential for this self-development, and Mill's book *On Liberty* (1859) is an eloquent and powerful plea for the liberty of the

---

[1] *Liberty, Equality, and Fraternity*, p. 244.   [2] *Utilitarianism*, p. 23.

individual. Mill thought it likely to survive longer than anything he had written. Morley thinks it worthy to stand with Milton's *Areopagitica*. He demands liberty of thought, of expression, and of action, not only against legislative interference, but also against the pressure of public opinion and convention. His claim for liberty of action is not so convincing as for opinion and expression. It is based on an untenable distinction between self-regarding acts and acts that concern others. " A man," he says, " should be free in all acts that ' concern himself alone.' " But are there any such? Very few indeed. There are regions of human experience which ought to be free. He pleads for the independence of the individual against the " despotism of a collective mediocrity," and who shall say it is not needed in our day? Reform and progress are usually initiated by the wise few—or one; let us therefore have individual enterprise and manifold diversity—an enriched and positive individualism.

Mill's later views on politics are expressed in the little book *Considerations on Representative Government* (1861). He was a democrat, but this book reveals his disappointment, doubts, and difficulties about self-government. The paradox of his view was that the majority ought to rule, but the minority is probably right. The majority has power, the minority wisdom. The extension of the franchise tends to outstrip the extension of education, which is slow in its results. Hence the danger of the tyranny of the majority. He is now anxious to curb and check it. His optimism survives in the belief that voting is educative, but he would protect the educated minority by giving them plural votes, and by restricting voting power to those adults (men and women) who are taxpayers, and who can pass some educational test—*i.e.*, who can read, write, and count. He still thinks democracy is the ideally best form of government, but admits that it is not suitable for all races and times. Three conditions should be fulfilled. The people should be (1) willing to accept it, (2) willing and able to maintain it, and (3) willing and able to do what it requires of them. Unless, however, minorities can be protected it is a bad form, and may be the worst. Looking into the future, Mill saw that the majority may demand class legislation and even spoliation for their own apparent (though not their real) interest. The result would be poverty and chaos. His remedies were extra votes to the educated classes, open to all by voluntary examinations, and Hare's scheme for representation of minorities by a transferable vote—what we know to-day as Proportional Representation. Both these remedies seem inadequate. He was strongly opposed to payment of Members as "the calling of the demagogue would be formally inaugurated," but election expenses should be paid by the State. He disliked vote by ballot (on which he had changed his mind) as being no longer needed. He felt the value of publicity and the responsibility for conviction. He strongly advocated votes for women on the same terms as men. This was his strongest political conviction. The proper business of the House of Commons is control, criticism, and discussion, *not* administration or legislation. These are for experts, the Cabinet and professional legal draughtsmen—he suggests the Law Lords! Parliament cannot make good laws, but it can see that good laws are made. He considered Members of Parliament to be representatives, not delegates; and he disliked pledges of any kind. These are rather conservative views, and indicate the measure of his disappointed hopes. "He was," says Graham, "too ardent a believer in progress. He looked for more than was possible, and expected it sooner than was possible. He wanted quick results." [1]

VI

After his death the *Autobiography* appeared (1873) and the *Three Essays on Religion* (1874), and later his *Letters*, edited by H. Elliot, in 1910. The *Autobiography* is a frank and illuminating record of the growth of his mind and the change in his opinions. It is the self-revelation of an anxious and over-serious mind eagerly searching for the truth. It was written mainly in 1861, and breaks off

[1] *English Political Philosophy*, p. 345.

abruptly. The *Essays on Religion* astonished his disciples
when they appeared a year after his death. He had
abandoned his lifelong rationalism, and declared his belief
in a modified theism—a God who was good, but not
almighty. It was a Manichæan attitude, satisfactory neither
to his friends nor to his opponents. The *Autobiography* and
the *Letters* reveal a sensitive and complex mind, a modest
and sincere personality, torn between loyalties—on the one
hand to his father and Bentham, and on the other to new
truth from many quarters. He was always trying to reconcile conflicting views, to see the good in his opponent, to
combine opposites in a higher synthesis, to admit light from
every quarter. He shows always a love of knowledge, a
search for truth, a willingness to learn, that are most
admirable. They led him to inconsistencies, but these are
more attractive than the narrowness and rigidity of his
father and Bentham. He was inspired by a magnificent
devotion to the welfare of humanity and the elevation of
character. He was greater as a man than as a thinker.
His character will live when his views are forgotten. Lord
Morley's tribute is a fitting one :

> Men will long feel the presence of his character about them,
> making them ashamed of what is indolent or selfish, and encourag-
> ing them to all disinterested labour, both in trying to do good and
> in trying to find out what the good is—which is harder.[1]

So Mill remains something of an enigma. He was an
empirical philosopher who became almost an idealist, a
Utilitarian who undermined the creed, a determinist who
yearned to believe in the freedom of the will, a hedonist who
taught self-sacrifice, an individualist who became a kind of
Socialist, a democrat who distrusted democracy, a rationalist
who embraced a limited theism. Yet in spite of these
inconsistencies his abiding and fundamental message to his
age was the value of freedom. He believed intensely and
persistently in liberty, free competition, free trade, freedom
of opinion, of speech, of writing, and of action. He wrestled
with the problem of reconciling the freedom of the individual

---

[1] *Miscellanies*, vol. ii, p. 250.

JOHN STUART MILL

with the claims of necessary collective action, and we are wrestling with the problem still. His vindication of liberty was valuable in his own day, and it is even more necessary now, when the pendulum has swung so far in favour of the State. If, as the Italian philosopher, Croce, said recently, the chief meaning of history is the victory of freedom, then Mill is one of the heroes of the fight. He has gained a permanent place in political and social philosophy by his love of liberty and his supreme devotion to the welfare and happiness of mankind.

ROBERT S. DOWER

BOOK LIST

A. PRIMARY AUTHORITIES

Works of John Stuart Mill, especially the *Autobiography*, *On Liberty*, and *Considerations on Representative Government*.
ELLIOT, H. (ed.): *Letters of J. S. Mill.* 1910.
CARLYLE, A. (ed.): *Letters of Carlyle to Mill.* 1923.

B. SECONDARY AUTHORITIES

COURTNEY, W. L.: *Life of J. S. Mill.* 1889.
MACCUNN, J.: *Six Radical Thinkers.* 1907.
DAVIDSON, W. L.: *Utilitarianism : Bentham to Mill.* 1913.
STEPHEN, SIR LESLIE: *The English Utilitarians.* 1900.
GRAHAM, W.: *English Political Philosophy.* 1899.
STEPHEN, J. F.: *Liberty, Equality, and Fraternity.* 1873.
DICEY, A. V.: *Law and Opinion in England.* 1905.
DOUGLAS, C.: *J. S. Mill : a Study of his Philosophy.* 1895.
KENT, C. B. ROYLANCE: *The English Radicals.* 1899.
SETH, A.: *The Philosophical Radicals.* 1907.

VII

AUGUSTE COMTE AND THE POSITIVE PHILOSOPHERS

THE reputation of Auguste Comte has taken a turn which would undoubtedly have surprised and distressed him if he could have foreseen it. It is based not on his social and political ideas, but on his classification of the sciences, on his so-called philosophy, on his development of the science of history. Yet Comte was the man who invented the term ' sociology,' and his mirror always reflected to him the face of a social reformer. To consider him, for once, as primarily a teacher of social science is, therefore, to do no more than accept his own idea of his true character. Whatever importance has been ascribed to his contributions to knowledge, those contributions were for him entirely subsidiary to another purpose. He had, indeed, no sympathy whatever with the disinterested pursuit of knowledge for its own sake. He valued knowledge solely for its possible application to practical life and to the service of humanity. In the great Western republic which he confidently expected to be established by the beginning of this century there were to be no such institutions as universities where specialists could pore over books or pursue pure research. He detested scholars who wanted to shut themselves away from the world of working men and women. In the place of universities he wished to build temples dedicated to the religion of humanity. In those temples he expected to be honoured and remembered not as a man of learning, but as the original high-priest of humanity. Comte was, in fact, a social reformer on a heroic scale. He made a stupendous attempt to provide mankind with a complete guide to conduct. That was the very essence of what he called religion, for he knew little or nothing of those irrational, timeless, absolute values

134

which are for many people the real meaning of religion. Unlike Spinoza, he was not a God-intoxicated man. But he was, as John Stuart Mill put it, a morality-intoxicated man. He yearned to make his fellow-creatures good and useful members of a great society of the living, the dead, and the unborn.

This intense and ever-increasing desire to improve the world was the guiding impulse of Comte's laborious life. But in pursuit of his dominant purpose, the reorganisation of society on a scientific basis, he found himself obliged to give all the best years of his life to a vast, comprehensive, preliminary study. His philosophy and systematisation of the sciences, the establishment of the hierarchy leading up from mathematics, through astronomy, physics, chemistry, and biology, to sociology, and his remarkable survey of the social evolution of Western Europe, were for him no more than the necessary spadework for the foundations of the new social order. All this preliminary work is contained in the volumes of the *Cours de philosophie positive*, admirably condensed into English by Harriet Martineau. His later volumes—constituting the *Système de politique positive*—are essentially a series of regulations for life in the ideal Positivist state and a sketch of the methods by which Positivism might peacefully supersede the political *régime* of the day. Opinions have differed as to the relative value of the two very distinct parts of his work, but, broadly speaking, commentators have attended to the earlier work and neglected the later. Recently, however, there has been some evidence of a tendency to consider that there is, after all, a system in the *Positive Polity* consistently developed from the earlier writings, and some allowance has been made for the fact that the system was left incomplete. Comte was surprised by death at the age of fifty-nine, and his last words were, " *Quelle perte irréparable !* " He had confidently anticipated many more years of active work, and had committed himself to dates for the publication of three more volumes to round off his plans for the Positivist state. Two of these unwritten works were to deal with the moral basis of education, and one with industry.

He would certainly have seen in the premature end of his own life a typical example of the wasteful brevity of human existence. While he was ready to admit that the death of the individual, the continual replacement of the conservative old by the more experimental young, is a necessary condition of that social progress in which he firmly believed, he thought the rate of replacement too rapid for true economy. Ninety-one years—*i.e.*, seven multiplied by thirteen—he considered to be the proper span of human life. " No one," he wrote while he was still a young man,

> has ever nobly devoted himself to the direct advancement of the human mind without bitterly feeling how time, employed to the utmost, failed him for the working out of more than an insignificant part of his conceptions.

No one, we might add, devoted all the time he had more incessantly and doggedly to the education of mankind than Auguste Comte.

The social and political ideas of any thinking man—and even as a student Comte was nicknamed " the thinker "—are bound to show the influence of his place in time and space, and to reflect his acquaintance with persons and books, as well as to express something of his innate disposition. Comte was a Southern Frenchman, born in 1798. He lived all his life in France and nearly all his adult life in Paris. Like other Frenchmen and Parisians, he took for granted that France was the most civilised country in the world and Paris the natural centre of all intellectual life. The social and political conditions of France and Paris during the earlier part of the nineteenth century were distinctly kaleidoscopic. Comte passed his boyhood under the developing Napoleonic system. But the double influence of Royalist parents and Revolutionary schoolmasters preserved him from any hero-worship of the Emperor. As a boy of ten or eleven he was an open partisan of the Spaniards during the Peninsular War. When he went to the École Polytechnique in Paris at the age of sixteen, Napoleon was insecurely tucked away on the island of Elba. Comte saw him once during the Hundred Days, when he appeared before the Polytechnique students in the guise of saviour of the country and stirred them to enrol in his army for national defence. Comte too was enrolled, and took part in the defence of Paris against the allies. But this brief moment of faith in Napoleon soon gave place to his earlier prejudice against military tyranny. He always declared himself a republican, although the republic of his dreams was not very much like any republic which has yet been organised. He protested against the Bourbon restoration. He had no affection for the subsequent Orleans monarchy. He had more sympathy with the ideals of Napoleon III, because he saw in them a possible turn in the Positivist direction, but as time went on, and he became more and more absorbed in a philosophical contemplation of the past and a prophetic vision of the future, he had less and less attention to spare for the political events of the moment. Kings and Governments, any Governments in actual existence, were for him no more than makeshift necessities, machinery for carrying on administrative work until he should have opened up the path along which not only the French nation, but all Western Europe, and eventually all the nations of the world, would proceed in peace and safety to the earthly paradise of Positivism.

Comte's mind was, in fact, impervious to new ideas in his later life. As a working instrument to chew the cud of a mass of material swallowed in large gulps in his youth it remained in excellent condition, except for the short period of insanity caused by his wife's infidelities coupled with the strain of embarking on his first series of lectures. But it received no fresh nourishment. Indeed, Comte deliberately protected himself from contemporary ideas by what he described as his system of " cerebral hygiene," which meant a strict limitation of his reading to books which had no connection whatever with his work, and a refusal to read any newspaper. His behaviour when he was sentenced to three days' imprisonment for refusing to serve in the National Guard of Louis Philippe was very characteristic. He marched off to prison armed with paper, pens, ink, sealing-wax, and books of poetry. He went on with his usual work, and he gave his mind its usual recreation. He had formed all his fundamental conceptions by the time he was twenty-four. For the rest of his life he elaborated those conceptions. It is, therefore, useful to know what were the influences to which Comte was exposed when he was young, but not important to take much into account what was happening to France and the world generally when he was older. It meant very little to him. The great emotional disturbance of his middle life—his encounter with Clotilde de Vaux—is, indeed, reflected in his work to an extent which amounts for some critics to a serious distortion. But to fall in love is an accident which may happen under any system of government.

The earliest influences, the family influences, were Catholic and Royalist. His mother was a devout Catholic, and, although Comte reacted against her teaching and declared himself an atheist at the age of fourteen, he was well prepared to understand and appreciate the institutions of the Catholic Church without any effort of adjustment. When he was nine he was sent to the *lycée* at Montpellier. There he drank up knowledge and revolutionary principles with eagerness, and displayed a precocious aptitude for mathematics. He had a passion for numbers, and the influence of certain sacred numbers, such as three, seven, thirteen, and their multiples, is only too evident in his work. Students of Positivism may, indeed, sometimes be tempted to imagine that the celebrated Law of the Three States really owes its genesis to Comte's inner conviction that three was a perfect number, and that the states must accommodate themselves. And the nine sacraments to be administered at intervals of seven years to the male members of the Positivist state are only one example out of many of his belief in the magic properties of certain numbers.

At the École Polytechnique, the school for higher education in science and technology, Comte worked hard and read tremendously. He studied biological science, absorbing the evolutionary theories of Lamarck as well as the phrenological teachings of Gall. He was well acquainted with the works of Descartes and the mathematicians who

138

followed him. He read Condorcet, and took into his own mind the idea that generalisations from the past must supply data for prevision of the future in historical as well as in physical science. He was very much impressed by Montesquieu's brilliant exposition of the spirit of laws. He knew something of the work of the Scottish philosophers, and was struck by Hume's comparison between the industrial civilisation of modern life and the military organisation of the ancient world. He read the Traditionalists, and gave sympathetic attention to the theocratic theory of the state. De Bonald and Joseph de Maistre taught him to respect the past. De Maistre, in particular, gave him his exaggerated estimate of mediæval institutions and the mediæval Church.

During this period of intense intellectual ferment Comte was expelled from the Polytechnique for insubordination. It was like him to be insubordinate. He was a difficult young man, intractable, inordinately proud, impatient of all external discipline, obstinately set upon going his own way, and absolutely uncompromising. For most of the remainder of his life he struggled to earn enough to live on by giving private lessons in mathematics, varied by a short period as entrance examiner to the Polytechnique. Towards the end he was assisted by the voluntary subscriptions of his disciples. He never held any post at all adequate to his abilities, and, considering his gifts and his temperament, it is hardly surprising that he came to believe that he was surrounded by enemies who plotted to keep him out of high positions. Very possibly his suspicions were to a great extent justified. He would have been a difficult colleague.

It was only a short time after his expulsion from the Polytechnique and while he was still open to impressions that Comte came into contact with the dominating influence of his intellectual life, the real source of Positivism. This influence was the reformer Claude-Henri de Saint-Simon, who had settled down, after an adventurous life, to be the saviour of a people lost amid the ruins of the Revolution. Saint-Simon was fifty-seven ; Comte was nineteen. Saint-Simon was preaching the necessity for a reorganisation of society on an industrial basis under the control of scientific

139

law. The doctrine of equality and the rights of man was to make way for fraternity and mutual obligation. The cold-blooded teachings of the political economists were denounced. No society, said Saint-Simon, can progress if its economic organisation is not in harmony with good moral principles. Discord and hypocrisy are bound to prevail if brotherly love and unlimited private competition are harnessed together between the shafts of the social omnibus. Comte, overcome by affection and admiration for Saint-Simon, vowed eternal friendship, and unhesitatingly placed his very considerable gifts and his educational training at the service of his new friend and master. Saint-Simon found him extremely useful. He engaged him as his secretary and later as a collaborator in his publications. The young disciple brought to their common work just the qualities lacking in the elder prophet—clarity, order, knowledge. Until then Comte's studies had been kept in different compartments, science in one, history and politics in another. But Saint-Simon's schemes linked science and politics together, and it was from Saint-Simon that Comte caught his faith in the sovereign virtue of what his master taught him to call Positive philosophy, and in the necessity of applying scientific methods to the study of mankind. He adopted, too, Saint-Simon's view that some moral equivalent for the teaching of the Church must be provided for the people, and that this service might usefully be performed by scientists.

Saint-Simon, once he was possessed by a new idea, burned to translate it into action. Having decided that industrial organisation ought to replace both feudal organisation and the succeeding revolutionary disorganisation, he wanted to industrialise society by a wave of his wand. Here Comte refused to follow him. He insisted that a general conversion must precede reorganisation. He thought, rather naïvely, that men would be convinced that their only path to social salvation lay through science and industry, once he had clearly demonstrated the necessity of that doctrine. In later life he modified his demand for preliminary intellectual assent and admitted that a change of heart must generally precede a change of mind. In Saint-Simon's day he was still intent on victory by argument, and he urged the need for time—time to work out the scientific bases of the needed social reorganisation, and then more time to get them accepted. But Saint-Simon had no time to spare. He ran on while Comte sat down to work out his bases. He grafted socialism on to industrialism. He preached the romantic doctrine of the natural goodness of the human heart. He suggested that women should enjoy equal political rights with men. Comte, who still believed in capitalism, who distrusted the undisciplined impulses of the human heart and was more than doubtful about the propriety of women playing any part whatever in public life, was left a long way behind.

He broke with Saint-Simon definitely in 1824, only a year before the death of that inspired publicist. It was inevitable that two such self-confident Messiahs should split apart sooner or later. Both had complete faith in themselves and in their schemes for the salvation of the world, and both advanced personal claims of a sufficiently remarkable character. Saint-Simon declared himself to be a second Socrates and the appointed Vicar of God. Comte announced that the scientific genius of Aristotle and the organising genius of St Paul were united in himself, and assigned himself a place equivalent to that of the Pope as supreme high-priest in the Positivist hierarchy. It is true that these announcements were made at a later stage in his career. In his twenties he was not consciously and completely a Messiah, but he was quite consciously and increasingly aware of the outstanding merit of his contributions to Saint-Simon's publications, and he wanted this merit recognised. In other words, he wanted, very naturally, to sign his articles, and it was the fact of his having signed a brilliant essay—the *Prospectus des travaux nécessaires pour réorganiser la société*—which precipitated the final crisis. Saint-Simon was jealously anxious to minimise the importance of his collaborator's work, Comte was mistakenly convinced that the ideas he was expounding were his own. During the remaining thirty years of his life he repudiated with increasing vehemence any suggestion that he had learned something from Saint-Simon. But recent investigations, particularly the able work of Professor Georges Dumas, make it clear that Saint-Simon was the real originator of Positivism. The disciple was, however, a greater man than his master. The philosophy of the sciences and the theory of society so remarkably developed by Comte would have been entirely beyond Saint-Simon's capacity.

The *Prospectus*, written by Comte in 1822, is a plan for the reconstruction of society on a scientific basis, with the aim of establishing social solidarity. It contains the germ of most of the ideas developed in Comte's later and larger works. He announces in this essay that the new order is to be founded on the rock of principles deduced neither from the imagined nature of God nor from the supposed necessity of abstract justice or liberty. These principles are to be discovered by the methods of investigation and proof which have served to establish the laws of the natural sciences. The work of discovery has still to be done, for hitherto reformers have merely destroyed the religious basis of unity and provided nothing more solid than the shifting sands of metaphysics in its place. The establishment of the laws of society must be entrusted to very different persons from the previous reformers, to men of learning and vision, not to lawyers or journalists and not to scientific specialists. His personal experience of *savants* had given Comte a particular dislike for them, and he never loses an opportunity of girding at " the vicious intellectual habit " of specialisation. The pioneers of sociology must be men of wide general culture coupled with strictly scientific methods of work.

Considering himself to be, at the moment, the only properly equipped pioneer in sight, Comte settled down to the task of discovering the laws of society single-handed. He began by the systematisation of the sciences which has made him famous. He passed on to a study of the nature, the history, and the social prospects of mankind. Regarding sociology as a science like the physical sciences, Comte presumed that when the governing laws were once discovered the future of society would be perfectly predictable. He

142

started with the happy confidence that he would find the laws of society to be as rigid in their action and as measurable in their results as the law of gravitation, then regarded as the ultimate physical certainty, but as his investigations progressed he was driven to admit that social movements are a good deal more modifiable than the rate of acceleration of a falling stone. Under the influence of the analogy of physical science Comte divides the science of sociology into two parts—" social statics," dealing with the conditions of existence of societies, and " social dynamics," treating of the laws of the movement of societies. It is the second section of his study which really engrosses him, but before he yields completely to its fascination he gives a brief exposition of social statics.

The elements of society are for Comte not individuals, but families of monogamously married men and women, with or without children. The ideal family, as envisaged in his later work, contains seven members—two parents, three children, and the parents of the husband. He entirely ignores other and less monogamous forms of union customary in other parts of the globe and at different epochs, as well as those advocated in France by the Saint-Simonians and Fourier. Comte's family is founded on Christian principles, and is, in its ideal state, subject to regulations even stricter than those of the Catholic Church, for Comte expects not only unbreakable union during life, but perpetual singleness after the death of the partner.

Not less than a family is Comte's unit, and certainly not more. He has no faith in any other type of communal life. " The common experience of human life," he says, " teaches us only too well that men must not live too familiarly together if they are to bear, in mutual peace, the infirmities of our nature." Nothing like a monastery or convent can flourish in Comte's world, and children never leave home for a boarding-school. Nor can men live alone. Human beings are sociable by nature, not, as Comte is careful to emphasise, by contract; and the family is the proper expression of this innate social disposition. " It is," he says, " and will ever be, the basis of the social spirit." The family owes this enduring quality to its blessed freedom from the intrusion of that false doctrine of equality which works havoc in public life. Men and women are not, and for immutable biological reasons never can be, equal. It is the duty of the stronger, ruder, more intellectual man to support and protect the gentler and more childlike woman, who should be debarred from either earning or inheriting any wealth, her husband, father, son, or brother being bound to maintain her. Husbandless, fatherless, brotherless, and childless females are the proper charge of the State. In these views about women and their place, which is, of course, the home, Comte is in sharp opposition to the Saint-Simonians, and comes into conflict with his distinguished English admirer, John Stuart Mill. But he does not neglect the education and occupation of women. They are to be educated in the same way and up to the same level as their brothers, and are themselves to be the teachers of all children up to the age of fourteen. It is true that women are denied any direct voice in public affairs, but they share this disability with all the men of the working classes and all the members of the teaching profession. Comte's state is not in any sense a democracy.

Having settled the family unit, Comte goes on to consider society as composed of families living in co-operation. Division of labour was already a familiar phrase, thanks to the early political economists, but Comte had no respect for their theories and detested the doctrine of *laissez-faire*. Something more is needed, he insists, than multiplied production of material goods by division of labour. Diversities of gifts must be used for the service of all, in more ways than is involved in manufactures and agriculture, and this comprehensive co-operation must be directed and controlled. The social function of government is to direct co-operation and, in particular, to ensure that the various and divergent interests and occupations of the community shall not split society into antagonistic classes ready to destroy or to enslave each other. How is this to be done, and who are to govern? How is a sense of unity to be preserved in a world of diversity? Comte concludes that it cannot be preserved on a material basis. Interests do conflict, and nothing will

144

harmonise them but the introduction of ideas of another order than the purely material. There must be a common belief, a common scale of values—in short, something like a common religion. Government, to be effective, must not confine itself to the protection of material interests. It must do more than secure the undisturbed possession of life and property to law-abiding citizens. It must see that sound doctrine is taught with an authority at least equal to that of the mediæval Church. What that doctrine should be is to be discovered by the study of social dynamics.

Comte's department of social dynamics includes a biological and an historical study of the social capacities of human beings. He fell foul of several critics in his own day and for some little time afterwards because he exhibited a hearty contempt for one method of studying mankind then in vogue and known as psychology. The psychology of that age was the analysis of the ego by introspection. Comte distrusted the process. Not so, he says, will you ever learn to know yourself. He anticipates some of the teachings familiar enough to twentieth-century students by insisting that the practice of sitting down to contemplate the workings of one's own mind is bound to lead its deluded devotees to suppose themselves to be far more thoughtful and reasonable animals than in fact they are. Man is not so much a reasonable being as a bundle of affections, passions, and desires. He only becomes to some slight extent reasonable because he learns to make use of his brain to gratify his instincts, and he usually finds this mental labour intensely disagreeable. Comte, who lived mainly by coaching students in mathematics, had been struck by the fact that most men will do anything rather than think. They enjoy being active, but action, to be enjoyable, must not be too monotonous and must not involve much brain-work. Society must not, therefore, be organised on the assumption that its members are by nature intelligent and studious.

Human behaviour, urges Comte, should be studied comparatively, the illumination shed by the behaviour of animals and the phenomena of double consciousness, lunacy, and other diseases of the personality not being neglected.

Like a number of other educated and progressive persons of his time, he extended an over-eager welcome to the theories of cerebral localisation put forward by the phrenologists, but he recognised their provisional nature and regarded phrenology chiefly as a step in the right, the Positive direction, a step towards the explanation of mental processes by physiology. Physiology by itself, however, cannot be enough. There is very little difference, Comte points out, between the structure of the brain and body of a man living under primitive social conditions and that of a Frenchman of 1840, not nearly enough difference to account for the later man's different way of living. To know yourself, therefore, you must know not only comparative physiology, but social history. And so Comte passes to his great survey of social evolution.

He achieves in this survey a magnificent piece of work. It is not wholly original. He takes his idea of progress, which is fundamental to the whole scheme, from Condorcet, his exalted vision of mediæval Catholicism from de Maistre, his views on industrial organisation from Saint-Simon. But these elements are fused into a harmonious construction by the glow of genius.

The vast panorama unrolled at this point is confined to the history of the white races and chiefly to Western Europe, a limitation which enables Comte to evade the difficulties of fitting Asiatic social experiments into his scheme in conformity with his Law of the Three States. The Three States are three periods, differentiated from each other by the nature of men's beliefs about the government of the world and their consequent organisation of society. First comes the theological period, subdivided, like so many of Comte's headings, into three, the fetishistic, the polytheistic, and the monotheistic. The theological period is followed by the metaphysical, and this, in turn, gives place to Positivism. This is not the place to dwell on the speculative ingenuity and the historical ignorance of Comte's account of the earliest, fetishistic phase, or on the insight and justice of his appreciation of the polytheism of Egypt, Greece, and Rome. The fine flower of the theological period is the

146

monotheistic mediæval Catholic Church, associated with feudalism. He ascribes all the good of this period to the actual organisation of the Church and the wisdom of its priests, and allows nothing whatever for the Christian doctrine on which that Church was founded. For Comte the Catholic Church is a fine institution unfortunately linked to an absurd theological fantasy which must shortly perish. It is the discipline and order of the mediæval world that he admires and would repeat if he could in the Positivist state to be inaugurated. But between the theological state and the Positivist is another, the metaphysical and anarchical. Properly speaking, this is not so much a state in itself as the breakdown of the theological state, but Comte's peace of mind requires three states, not two, and the Positive state must be the final one. In its earlier phase the metaphysical state appears as Protestantism, which means, for Comte, very little beyond the destruction of authority and the break-up of order and discipline by the poisonous corruption of the pernicious doctrine of individual liberty of judgment. In its later phase the metaphysical period becomes the period of deists and Encyclopædists, paving the way for the Revolution. But, indeed, as Mill puts it,

> Whatever goes by the different names of the revolutionary, the radical, the democratic, the liberal, the free-thinking, the sceptical, or the negative and critical school or party in religion, politics, or philosophy, all passes with him under the designation of meta-physical, and whatever he has to say about it forms part of his description of the metaphysical school of social science.

Since every historical fact is, for Comte, inevitable and neces-sary, the metaphysical state is admitted to have its proper place, but its function is essentially negative. Revolutions are its appropriate expression, and such ignoble creatures as lawyers and writers its worthy instruments. But once the field is cleared its function is fulfilled. The way is prepared for the entry of Positivism, a state without kings tyrannising by divine right and without a people puffed up to consider their voice as the voice of God.

Comte's reading of social history is, of course, anything

but impartial. He starts with the hypothesis that all roads must lead to Positivism, and he assumes that he has proved the inevitability of the third state when he has done very little more than protest its necessity. We have to take his word for it that the Positivist state is not another Utopia, but the fixed and predestined future which must sooner or later be upon us. If we do take his word we must agree that we can do nothing to prevent its arrival, though we can hasten the day of its general adoption, never losing sight of the fact that one of the distinguishing marks of the preliminary social reorganisation will be the union of the progress acclaimed by the spokesmen of the metaphysical state with the order characteristic of the theological. The kingdom of Positivism is not for the violent to take by storm, but for the meek to institute by consent and co-operation.

The end of the *Positive Philosophy* brings Comte and his readers within sight of the promised land, but still too far off for the landscape to be very clearly visible. The next piece of work to be undertaken was the *System of Positive Polity*, which measures out every inch of the new republic and gives explicit directions for the transformation, in France, of the Government of the Second Empire to the Government of the Positivist state. But between the issue of the last volume of the *Positive Philosophy* in 1842 and the publication of the first volume of the *Positive Polity* in 1851 Comte suffered an experience which profoundly affected his conception of the good life and his plans for ensuring it. In particular, it affected his view of the place and importance of women under a Positivist *régime*, giving them a greatly enhanced prestige. This change of heart was inspired by his passionate attachment to Clotilde de Vaux and his constant devotion to her memory. Clotilde de Vaux was a good and amiable young woman whose husband had abandoned France in a great hurry to escape conviction for the embezzlement of public funds. She was the sister of a student at the Polytechnique who had become a friend of Comte's. Already fast in the grip of tuberculosis, Mme de Vaux was occupying her time with reading, with writing melancholy and not very extraordinary tales, and with the pious duties

148

of a good Catholic. Comte, seventeen years her senior, and himself separated from his wife for several years, fell in love with her at sight and completely. Clotilde was not attracted by him as a lover—she was, indeed, struggling with a hopeless passion for another man—but she was sorry for his loneliness, and very ready to be his friend and confidante, to listen with sympathy to his expositions of the Positive religion, and to serve as a focus for his adoration. Comte wrestled with his emotions, controlled his desires, and offered himself to Clotilde on whatever terms she liked to impose. His worship of her person led, naturally, to excessive admiration of her mediocre literary gifts and to increased respect for the Catholic Church, which she did not abandon for Positivism. Clotilde died within a year of Comte's first acquaintance with her, and for the rest of his life all his work was inspired by and dedicated to her memory. He communed with her in long daily prayers, and wrote her long letters which he read aloud, each year, by her tomb. He appears, indeed, to have acquired the power of calling up her image before him by voluntarily induced hallucination, but he recognised these appearances for what they were, and did not take them as proofs of her continued existence in any world except that of his own mind.

When Clotilde died Comte had been at work for some time on his scheme for the *Positive Polity*. But in the light of his amazing experience as her friend he tore up all that he had written and rewrote it with a new accent, subordinating intellect to affection. The essence of the message he finally found himself driven to deliver, complicated as its expression may be, is the simple injunction to us to love one another. And since Clotilde had taught him to love he concludes that the supreme and all-important function of women in the state is to kindle and nourish the pure flame of affection and sympathy. Contact with Clotilde had not led him to imagine that women ought to play any part in public affairs. Clotilde de Vaux was not a claimant for women's rights, though she did write a novel to show up some of the miseries entailed by lack of facilities for divorce in such cases as her own. Comte's one desire was to shelter and protect

149

Clotilde, and it was as sheltered and protected goddesses of the home that he saw the women of the perfected state.

As for the business of government, it seems to Comte obvious that it should be entrusted to experts, in much the same way as the business of building bridges or curing diseases. It is only the ignorant who suppose that they can build or heal without being trained for the job, and the better educated one is the more one respects vocational training and the less competent one thinks oneself even to select engineers and physicians without advice. To give political control to the masses by a system of universal suffrage is to encourage the false belief that any man can know, without taking the trouble to learn, how he ought to be governed and who his governors ought to be. A better educated public would spontaneously renounce so dangerous a practice.

" All that is wanted," says Comte, " is to reconcile once for all dictatorial government and liberty." But who is to dictate ? Comte replies that in the sphere of industrial organisation the dictators must be the men most capable of applying general laws to special industrial conditions. But there must also be dictators in the sphere of morality, to ensure unity of interests by the common adoption of an altruistic standard. The good society must, therefore, be governed by two powers, corresponding to the temporal and the spiritual of an earlier age. Comte refuses to separate social from political questions. He is ready to hand over to the temporal dictators the management of all material interests. From this point of view the state is to act as a general benevolent providence for its citizens. And as in the best period of the theological state the material power was military and the moral power was the priesthood of the Catholic Church, so in the Positivist state the material power will be industrial and the moral power scientific. The right people to govern are thus indicated as, on the material side, the industrial chiefs, and, on the moral side, men of wide scientific culture, who are called priests by Comte. The social pyramid is constructed on a large solid base of ' proletariate.' Above them come farmers, then manufacturers, then merchants, and finally bankers. The temporal government of the state is to be carried on by a small committee of three bankers, representing respectively agriculture, industry, and commerce.

But the state of the future is not to be of anything like the same size as France. What Comte calls the "factitious agglomerates" of France, Germany, England, Italy, and Spain are to be divided into small territories, about the same size as Belgium, with populations of two or three millions. It will be comparatively easy for the Government to take care of the interests of all the citizens of so manageable a state as this. "The approaching separation of Ireland," Comte writes in 1852, "will naturally lead on to the rupture of the artificial bonds which now unite Scotland and even Wales with England proper." A similar process of decomposition will take place in other overgrown states—we may imagine Comte pointing with satisfaction to Latvia, Estonia, and Lithuania. These small republics, living side by side in peace—for Comte believes that war is impossible to an industrially organised state—are peopled by two sharply divided classes, the rich and the poor, or, as he prefers to call them, the patricians and the proletariate. The main object of the Positivist scheme of government is to ensure that the proletarian masses shall live as a contented herd. In Comte's view improvement in the conditions of life for the masses is far more important than any provision of what are called equal opportunities—chances for bright young men to climb over the heads of their fellows, leaving in their wake envy and jealousy. The provision of sufficiency and security for all is more urgent and necessary than the offer of rewards to the gifted, who are already better off by those very gifts than their comrades. In the Positivist state each family will own a house or flat with an adequate number of rooms (seven is the minimum), and each labourer will be paid wages divided into two unequal portions. One portion is fixed and is independent of the amount of work performed; in times of unemployment it is still paid by the industry for which the labourer is trained. The other and larger portion is dependent on the work accomplished. But

Comte is always emphatic in pointing out that labour is in fact the free service owed by each individual to humanity, and that wages and salaries are merely the condition of the labourer's existence and not the price of his labour. That labour is directed by a comparatively small body of capitalists. It matters very little, says Comte, in whose hands capital accumulates so long as it is used for the benefit of the mass of the population. Its proper use depends more upon moral standards than upon political measures.

The position of the masses is, clearly, that of entire dependence on a dominant capitalist class. In the Positivist state they will have no representation in the Government. They have the right to strike as trade unionists. The population as a whole has the right to revolt. But it is not expected that these rights will be freely or frequently invoked. What safeguards does Comte propose against the exploitation of the workers by greedy and powerful masters?

The power to which he chiefly trusts is educated public opinion. Each boy and girl in the state receives a good and comprehensive education. Up to the age of fourteen they are educated at home by their entirely competent mothers. For the next seven years they attend the lectures of the so-called priests, who expound the sciences and examine them at the conclusion of their courses. At the age of twenty-one each citizen will have been instructed in the arts, in languages and history, in philosophy and comparative religion, and in the fundamental sciences, ending with a year's work in sociology. With this mental training behind them labouring men will be well qualified to discuss social and political questions in working men's clubs, or in *salons*, presided over by women, and they will be free to publish their views in any way they like. Comte imagines them placarding the walls rather than publishing articles in newspapers, which he hopes will disappear. This liberty of speech and publication is one check on the possible abuse of material power. The other is the authority of the priesthood. Side by side with the temporal power in the small republics is the more universal power of a Church dedicated

to the service of humanity. The priests of this Church
have their sacerdotal functions. They administer the nine
sacraments, for instance. But their chief work is to teach
and to advise. To ensure the purity and disinterestedness
of their teaching and their advice priests are to be as strictly
preserved as women from the contaminating influence of
material possessions, beyond a modest salary supplied by
the state. Any priest discovered to be adding to his income
by writing popular articles, or by giving private lessons to
rich pupils for a consideration, would run a serious risk of
expulsion from office. Like the industrial world, the priesthood is organised in a hierarchy, but this culminates not in
a committee of three, but in a single figure, a supreme high-
priest, enthroned, naturally, in Paris, and wearing the
features of Auguste Comte. The priests are envisaged as
acting as arbitrators in industrial disputes, and as public
censors of conduct inimical to the interests of the people.
They are also to continue the work on sociological laws
initiated by Comte, in order that they may always be in a
position to guide their fellow-citizens towards the future in
peace and safety. The ultimate weapon of the priesthood
is excommunication from human society, which is to be as
effective as any mediæval sentence in reducing its object to
the condition of a social leper. But the priests are not
independent of the state. They are materially dependent
on the capitalist Government, which can, if necessary, cut
off supplies. It is part of Comte's scheme to balance these
powers against each other. He externalises in them the
two principles which he finds in mankind, the active,
grasping, egoistic, and the sympathetic, altruistic. Although
he refuses to support the doctrine of the perfectibility of
man, he sees social history as a record of advance towards
altruism, and he considers it to be the duty of the Government to encourage a social, generous, expansive attitude
towards life. He detests thrift and the savings-bank for
the working classes. Although himself a water-drinker, he
does not hesitate to proclaim that the wine-shop is a better
place for one's money than the savings-bank. Thrift is a
virtue for the rich, but a vice for the poor. It encourages

153

an egoistic and narrow state of mind which is quite strong enough without any encouragement. It must, indeed, for the continuance of life, be stronger, have more " intrinsic energy," than the more civilised emotion, but altruism must be assisted by all possible means to hold its own. Comte has no idea of combining the two antagonistic sets of instincts in any kind of higher synthesis. His aim is to keep them in equilibrium, and the two hierarchies in the Positivist state, one representing industry and material interests, the other morality and unselfish ideals, reflect his view of the dual nature of man. This nature he sees externalised too, to some extent, in the two sexes, man representing the active, egoistic, material instincts, and woman the altruistic and spiritual. The morality of the state is in the hands of the priests and women, who are to the family what priests are to society as a whole, teachers and counsellors.

In constructing his social system it was Comte's belief that he was leaving to the world something more than " a sterile collection of facts," like other philosophers. He thought that he had laid down practical and sound regulations for the conduct of life, and a large portion of the *Positive Polity* is concerned with directions for an orderly passage from the governmental system of the day to Positivism. But the inevitable question which every reader of the *Positive Polity* is bound to ask is whether Comte's system obeys his own law that it must be adapted to the capacities of men and women to live by it. It is dictatorial enough, but where is the liberty he so rightly regarded as an equal necessity ? Life under the Positivist *régime* is likely to be organised for us as minutely as in a convent or a monastery. The size of families is prescribed, and so is the size and content of family libraries. The trade or profession of any man is determined in early life and can scarcely be changed later. Families are not free to move house or to change their tradesmen. Artists are bound to the service of the religion of humanity, and must use their gifts to adorn the ceremonies and the temples of that religion. The doctrine made very little appeal to the Romantics of the last century,

154

with their passion for individual liberty. Positivism did not conquer the world, or even the West. The gospel of order and altruism was knocked out for the time being by the Darwinian slogans, " survival of the fittest " and " the struggle for existence," popular expressions which gave a long period of expansion with prestige to those personal, egoistic impulses which Comte set out to control. His attempt to associate Positive sociology with a religion, accompanied by saints and sacraments and rites adopted and adapted from those of the Catholic Church, had very little success. For the Church, instead of sinking in honourable decrepitude to final dissolution and oblivion, as provided for in Comte's scheme, has shown itself to be alive and vigorous and capable of carrying on a proselytising campaign of its own very much more effective than the missionary labours of the Positivists.

Comte's influence on scientists and on historians of all kinds has been incalculably great. Professor Robert Flint, writing in 1893, maintained that Comte's mode of thought had been for half a century more powerful and prevalent than any other. His influence on social and political ideas has been comparatively slight. The tide of democracy was in flood and was not to be turned back by Comte. But times and ideas change. Town-planning is slowly invading the province of the individualist jerry-builder. Councils of Five are seriously proposed as necessary and practicable alternatives to Parliamentary government. Comte has been adopted in France as the prophet of the *Action française* group, who hope to abolish democracy and establish order. It is not likely that his practical schemes will ever be adopted whole, for, as Comte himself said, " even the wildest dreamers reflect in their dreams the contemporary social state," and he would be the first to admit that the social ideals of Positivism, like others, are relative and progressive. The state he envisaged was for realisation in 1850. Its regulations would need revision for 1932. But are we not approaching a Positive state when Mr Maynard Keynes urges us to entrust to science those things which are properly the domain of science, and not to " overestimate the importance of the economic problem or to sacrifice to its supposed necessities other matters of greater and more permanent significance " ? " It should," he says, " be a matter for specialists, like dentistry." If Comte could have brought himself to write as simply and easily as Mr Keynes is not that very much what he would have said ?

THEODORA BOSANQUET

BOOK LIST

A. WORKS OF COMTE

Cours de philosophie positive. 6 vols. 1st edition, 1830–42.
Système de politique positive. 4 vols. 1st edition, 1851–54. The first of these volumes contains the *Discours sur l'ensemble du positivisme,* originally published in 1848. The fourth volume contains, as appendices, six *Opuscules de philosophie sociale,* written between 1819 and 1828.
Catéchisme positiviste. 1852.
Synthèse subjective, vol. i, containing the *Système de logique positive, ou Traité de philosophie mathématique.*

English Translations

The Positive Philosophy of Auguste Comte. Freely translated and condensed by Harriet Martineau. 2 vols. 1853.
System of Positive Polity. Translated by J. H. Bridges, Frederic Harrison, E. S. Beesly, and others. 4 vols. 1875–77.
The Catechism of Positive Religion. Translated by Richard Congreve. 1858 ; revised edition, 1883.

B. BIOGRAPHICAL AND CRITICAL STUDIES

Testament de A. Comte, avec les documents qui s'y rapportent. Translated as *The Will of Auguste Comte with the Documents which relate to it.* (Published by the Positivist Society, 1887.)
ROBINET, J. F. E.: *Notice sur la vie et l'œuvre de A. Comte.* 1st edition. 1860.
LITTRÉ, A.: *Comte et la philosophie positive.* 1st edition. 1863.
MILL, JOHN STUART: *Auguste Comte and Positivism.* 1865.
CAIRD, EDWARD: *The Social Philosophy and Religion of Comte.* 1885.
LÉVY-BRUHL, L.: *La Philosophie de A. Comte.* 1900. English translation, *The Philosophy of Comte,* by Kathleen de Beaumont-Klein. 1903.
FAGUET, ÉMILE: *Politiques et moralistes du dix-neuvième siècle.* Deuxième série. 1903.

156

AUGUSTE COMTE

MAURRAS, CHARLES: *L'Avenir de l'intelligence.* 1905.

DUMAS, GEORGES: *Psychologie de deux messies positivistes.* 1905.

WHITTAKER, THOMAS: *Comte and Mill.* 1908.

DE ROUVRE, CHARLES: *L'Amoureuse histoire d'Auguste Comte et de Clotilde de Vaux.* 1920.

GOULD, F. J.: *Auguste Comte.* 1920.

CANTECOR, G.: *Comte.* Undated.

VIII

JOHN AUSTIN AND THE ANALYTICAL
JURISTS

THE fifty years of punctuated peace that followed the Napoleonic wars—the period that has been named "the era of reaction and reconstruction "— was divided into two unequal portions by the *annus mirabilis*, 1830. Up to that date reaction was dominant throughout Europe: after that date reform, revolution, and reconstruction became ascendant. The outstanding events that marked the turn of the tide were, first, the final expulsion from Paris of the Bourbon dynasty, which failed and fell because of the proved incapacity of its members either to learn anything or to forget anything ; secondly, the successful revolt of the Belgians against the Dutch ruler of the United Netherlands—a revolt that initiated the disintegration of the treaty system elaborately constructed at Vienna in 1815 ; thirdly, the death of the obstructive George IV, and the accession of his more mobile brother, William ; and, finally, the resignation of the Wellington Ministry in November, followed by the return of the Whigs, under Grey and Russell, to office and to power, after a long and weary period of exclusion.

In respect of England the period of reaction may be said to have begun as far back in history as the accession of George III in 1760. For not only did George III himself —trained as he was by Bute in the principles of Bolingbroke—make it his prime endeavour to drive out the Whigs, and to emancipate himself from the control of their Cabinet ; but Whigs and Tories alike were taught by such high authorities as the French Montesquieu, the Swiss de Lolme, and their own countryman Blackstone that the English constitution was, by reason of the division and balance of its powers, perfection, and that the cry for reform was but

158

the voice of ignorance or perversity. On the Continent, however, where despotism—occasionally benevolent, but more often the reverse—prevailed till 1789, reaction did not set in until, near the end of the century, the failure of the Revolution to fulfil its promises drove the disillusioned majority to turn its eyes and fix its hopes once more on the overturned thrones, the desecrated altars, the despoiled nobilities, and the disendowed priesthoods of the Ancien Régime.

No three writers better represent the composite spirit of the reaction than the French Chateaubriand, the German Hegel, and the English Coleridge. The first sought to stem the rising tide of secularism by re-erecting the demolished dam of mediæval faith ; the second endeavoured to counter the encroaching anarchy by exalting the authority of the State ; the third strove to provide an antidote to revolutionary novelty by reviving and re-interpreting all " the old perfections of the earth." In a striking manner, indeed, Coleridge resembled the Neo-Platonic philosophers of the days of dying Rome, the men who endeavoured to put the new wine of rationality into the old bottles of pagan superstition.

Similarly, no three writers more adequately typify the varied aspects of the genius of reconstruction than do Owen, Mill, and Comte. The enthusiastic but unbalanced manufacturer of New Lanark, who dreamed of building a new society on the four pillars of communism, co-operation, culture, and currency reform, stood for all that was most representative of the wild utopianism of the age. The Utilitarian servant of the East India Company, who employed his ample leisure in demonstrating how a new world could be peacefully evolved out of the old by means of education, freedom, and democratic government, stood for all that was most representative of the mild meliorism of the age. The religious and philosophical Frenchman, who denounced and repudiated both theology and metaphysics, and yet founded a school and initiated a cult, stood for all that was most representative of the agnostic materialism and positive science of the age.

For the age—roughly 1830–65—was one in which profound and numerous changes were rapidly taking place. The Industrial Revolution was transforming the arts and crafts not only of England, but of all Continental countries, and of America; the vast economic upheaval that ensued was transmuting the face of society, giving rise to a new middle class, converting also, as by the spell of an evil magician, the peasantry into a proletariat, and herding it into pestilential urban slums. On the other hand, the spread of education and the consequent " march of mind " were generating a new speculation into the meaning of life. Biblical criticism was shaking men's faith in orthodox religion. The revelations of natural science—in particular geology and biology—were opening up new vistas of probability to the imagination of thinkers. The dreams of political reformers and social revolutionaries were stimulating in the minds of the unhappy and oppressed proletariat visions of a radically regenerated earth. On the Continent men undisciplined in intellect and inexperienced in the conduct of affairs were carried away by the wild fantasies of Saint-Simon, Fourier, Proudhon, Cabet, Lassalle, and Marx. In England, on the other hand, although the writings of men like Charles Hall, William Thompson, and Thomas Hodgskin show that fantastic speculation was not unknown, the dominant progressive influence was that of Jeremy Bentham and his school of Philosophical Radicals.

Jeremy Bentham was not a great original thinker. His Utilitarian ethics, which taught that the ultimate test of conduct is its consequences, he learned from Hume, and from Hume's great predecessor, Hobbes. His Utilitarian politics—between which and the ethics a deep logical gulf yawned—he picked up from Beccaria, Helvétius, Priestley, Paley, and other contemporaries: it was in the air. It taught that the aim of government *ought to be* " the greatest happiness of the greatest number "; but, since the idea of obligation is absent from Utilitarian ethics, why the Government should have this aim, or, indeed, how its individual members could conceivably have so altruistic an aim, is not evident. Man, however, or at any rate the Englishman, is not a severely logical animal, and the "greatest happiness" formula, with its implication of human equality, exactly suited the requirements of the time. It provided the magic phrase—the "Open Sesame" —before which the barriers of privilege and prerogative, of monopoly and nepotism, of iniquity and inequity, went down, leaving the way free for the unimpeded advance of individual energy and initiative.

Bentham had disciples in many walks of life, and of many shades of politics. His most wholehearted admirers and enthusiastic followers were, of course, the so-called Philosophical Radicals, headed by James Mill and his eldest son, John Stuart Mill: they shared both his zeal for drastic political reform and his rejection of intuitional religion. The Manchester School of economists, also, were Benthamites in their denunciation of Government interference and their advocacy of *laissez-faire*. Sir Robert Peel and his favourite pupil, the young Gladstone, were profoundly influenced by Benthamite humanitarianism. Nearly all moderate English opinion in the early Victorian age was, indeed, Benthamite. Only the more extreme opinion remained alien—on the one side the Conservatism of Benjamin Disraeli, and on the other side the Communism of Karl Marx. Numerous, however, as were the groups of Benthamites, solitary and unique among them stood the figure of John Austin.

II

Of John Austin's career it is not necessary to say much. Unlike Rousseau, Austin was not a man whose opinions reflected mirror-like the changes and chances of an ever-shifting environment. Unlike Burke, he did not play a great part in practical affairs, or express his ideas in forms determined by the exigencies of the political problems of the moment. He lived, indeed, a life singularly remote from the common ways of men; his habitual abode was the spaceless and untimely realm of thought. He himself

161

once remarked, " I was born out of time and place; I ought
to have been a schoolman of the twelfth century or a
German professor." It is doubtful, however, whether he
would have felt at home even in a mediæval Benedictine
monastery or in a modern German university; for his
intense individualism would have rebelled against the rigid
curriculum of the cloistered school, while his ingrained
lethargy and untidiness would have sought and found
escape from the systematised labour expected of a Teutonic
professor. He was, in fact, according to any terrestrial
standard, a failure. He had, in the judgment of all who
knew him, great, though slow-moving, powers of mind;
but they were rendered inoperative by defects of character
—by laziness, by unpunctuality, by lack of a sense of proportion, and by a curious incapacity to bring to a conclusion
any work that he attempted. His only chance of success
would have been to be compelled to earn his own living;
but from this saving chance he was excluded by the too
kind Providence that gave him a wealthy father, a prosperous brother, and a capable wife. " It is doubtful," says
his biographer, " whether he even made in the last forty-
two years of his life, by his profession, by his pen, or as a
lecturer, a hundred pounds." [1]

Born in 1790, the eldest son of a Suffolk miller who
became rich by means of war-contracts, he entered the Army
with a purchased commission in 1807, and served for five
years in Malta and in Sicily under Lord William Bentinck.
These years—the period of the great Napoleonic struggle
that began at Tilsit and ended at Moscow—were a lustrum
of intense agitation; but almost all we know of the young
Lieutenant Austin's share in the hurly-burly is that during
his term of service in the Mediterranean he managed to
get and to read Dugald Stewart's *Philosophical Essays*,
Drummond's *Academical Questions*, Enfield's *History of
Philosophy*, and Mitford's *Greece*. Having learned so much,
we are not surprised that the next information we receive
is to the effect that in 1812 he himself and the military
authorities concurred in thinking that he had completed

[1] Sir John Macdonell in the *Dictionary of National Biography*, vol. ii, p. 268.

such contribution as he was qualified to make towards the resettlement of Europe, and that he might therefore with advantage be released for civilian pursuits. Consequently, at the age of twenty-two, he sold his commission and began to read for the Bar. That is one reason why he could not claim to share with Bill Adams the glory of winning the battle of Waterloo! Soon his military experiences faded into the dim, indefinite background of his life; but they probably impressed upon his mind a permanent tendency to over-emphasise the element of command in law, and to stress unduly the indivisible and illimitable character of supreme authority. His jurisprudence always smacked of the drill-sergeant.

In 1818 he was called to the Bar by the Inner Temple, and for seven years he strove to secure a practice, partly on the Norfolk Circuit, and partly in chambers at Lincoln's Inn. But practice eluded him. He was too slow, too heavy, too meticulous, too conscientious, too much behind time, too unpractical. In 1825 he gave it up for ever. At that date his younger brother, Charles, then twenty-six years of age, was just at the beginning of his brilliant and unprecedentedly successful forensic career. It would be difficult to conceive two brothers more strikingly different: John, ponderous, laborious, hesitant in judgment, ineffective; Charles, light, facile, even more cocksure than his friend Macaulay, overwhelmingly decisive in argument or debate.[1]

Charles Austin, called to the Bar in 1827, took silk in 1841, made over £100,000 in the one year of the railway crisis (1847), retired with a fortune at the age of forty-nine, and lived for another quarter of a century in cultured comfort. Concerning his brother, nine years his senior, Charles remarked, " John is much cleverer than I, but he is always knocking his head against principles." Every one seems to have been impressed by John's cleverness. " He was a man of great intellectual powers," said the younger Mill, who had him as a tutor, and attended his lectures.

[1] See the sketches of Charles Austin given in Mill's *Autobiography* and Trevelyan's *Macaulay*.

" If John Austin had had health," said Lord Brougham, " neither Lyndhurst nor I would have been Chancellor." But no two critics could agree as to precisely why so much talent should have resulted in such complete futility. His brother attributed his failure to conscience; his wife to shyness and reserve; Mill to melancholia; and Brougham to indigestion. Whichever of the four was correct, the fact remains that (if the logical process of rule of three be sound) it would have taken him, at his rate of earning, 42,000 years to make the sum of money that Charles made in 1847.

The success of a thinker, however, is not measurable in terms of cash. Charles is now forgotten, save as a name associated with the more enduring names of Mill and Macaulay. John lives, by his own merit, as a legal philosopher who, as the result of much-protracted, often-intermitted, intolerably prolix, and never-completed labours, did a permanently valuable piece of work in determining the province of jurisprudence, defining its vocabulary, and clearing away the fogs of many bewildering misconceptions that clung around it. His main tasks as a jurist were accomplished during the eight years 1826–34. In the first of these years he was appointed, through the influence of Jeremy Bentham and James Mill, to the chair of jurisprudence in the newly constituted University of London (University College). Since the college was not to be opened until the autumn of 1828, Austin had two years in which to think of what to say. He occupied the time in going to Germany and—particularly at the Universities of Heidelberg and Bonn—in sitting at the feet of the great modern civilians who there taught the revived and rejuvenated Roman law. His wife accompanied him, and helped him with the language.

John Austin's wife, Sarah, has already been mentioned twice, and it is necessary here to pause a moment in order to note a few things about her. She was a remarkable woman—beautiful, talented, brilliant, fascinating, high-souled. That she was attracted by the judicially minded John is the best evidence we have that he was possessed of a charm which he conspicuously failed to impart to his

164

writings. She herself secured, and continues to hold, an independent place in English literature. As translator of Ranke's *History of the Popes* and of Guizot's *English Revolution*, as author of a work on *Germany from 1760 to 1814*, and as editor of her husband's unliterary remains, she displayed abilities of a high order. John and Sarah (three years his junior) were married in 1820. They settled in Queen Square Place (now Queen Anne's Gate), Westminster, close to Bentham and the Mills, and there in 1821 was born their only child, Lucie, who became Lady Duff Gordon.[1]

From Queen Square in 1826 John and Sarah set out for Germany, and in Germany they remained for nearly two years—that is, until it was time for John to begin his course of lectures. The lectures, on the province of jurisprudence —toilsome, slow-moving, over-elaborated, arid, burdened with irrelevancies, and incalculably remote from the practice of the law—in spite of their novelty, originality, and high logical power, failed to attract students. And since the professors at University College were at that time dependent for their salaries on the fees paid by their pupils, after four years, when the class had dwindled to five, Austin had to resign. His pupils, however, although few, had included a striking proportion of young men destined to eminence in the worlds of law and politics—*e.g.*, J. S. Mill, G. Cornewall Lewis, Lord Belper, Lord Romilly, Charles Villiers, Charles Buller, and Sir W. Erle. They all spoke with profound respect for their teacher, and all confessed that they owed him an incalculable debt for the clarification of their legal ideas.

Nevertheless he had, for the third time, failed. Sarah Austin, in the memoir which she prefixed to her husband's posthumous works, says:

Such was the end of his exertions in a cause to which he had devoted himself with an ardour and singleness of purpose of which few men

---

[1] It is a curious coincidence that precisely at the time when Sarah Austin in Queen Square Place was encouraging and befriending the young John Stuart Mill, in Guilford Street, not very far away, Sara Austen, wife of a prosperous solicitor, was assisting the youthful Benjamin Disraeli, of Bloomsbury Square, to get his first novel, *Vivian Grey*, into shape for publication.

are capable. This was the real and irremediable calamity of his life—the blow from which he never recovered.

The remaining failures of his career can soon be chronicled. In 1833 he was made a member of a commission to inquire into the criminal law: the report, issued in June 1834, showed that he had failed to convince the Commissioners that a code and not a mere digest was requisite. In 1837 he was appointed to lecture in the Inner Temple on " the general principles of jurisprudence and international law," but he failed to keep an audience, and the course was suspended within a few weeks. In 1836 he went to Malta, the scene of his early military inactivities, together with his old pupil G. Cornewall Lewis, in order to inquire, on behalf of the Government, into the condition of the laws and into the grievances of the natives. In his search for the ideal constitution he failed to keep in contact with the realities of the situation, and his report (1837), though juridically interesting, was practically useless. Then his health failed, and for ten years he was taken about by his devoted wife from one resort to another—Carlsbad, Dresden, Berlin, and Paris. Finally, the 1848 upheaval in Paris drove him back to England. He settled at Weybridge, and, failing to find anything to do, he spent the concluding eleven years of his life in placid, and not unhappy, idleness. In December 1859 he failed to remain alive.

III

Seeing that John Austin lived to the mature age of sixty-nine, and considering that during two-thirds of his existence he was supposed to be studying law, we must admit that his output was surprisingly small. In 1832 he published the substance of his University College lectures under the title of *The Province of Jurisprudence Determined*. The book, described by Lord Melbourne as the dullest he had ever read, fell flat; few lawyers took any notice of it; no second edition was called for during its author's lifetime; even to-day it is scarcely known outside the English-speaking world. Nay, in England itself its solid worth has been recognised only since, in the sixties, it began to be vehemently attacked. No other book than this ever came from his pen. He wrote, however, occasionally for the reviews. Mill tells us in his *Autobiography* that Austin contributed one article to the *Westminster* criticising McCulloch's defence of primogeniture. He published at least two in the *Edinburgh*; one (1842) adversely reviewing List's *National System of Political Economy*, and the other (1847) advocating a strong central Government, supplemented and moderated by an extensive system of local devolution. Towards the close of his life (1859) he was invited by the editor of the *Quarterly* to furnish an article opposing Russell's projected scheme of Parliamentary reform. He produced the article; but he prefaced it with so voluminous a survey of the whole English constitution that the editor had to decline to publish it. Austin therefore issued it as a separate pamphlet (Murray, 1859). It is extremely interesting as showing how a good Benthamite Utilitarian could be a sound and thoroughgoing Tory. In the pamphlet Austin, after completing his survey of the constitution, expatiated on the inexpediency of any change, enlarged on the evils which any extension of the franchise would entail, dwelt (with obvious recollection of Paris in 1848) on the horrors of mob-rule, and concluded by showing the beneficent consequences of even the anomalies of the existing system of representation. After his death his devoted wife, with infinite toil, collected and arranged his chaotic manuscripts, supplemented them from the old note-books of quondam pupils (especially those of Mill), and produced the two-volumed *Jurisprudence* (Murray, 1863) which remains the chief monument to his fame.[1]

Austin's *Jurisprudence* is a curious work, unique of its kind. It consists of four completed sections, and a collection of *disjecta membra*. Of the completed sections the first and incomparably the most important is the old (1832) *Province of Jurisprudence Determined*. The other three sections deal respectively with (1) pervading notions—that

[1] *Cf.* John Stuart Mill's "Austin on Jurisprudence," originally published in the *Edinburgh Review*, October 1863; reprinted in *Dissertations and Discussions*, vol. iii (1867).

is, the connotation of legal terms such as right and duty, person and thing, will and intention, negligence and inadvertence; (2) law considered in relation to its sources; and (3) law considered in respect of its purposes and subjects. The defects of the book, apart from its intolerable style, are numerous and glaring. Its arrangement is imperfect; its basis of classification indefensible; its omissions numerous; its repetitions tedious beyond measure; its over-elaboration ridiculous; its irrelevancies many and protracted; its disfigurement by italics excessive; its occasional truculence of language disturbing, if now and again diverting. But over against these defects it had merits which those who first read it in the sixties were more ready to recognise than some of the pundits of this later age. It clarified once for all some of the fundamental notions of law; it swept away finally many pernicious confusions, the practical consequences of which had been serious; it dammed certain current metaphors whence for generations had flowed streams of nonsense whereby, as he expressively remarks, "the field of jurisprudence and morals had been deluged with muddy speculation."

Mill had no doubt as to the value of Austin's work. He considered that it " placed him in the estimation of all competent judges in the very highest rank of thinkers." He regarded it as an incomparable discipline in " the difficult and precise art of thought," adding that, "though the merit and worth of his writings as a contribution to the philosophy of jurisprudence are conspicuous, their educational value as a training-school for the highest class of intellects will be found to be still greater." His reasoned conclusion was that " no one thoroughly versed in these volumes need ever again miss his way amidst the obscurity and confusion of legal language."[1] Sir Henry Maine, twelve years later, although he dissented emphatically from some of Austin's views, agreed with Mill as to the sterling value of Austin's analysis. " There is not," he said,

the smallest necessity for accepting all the conclusions of these great writers [i.e., Bentham and Austin] with implicit deference;

[1] J. S. Mill, *Dissertations and Discussions*, vol. iii, pp. 206–274.

but there is the strongest necessity for knowing what these conclusions are. They are indispensable, if for no other object, for the purpose of clearing the head.[1]

Sir Thomas Erskine Holland, no more a disciple of Austin than was Maine, concurs in Maine's eulogy. The *Jurisprudence*, he asserts, is

a book which no one can read without improvement. It presents the spectacle of a powerful and conscientious mind struggling with an intractable and rarely handled material, while those distinctions upon which Austin after his somewhat superfluously careful manner bestows most labour are put in so clear a light that they can hardly again be lost sight of.[2]

Austin, in short, had a mole-like mind. Its operations were subterranean, tedious, and obscure. It rarely ascended to the surface, and it never rose into the air. Hence it remained oblivious to scenery, and failed to see things in their entirety. But it did invaluable work in grubbing about among the roots of thought, and in tracing ideas to their sources. Nevertheless a mole-like mind is a muddled mind; and Austin, if with wearisome burrowing he succeeded in unravelling some of the radical tangles that he found in the legal underworld, undoubtedly himself created others. To be specific: if he elucidated the meaning of ' law ' he still further confounded for us the connotation of ' sovereignty.' But of that more anon. Suffice it here to say that his influence as an analyser of fundamental legal ideas was far-reaching and beneficent. His book opened a new era in the science of jurisprudence—that is to say, in the study of the abstract or formal philosophy of positive law. It served, moreover, as a model to all workers in the realm of the moral and social sciences, impressing them with the supreme importance of the exact use of words and of the employment of rigid logical processes. In the world of legal practice it powerfully assisted the causes of simplification, codification, and reform. Above all, it stimulated further research into the meaning of the three great terms,

[1] Maine, *Early History of Institutions*, p. 343 (1875).
[2] Holland, *Jurisprudence*, preface to first edition (1880).

law, sovereignty, and State. And if it be argued that research into the connotation of abstract nouns is an insignificant occupation for all persons except infants at school, the reply is that there have been few graver causes of civil conflagrations and international conflicts than precisely these terms which are so hard to define. One could draw many parallels from the realm of theology; for all theological controversies are logomachies. For example, as is well known, the difference of meaning between *homo-ousios* and *homoi-ousios* caused the streets of Constantinople, in the fourth, fifth, and sixth centuries of the Christian era, to flow with blood. It is, however, sufficient for our purpose to note, by way of illustration, that the Hundred Years War between England and France was fought to decide the question whether the Salic Law was a law or not a law; that the Civil War between Charles I and his Parliament was fought to decide the question whether the English sovereign was a sovereign or not a sovereign; and that the great nineteenth-century struggle between the North and the South in America was fought to decide the question whether an American state was a state or not a state. In other words, the conceptions represented by the terms law, sovereignty, and state lie at the very foundation of political principle and governmental institution. Just as Tennyson truly says, respecting the " flower in the crannied wall " which he has plucked and examined (reversing the process followed in respect of students at universities):

> Little flower—but *if* I could understand
> What you are, root and all, and all in all,
> I should know what God and man is,

so if political idealists could but say precisely what are the nature, the source, and the sphere of supreme authority they would have solved the problem of the governance of men.

IV

The Theory of Law

The term ' law ' has from the first been an ambiguous one: it has connoted two ideas, closely connected, yet distinct—namely, (1) a causal authority and (2) a consequent uniformity of behaviour. In other words, it has stood for both force and order; for both will and regularity; for both general command in the imperative mood and general statement in the indicative. Not until the dawn of the modern scientific age did this ambiguity cause much inconvenience. For, on the one hand, among men general commands resulted in general conformities of conduct; and, on the other hand, in the realm of nature the undeviating regularities of the behaviour of such bodies as the sun and the moon were regarded as consequent upon the direct fiat of some supernatural will. The development of physical science, however, from the time of the Renaissance, necessitated the bifurcation of the term. (*a*) '*Law*,' *in the scientific sense of the word*, became simply and solely a general statement, entirely devoid of any implication of command. A good example is the so-called law of motion, which runs: " Action and reaction are equal and opposite "; or the law of gravitation, first formulated by Newton and now modified by Einstein, to the effect that " Every particle of matter in the universe attracts every other particle with a force whose direction is that of the straight line joining the two, and whose magnitude is proportional directly as the product of their masses, and inversely as the square of their mutual distance." General statements such as these may be true or may be false; but either to obey them or to disobey them is impossible. They lie wholly outside the sphere of the will. They are nothing more than provisional hypotheses, based on observation and experiment, which men of science accept as true pending further investigation. (*b*) '*Law*,' *in the juridical sense of the word*, on the other hand, gathered to itself exclusively the idea of command, authority, and force. It came to connote a general injunction addressed to the will, without any implication whatsoever as to any consequent uniformity of behaviour. Austin well defines it as " A rule laid down for the guidance of an intelligent being by an intelligent being having power over him."

It is decidedly unfortunate that, since ' law ' in the

scientific sense and ' law ' in the juridical sense have come to mean things so wholly different and distinct, a new term has not been adopted in place of one or other of them. For confusion between the two connotations has persisted in spite of all the efforts of grammarians and logicians to keep them apart. Even in the eighteenth century eminent thinkers like Montesquieu in France and Blackstone in England gave general definitions of ' law ' in which the two uses of the words were hopelessly confounded. It was, indeed, directly due to their copious effusions of muddled nonsense respecting ' law ' that Austin was compelled to remark, as before noted, that " the field of jurisprudence and morals had been deluged with muddy speculation." Austin did much to clarify the flood and to separate its elements. Yet even to the present day it is possible to hear occasionally, mainly from the pulpit, such expressions as " a violation of the law of gravitation "—expressions as devoid of rational meaning as any in *Alice in Wonderland*, and unredeemed by Alice's charming irresponsibility and humour.

The jurist, then, regards laws scientific as laws in a merely metaphorical sense, and he dismisses them from his purview. But, even so, within the proper limits of his subject there are so many laws claiming to be imperative as to give him plenty to do when he attempts to define and to classify. There are laws divine and laws human; laws revealed and laws unrevealed; laws customary and laws statutory; laws moral and laws social; laws municipal and laws international; laws civil and laws criminal; laws natural and laws conventional; laws of honour; laws of fashion; and countless other varieties. How can he reduce these numerous categories to system and simplicity? How can he grade them in order of authority?

The task of the modern jurist has been immensely facilitated by the labours of a long line of eminent predecessors. For us it is unnecessary to go back beyond the great Roman Imperial lawyers who flourished in the early centuries of the Christian era; although it is true that they themselves owed much to the ancient Greeks, as the Greeks owed much to still more venerable Oriental *prudentes*. The Roman lawyers distinguished three kinds of authoritative commands—namely, (1) *jus civile*, (2) *jus gentium*, and (3) *jus naturæ*. The *jus civile* was the law peculiar to Roman citizens, and inapplicable to any other persons. The *jus gentium* may roughly be described as the highest common factor of the laws that prevailed among the *peregrini*, or strangers, who frequented the great city : it was a system of rules marked by simplicity, equity, intelligibility, and freedom from technicalities and traps. The *jus naturæ* was essentially the dictates of conscience and common sense sublimated by the Stoic philosophy into an authoritative system of precepts regarded as emanating from the primal and universal reason. It tended to be identified with the *jus gentium*, and probably would have become merged and lost in it, but for the fact that the *jus gentium* recognised the ubiquitous institution of slavery, while the Stoic conscience repudiated and denounced it as incompatible with the natural liberty and equality of men.

Mediæval Christendom—in law, as in so much else, the heir of Imperial Rome—accepted the classification of the great Latin jurists, but supplemented it and redefined its terms. First and foremost, it added the category of *jus divinum*, the supernaturally revealed law of God. Secondly, it explained the *jus naturæ* as the unrevealed law of God, the law made known to all men in all lands and in all ages by means of the inner monitor of conscience.[1] Thirdly, it regarded the *jus gentium* as the nearest actual approach among sinful men to the ideal standard of the *jus divinum atque naturale*. Finally, it relegated the *jura civilia*, the numerous and varied legal systems of the many peculiar peoples within the pale of Christendom, to the lowest grade of commands, treating them with contempt, and denying to them all validity when they conflicted with the precepts of the higher laws. The best epitome of the mediæval conception of law is that given by St Thomas Aquinas in the second part of his great *Summa Theologiæ*.

The early modern jurists, such as the Spaniard Suarez

[1] *Cf.* Romans ii, 14–15.

and the English Hooker, were ecclesiastics brought up in the school of St Thomas. Hence they accepted in the main the mediæval legal categories. That is to say, they regarded the *jus divinum* as the most authoritative, and the *jus civile* as the least authoritative, of the commands that regulated human conduct. The first important thinker radically to dissent from this view was Jean Bodin, the author of that remarkable work, *De Republica Libri Sex*.[1] The cause of his dissent was that since 1562 he had seen his country, France, torn by ferocious civil wars and disgraced by such appalling atrocities as the Bartholomew massacre, simply because Catholics and Calvinists could not agree in their interpretation of the *jus divinum*. When he had come to the conclusion that no concord was possible he wrote his book to show that the only way of peace and national salvation was the recognition of the sovereignty of the State and the primary obligation of its *jus civile*. Nevertheless, even though he exalted the *jus civile* to the highest place, he was so much still a denizen of the Middle Ages as to admit (with bewildering inconsistency) that the validity of the *jus civile* depended on its harmonisation with the *jus divinum*, the *jus naturale*, the *jus gentium*, and even with a novel class of peculiarly French *leges imperii*, by which he seems to have meant such constitutional fundamentals as the so-called Salic Law. Bodin prepared the way for Hobbes, Bentham, and Austin; but he did not himself advance far along the path of clarity.

Before Hobbes, however, brought his Leviathan on to the path to trample down with ruthless weight the lingering entanglements of mediæval ideology, the great Dutch jurist Grotius had boldly appropriated two of the four mediæval categories of commands, and had combined them to constitute a code of universally obligatory international law. He had taken the *jus gentium* and had converted it from a system of private law common to the peoples of all nations into a system of public law binding upon states *inter se*. He had also taken the *jus naturale* and, dropping its peculiarly

---

[1] Issued first in French in 1576, and secondly in a revised and improved Latin version in 1586.

Christian definition as the unrevealed law of the God of the Bible, had secularised and universalised it by describing it as " the dictate of right reason " (*dictatum rectæ rationis*), and as such imperative for Jew, Turk, infidel, and pagan, equally with Christians of all the warring sects.

Hobbes, however, was, as we have noted, the person who broke most completely with the mediæval and Roman tradition respecting law. He nominally accepted the four-fold classification of the schoolmen—just as he nominally accepted the Huguenot idea of the social contract as the basis of society and the State—but he turned it inside out and entirely emptied it of its former content. The *jus divinum*, he said (professing profound veneration), applied solely to the other world beyond the grave ; the *jus gentium*, in Grotius's sense of the term, was non-existent, since nations in respect of one another were in a state of nature—that is, of chronic war ; the *jus naturæ* consisted merely of the dictates of common sense tending towards self-preservation, and as such was devoid of all ethical or juridical character ; only the *jus civile* remained in any way imperative. The will of Leviathan is the only source of valid law on earth, and " no law can be unjust " !

It is not surprising that Hobbes's drastic treatment of the ancient and sacrosanct categories of law met among his mediævally minded contemporaries with general reprobation and repudiation. John Locke, in particular, who strove in his *Two Treatises on Government* (published in 1690) to steer a middle course between the divine right of Filmer's *Patriarcha* and the profane wrong of Hobbes's *Leviathan*, reasserted the reality and supreme authority of natural law, and contended that the very end and object of civil government was the formulation and protection of the natural rights of the individual to life, to liberty, and to property. In the eighteenth century, indeed, largely under the influence of Locke, the cult of nature and natural law had an immense vogue. It captured romancers like Defoe ; it took possession of sentimentalists like Rousseau ; it inspired a whole school of philosophers and theologians, among whom Bolingbroke and Voltaire stood eminent ; it served, in the hands of Pufendorf and his compeers, as the main source of international law. Nay, more, it even re-invaded the province of jurisprudence. Blackstone, in particular, freely re-admitted it. The law of nature, he said, " is binding over all the globe, in all countries, and at all times. No human laws are of any validity if contrary to this." [1] This was serious : in an English law-court could a person accused of violating one of the laws of England plead successfully that the law was invalid because contrary to the law of nature? What, again, of the divine law? Sir Thomas More, in the sixteenth century, when convicted of high treason had pleaded that the statute under which he had been condemned was " directly repugnant to the laws of God and His Holy Church." His plea had been disallowed. Ought it to have been so? In Blackstone's opinion, apparently not. For he said, " Human laws are of no validity if contrary to divine laws—all valid laws derive their force from that divine original." [2]

Here undoubtedly was a problem that needed clearing up. What laws could claim validity in the English courts? Could Acts of Parliament or cases adjudged be set aside by the plea that the law which they laid down was contrary to the divine law, or natural law, or customary law, or constitutional law, or international law, or moral law, or any other code of human conduct? Austin, who, like Bentham, was filled with intense disgust at the sloppiness and incoherence of Blackstone's thought, set himself to clarify the mess. And most effectively did he succeed in doing so. First he delineated the three features that, in his opinion, characterise all laws properly so called. They are as follows : (1) Every law properly so called must emanate from a determinate source; (2) it must be the expression of a command; (3) it must be enforced by a sanction—that is, by a penalty in case of disobedience. Applying this triune test, he discovered three great classes of laws proper— namely, (a) laws of God, whether revealed or unrevealed; (b) positive laws—i.e., laws of the State, whether enacted

---

[1] W. Blackstone, *Commentaries on the Laws of England*, vol. i, p. 41 (1765).

[2] Blackstone, quoted by J. Austin, *Jurisprudence*, vol. i, p. 214.

directly or enacted indirectly; (c) other commands—*e.g.*, the rules of clubs and similar voluntary associations. Outside the range of laws proper he placed such rules of human conduct as lacked either determinate source or one or more of the other marks of true law—*e.g.*, customary law, laws of honour, laws of fashion, and (shades of Grotius!) international law. Beyond these again, wholly beyond the pale of jurisprudence, he relegated to the limbo of mere metaphor the laws of science, political economy, etc.[1]

Of Austin's " laws proper " some are enforced by one kind of sanction, others by other kinds. Thus, the revealed law of God is enforced by religious sanctions; the unrevealed law of God, known to men partly by means of the moral sense and partly by means of the test of utility, is enforced by ethical sanctions; the rules of voluntary associations are enforced by social sanctions. But the only kind of law sanctioned by the State and enforced in its courts is positive law. And positive law is within the law-courts final and supreme even though it conflicts with all and every other code of law whatsoever. " To say," says Austin, rebuking Blackstone, " that human laws which conflict with the divine law are not binding—that is to say, are not laws—is to talk stark nonsense." [2] Austin, of course, is absolutely right. The courts of the land must enforce the law of the land, or legal chaos would supervene. If in the opinion of any subject the law of the land conflicts with the divine law, or with the moral law, or with any code of

---

[1] The following table summarises the Austinian scheme of law. Its relation to the mediæval scheme is indicated by means of the names printed in brackets.

    I. LAWS PROPER
        1. Laws of God : (a) revealed (= *jus divinum*).
                        (b) unrevealed (= *jus naturale*).
        2. Positive laws (= *jus civile*).
        3. Other commands.
    II. LAWS IMPROPER—*e.g.*:
        1. Laws of honour or fashion or custom.
        2. International law (= *jus gentium*).
    III. LAWS METAPHORICAL—*e.g.*:
        1. Laws of science.
        2. Laws of political economy.

[2] Austin, *Jurisprudence*, vol. i, p. 215.

law regarded as having superior authority, three courses lie open to him: (1) he may use his political power and his social influence to get the law changed; (2) he may refuse to obey and pay the penalty; (3) he may, if he regards the situation as serious enough, organise a rebellion and endeavour to destroy the State, in the hope of setting up a new one more in accordance with his conscience. But meantime the courts of the State must enforce positive law—the law, the whole law, and nothing but the law.

Austin rendered an inestimable service to the cause of clear legal thinking by sweeping away from the field of jurisprudence all the antiquated lumber of natural law and natural rights by which it had long been littered and encumbered. There are some who hold that, in his definition of law, he over-stressed the idea of force and understressed the elements of order and justice. There are others who resent his exclusion of international law from the category of laws proper. Others, again, maintain that, especially in respect of primitive societies, he underestimated the importance and authority of custom. But none of these criticisms carries much weight. All of them are of historical and philosophical, rather than legal, significance. They do not affect the main point—namely, that positive law is the only kind of law that can possibly be recognised as valid in the law-courts of the State. Let us note, then, Austin's definition of positive law. It is, he says, "law set by a sovereign person or body of persons to a member or members of the independent political society [i.e., State] wherein that person or body is sovereign or supreme."[1] This brings us to Austin's second great conception—namely, that of State sovereignty. To that we will now turn.

V

THE THEORY OF SOVEREIGNTY

It cannot be said that Austin was so successful in elucidating the theory of sovereignty as he was in elucidating

[1] Austin, *Jurisprudence*, vol. i, p. 177.

the theory of law or in defining the province of jurisprudence. He was successful in his delimitations of law
and jurisprudence because he was able to distinguish more
clearly than any of his predecessors the sphere of legality
from the sphere of morality. He was less successful in
his attempts to define sovereignty because he was not able
to distinguish with sufficient clarity between three separate
and distinct forms of sovereignty—namely, the legal, the
political, and the ethical. The only question which he, as
a jurist, was called upon to answer was the legal question :
What is the ultimate or supreme authority recognised by
the law-courts as the source of positive law? But he confused this simple, straightforward, and easily answered
question with the more complicated and difficult political
question : What, as a matter of fact, is the ultimate or
supreme power which actually controls or governs the
State? Nor did he wholly keep these legal and political
questions from confusion with the still more disputable
ethical question : Where *ought* the ultimate and supreme
sovereignty to reside? In respect of Great Britain, for
example, he said that the sovereign—legal, political, and
ethical—was the composite body consisting of King, Lords,
and electors—a body which no law-court could recognise ;
a body which demonstrably has never exercised actual
governmental control ; a body whose ethical claim to
supremacy no one has ever maintained.[1]

That Austin confused the legal sovereign with the
political sovereign and with the ethical sovereign is no
doubt due to the fact that his predecessors had done the
same. Bodin, the first thinker to deal systematically with
the subject, had accurately (if not adequately) defined
sovereignty, as a legal conception, in the statement : *Majestas
est summa in cives ac subditos legibusque soluta potestas.*[2] But

---

[1] It is worth noting that this amazing muddle perpetrated by Austin in 1832 was
repeated by him in the pamphlet which he published in the last year of his life
(1859). In his *Plea for the Constitution*, p. 9, he says that " the sovereignty resides
in the King, the House of Lords, and the electoral body of the Commons." The
more one reads of Austin the more one is impressed by the difficulty and slowness
with which he escaped from his mental confusions.

[2] J. Bodin, *De Republica, Lib. I, cap.* 8.

his further discussion of *majestas* showed that his prime concern was the political problem—where in France actual sovereignty resided—and the ethical problem—as to whom the ultimate loyalty of Frenchmen was properly due. Similarly Hobbes, the second great theorist to treat of sovereignty, had dealt with the matter almost wholly from the political point of view. He was concerned not so much to clarify the procedure of the law-courts as to save the Commonwealth from a devastating civil war due to the contentions (1) of Parliamentarians, that sovereignty could be divided; (2) of philosophers, that natural law took precedence of civil law; (3) of jurists, that the common law was unchangeable even by statute; (4) of democrats, that the limits of obedience were determined by an original contract between sovereign and subjects; and (5) of ecclesiastics, both Catholic and Calvinistic, that the State was subordinate to the Church. He vehemently maintained on prudential grounds the political supremacy of the State, and on utilitarian grounds its ethical claims to ascendancy. Finally, Jeremy Bentham, Austin's immediate predecessor and master, had been primarily a law-reformer and not a legal theorist. His *Fragment on Government* (1776), which is mainly an essay on sovereignty, had been devoted to a destructive attack upon the introductory sections of Blackstone's *Commentaries*, wherein Blackstone had eulogised the English constitution as almost flawless; had exalted English law as ideal; had deprecated change; and had attributed the virtues of the English system of government precisely to that division and separation of the sovereign powers of legislation, administration, and adjudication whose division and separation Hobbes had declared to be impossible. Bentham had demolished Blackstone and reaffirmed with striking emphasis the necessary indivisibility of sovereignty. But it had been political, not legal, sovereignty of which he had treated.

Since all Austin's great predecessors had treated sovereignty from the political or ethical point of view, rather than from the legal point of view, it is not astonishing that Austin did the same. Nevertheless it is a misfortune that

180

he was not able to emancipate himself from the influence of his masters, because, since he had determined the province of jurisprudence, it was essential for the completion of his system of thought—his philosophy of positive law, as he called it—that he should consider and define sovereignty purely as a legal conception, without any reference to either politics or ethics. His problem was simply, as we have already remarked: What is the ultimate or supreme authority recognised by the law-courts—the authority from which there is no legal appeal?

Now this is a problem which, as a rule, when once its limitations are recognised, is fairly easily solved. Rarely, indeed, is its solution more difficult than that of an ordinary cross-word puzzle. In Great Britain, for example, the legal sovereign is obviously the King in Parliament—that is to say, the composite body consisting of King, Lords, and Commons. A statute of this body passed in due form cannot be questioned in any British court; and if stress is laid upon the words " in due form " as limiting the legal omnipotence of the King in Parliament, the answer is that this sovereign body can determine its own form and procedure. In the case of such a federal body as the United States of America, which necessarily has a rigid constitution, the solution to the puzzle is not quite so simple. It is not, however, very difficult; and if a great deal of misapplied ingenuity has been expended over it, this has been mainly owing to the fact that the would-be solvers have tried to discover a legal sovereign which is at the same time the political sovereign. Those who can dismiss the irrelevant problem of political sovereignty from their minds will soon come to the perception that the legal sovereign in America is the composite body (part central, part provincial) which has power to amend or abrogate the fundamental constitution.[1] The fact that this body is for long periods of years dormant and inoperative; the fact that even when it is roused from slumber it finds it difficult in practice to

[1] Including that fifth article of the constitution which has caused theoretical jurists so much concern—the article which decrees that, without its own consent, no " state " be deprived of its equal suffrage in the Senate.

do anything—these facts, and other facts of the same sort, do not in the slightest degree affect the issue. Here, in the realm of law, is the sovereign—that is to say, the ultimate or supreme authority from which, in the realm of law, there is no appeal. The problem of locating the legal sovereign in countries which have a rigid constitution wherein no provision is made for amendment, or in invertebrate organisations such as the mediæval Holy Roman Empire, or in Oriental tax-gathering empires such as that established by Cyrus in Persia or Runjeet Singh in the Punjab, is no doubt considerably more difficult. But it can always be solved provided that the country or the community in question was really a State in the modern sense of the term. If in any country or in any community there was, or is, no positive law, with courts administering it, *cadit quæstio.*

If Austin had confined his attention to his proper task— namely, the definition and location of *legal* sovereignty— he might have noted the following as its most conspicuous marks : (*a*) it is necessarily determinate, (*b*) it is capable of precise location, (*c*) it may be dormant or in abeyance, (*d*) it is capable of division, (*e*) it is incapable of legal limitation, (*f*) it is omnipotent within its own sphere, and (*g*) it is unaffected by any question of obedience or disobedience on the part of its subjects. The first two marks require no comment. As to the third, the dormancy of the legal sovereign may be illustrated by the long intervals (in one case over sixty years) which elapsed between amendments of the American constitution ; the abeyance of legal sovereignty may be said to occur whenever there is no House of Commons in being in Great Britain—that is to say, during the process of any general election. The dormancy or abeyance of the ultimate or supreme legal authority causes no inconvenience, because the actual work of administering the law is carried on without interruption by countless bodies exercising delegated powers. Moreover, fourthly, legal (though not political) sovereignty is capable of division, and in Great Britain is actually divided. Montesquieu and Blackstone were not, in this matter of separation of power, so completely mistaken as Bentham and Austin supposed

182

them to be. The legal sovereign in Great Britain is, as we have noted, the King in Parliament—that is to say, King, Lords, and Commons. But the King is the supreme executive, and the House of Lords is the supreme judicature. Hence, although no doubt the King in Parliament can legally do what it likes with both monarchy and peerage, nevertheless every legislative Act of Parliament requires for its sovereign efficacy the consent of the King (the supreme executive) and of the House of Lords (the supreme judicature), and *in the sphere of law* there is no reason why either of them should give it. Of course, in the sphere of practical politics . . . but we are not treating of that at present. In the sphere of law, or at any rate of legal theory, Great Britain seems to have developed a specimen of that juridical rarity, a divided sovereignty. As to the next, the fifth, point, that the supreme legislature is incapable of legal limitation—though not of political or moral limitation—is a commonplace of jurisprudence : there is no need to labour it. The sixth point, however—namely, that the legal sovereign is omnipotent within its own sphere, *i.e.*, the law-courts—calls for a moment's comment. For it recalls two famous sayings respecting the British Parliament—*i.e.*, King in Parliament and its powers—that deserve repetition and comment. The first is that of Sir Thomas Smith, made in his *Commonwealth of England* (1583):

> All that ever the people of Rome might do, either *centuriatis comitiis* or *tributis*, the same may be done by the Parliament of England, which representeth and hath the whole power of the realm, both the head and body.

This is sound sense, and is remarkable as being the first definite formulation of the legal theory of Parliamentary sovereignty. The second is that of Jean de Lolme in his *Constitution d'Angleterre* (1771) to the effect that " it is a fundamental principle with English lawyers that Parliament can do everything except make a woman a man, and a man a woman." This may be funny; but it is sheer nonsense. Parliament can do nothing except make laws ; and it can as easily make a law to the effect that every man must become a woman and every woman a man as it can make any other law. If it does make such a law the law-courts can do nothing but regard it as valid. They cannot, of course, compel either men or women to do the impossible —although the spectacle of long-haired men and short-haired women at the present day raises doubts as to whether or not this particular feat *is* impossible. But, assuming it to be impossible for an interchange of sex to take place, the law-courts can still impose the legal penalties enacted against those who do not do the impossible. And to impose penalties is all they can do in the case of the infringement of any law whatsoever. For the law is equally satisfied by the rendering of obedience or by the payment of the penalty of disobedience : it shows no preference whatsoever for the one as against the other. This brings us to the seventh and last mark of legal sovereignty: it is unaffected by any question of obedience or disobedience on the part of its subjects. A law duly enacted is a law even if no one obeys it at all; it is and remains a law, indeed, even if no one can possibly obey it.

With these marks of legal sovereignty in our minds let us examine Austin's definition of sovereignty. It is couched in singularly circumlocutory terms. " If," it runs,

> a determinate human superior, not in the habit of obedience to a like superior, receive habitual obedience from the bulk of a given society, that determinate superior is sovereign in that society, and the society (including the superior) is a society political and independent.[1]

Here, it is obvious, is a hopeless confusion between the legal and the political sovereign—a confusion due, apparently, to the baseless assumption that the two are identical. The *legal* sovereign must be " a determinate human superior " : the law-courts must know precisely from whom emanate the commands which they are precluded from treating as invalid. The *political* sovereign, however—that is, the power which actually exercises supreme control in a State—need not be determinate, and, in fact, very rarely

[1] Austin, *Jurisprudence*, vol. i, p. 221.

is so. As the American jurist J. C. Gray well says, "The real rulers of a political society are undiscoverable. They are the persons who dominate over the wills of their fellows."[1] They may be a single crowd-compeller, such as Lenin or Mussolini; they may be a group of demagogues, such as the French Committee of Public Safety; they may be a gang of conspirators, or the leaders of an army, or the organisers of a general strike; they may be a band of newspaper proprietors; they may be the electors; or they may be a host of men, unknown even to one another, who by speech and writing mould that vague but potent thing called public opinion. Austin, then, starts his definition with his eye correctly fixed on the determinate legal sovereign, and not on the indeterminate political sovereign. But he immediately shifts it. For the requirements of habitual obedience within the State, and habitual freedom from obedience to extraneous authority, although vital to the existence of political sovereignty, are totally irrelevant to legal sovereignty.

If we ask what are the distinguishing marks of the *political* sovereign—that is, of the actual controlling power in the State, as distinct from the legal sovereign—the answer is that the *political* sovereign, as distinct from the legal sovereign, (a) is generally indeterminate; (b) is generally incapable of precise location; (c) cannot be in abeyance, any more than a mass can be devoid of a centre of gravity; (d) is incapable of division, just as the centre of gravity of a mass cannot be divided; but (e) is subject to all kinds of effective limitations and restrictions.

The last is, perhaps, the only point that calls for explication. Is not a limited or restricted sovereignty a contradiction in terms? No; in the sphere of politics it is not. For political sovereignty—the actual control of a State—is a shifting, unstable, impermanent thing. A stroke may incapacitate Lenin, a shot may remove Mussolini, a mistake in tactics may overthrow a trade union or newspaper oligarchy, a parrot-cry or a panic may revolutionise public opinion. Hence there are certain things which no political

[1] J. C. Gray, *The Nature and Sources of the Law*, p. 79 (1924).

sovereign-of-the-moment dare do, if he wishes to remain sovereign. Political sovereignty is always precarious. Not even Lenin dared to take the land from the Russian peasants. Not even Mussolini dared to break with the Papacy and occupy the Vatican. No political sovereign, in short, however highly exalted above all subjects he may be, can hope to retain supreme authority unless he recognises that there are certain things he cannot do, certain spheres into which he must not enter. The penalty for the ignoring of these restrictions and limitations is that he ceases to be sovereign. That is to say, he ceases to receive that " habitual obedience from the bulk of a given society " which Austin might have correctly noted as a mark of the *political* sovereign, even though it had no relevance to the *legal* sovereign to whom he seemed to apply it.

This sharp and all-important distinction between legal and political sovereignty, which Austin so fatally ignored, gives rise to three questions. First, if the doctrine of legal sovereignty has no significance outside the law-courts is it worth while to pay so much attention to it? Secondly, what, if any, is the relation of the legal to the political sovereign in a State? Thirdly, what is to be said concerning the ethical question, Where *ought* supreme power to reside? The answers to these questions must be brief and summary.

I. The problem of the nature and location of the legal sovereign is important simply because the law and the law-courts play so prominent a part in our communal life. Law lies at the very base of our civilisation; all our social and economic institutions are founded upon it; upon its existence and stability the continuance of all our liberties and felicities depend. Almost every act of our lives is conditioned by law; in the atmosphere of law we for ever move and have our being. Hence the law-courts and the rules they administer and enforce determine the ways of life of the whole community, even though but a small fraction of the community actually passes through their formidable portals. The main subject of Parliamentary debates and divisions, and the main object of general elections, is to decide the nature of the laws which the country shall impose. Thus the problem of legal sovereignty is not an abstract question, of interest only to philosophical jurists : it is a practical question of the closest personal concern to every subject.

II. Since the question of the nature and location of legal sovereignty is a matter of such urgent moment to every citizen, it is clear that the political sovereign—*i.e.*, the person or body of persons that actually exercises dominant control in the State—will not tolerate the continued existence of a legal sovereign (*e.g.*, in Great Britain a Parliament) that does not conform to its wish. If no constitutional means exist for keeping the legal sovereign in harmony with and— outside the law-courts, wherein alone it is supreme—in subjection to the political sovereign, a revolution is likely to ensue. In Great Britain the electors are assumed to be the political sovereign, and periodical general elections are the device adopted for the maintenance of harmony between them as a body and the legally sovereign Parliament. But the precise seat of political sovereignty, as we have already observed, is extremely difficult to locate, and the assumption that it resides in the electors as a body is by no means unchallenged. In 1926, for instance, it was challenged by the trade unions, or rather, by a certain company of trade-union officials, syndicalists, and communists, who acted in the name of the unions. If their general strike had been successful and they had destroyed Parliamentary government in this country they would have been compelled to institute a new legal sovereign, a new system of law-courts, and a new body of law. By some means or other, in short, the conventional sovereign within the law-courts must be kept in harmony with, and in subordination to, the political sovereign who actually exercises dominant authority in the world outside the law-courts.

III. What, finally, is to be said concerning the ethical question, Where *ought* supreme power to reside in a community? We have already remarked that the political sovereign, however great his power, is practically restricted by numerous limitations of a prudential kind. In other words, there are certain things which no despot, however autocratic, could possibly do with any hope of being allowed to retain his place and power. As David Hume well observed, " It is on opinion only that Government is founded ; and this maxim extends to the most despotic and most military Governments, as well as to the most free and most popular." [1] Political sovereigns who abuse their power are faced by rebellion, which, if it is sufficiently widespread, deprives them of their sovereignty and sets up another sovereign in their stead. And just as there are certain things that they cannot or dare not do, so there are other things which (on moral or religious grounds), they *ought* not to do. These things, no doubt, vary from age to age as ethical standards change. At the present time it would perhaps be generally agreed that the political sovereign *ought* not to persecute its subjects in the matter of religious belief, and, on the other hand, that it *ought* to seek so far as its power extends to secure " the greatest happiness of the greatest number " of those within the scope of its authority.

But, since political sovereignty cannot be divided, the problem remains, when all has been said concerning moral and other limitations of sovereignty, where in the last resort *ought* this supreme authority to reside? This is the problem that Austin discusses in his *Plea for the Constitution* (1859). He solves it in a conservative sense ; but he is as emphatic as the most convinced democrat that the ultimate sovereignty must reside, and ought to reside, in the State. For the State represents the community as a whole, and, as the world is at present constituted, it is the only institution that does so. Hence, however large an autonomy the State may leave to Churches, to trade unions, to universities, and to other voluntary associations of a sectional kind, in the last resort its authority must, in the interest of the community as a whole, override them all. So long as the primary division of mankind is the present division into nations, so long must each nation, organised as a State and acting through its Government, be supreme within the territorial limits of its jurisdiction in all causes and over all persons. Political sovereignty cannot be par-

---

[1] D. Hume, *Essay on the First Principles of Government* (1741).

JOHN AUSTIN

titioned. There cannot within one and the same territorial area be more than one authority employing the sanction of physical force. The conduct of international diplomacy and the power of waging war and making peace also demand a central and final authority. The right of levying taxes by compulsion cannot reside in multiple hands.

In short, in so far as the community of the nation is valuable as a maintainer of justice, a keeper of peace, an organiser of the conditions of the good life, it demands for its executive Government the obedience of all good men. But it must never be forgotten that the benefits of community are not the supreme values. The supreme values of truth and righteousness concern the individual conscience alone. As it has often happened in the past, so it may happen again in the future that the lonely soul will have to decide whether or not the ineluctable claims of truth and righteousness demand that the authority of the community be defied and the higher authority of the individual conscience be obeyed. No well-balanced mind will lightly challenge an authority upon which so much that is essential to human felicity depends as the State. No sane man will wantonly precipitate the anarchy that any formidable defiance of the will of the Government necessarily entails. Nevertheless, in the last resort the individual conscience is supreme.

> Whoso has felt the Spirit of the Highest
> Cannot confound nor doubt Him nor deny:
> Yea, with one voice, O World, tho' thou deniest,
> Stand thou on that side, for on this am I.

Postscript

Other questions concerning the sovereignty of the State have risen since Austin's day, questions which it would be irrelevant for us to discuss here. Such questions are, for example, the problem of the relation of the British Parliament to the Parliaments and other legislative assemblies of the Empire; and, still more vital, the place of the sovereign national State in general in a League of Nations or a Federated World. These are large and complex problems

189

of prodigious practical importance. All we can or need say about them here and now is that their solution will be immensely facilitated if those who have to deal with them come to their treatment with an adequate acquaintance with their Austin, and with clear ideas as to the true nature of law, of sovereignty, and of the State.

The Editor

BOOK LIST

A. Primary Sources

Austin, John:
1. *The Province of Jurisprudence Determined.* 1832.
2. *A Plea for the Constitution.* 1859.
3. *Lectures on Jurisprudence.* 2 vols. 1863. 5th edition, edited by Robert Campbell, 1885.

B. Secondary Sources

Anson, W.: *Law and Custom of the Constitution.* 1886.
Brown, W. J.: *The Austinian Theory of Law.* 1906.
Bryce, James (Lord): *Studies in History and Jurisprudence.* 1901.
Clark, E. C.: *Practical Jurisprudence.* 1883.
Dicey, A. V.: *Law of the Constitution.* 1885.
Gray, J. C.: *The Nature and Sources of the Law.* 1909.
Harrison, F.: *Jurisprudence and the Conflict of Laws.* 1919.
Holland, T. E.: *The Elements of Jurisprudence.* 1880.
Lewis, G. C.: *Use and Abuse of Political Terms.* 1832.
Maine, H. S.: *Early History of Institutions.* 1875.
Markby, W.: *Elements of Law.* 1871.
Mill, J. S.: *Dissertations and Discussions.* 1867.
—— *Autobiography.* 1873.
Pollock, F.: *A First Book of Jurisprudence.* 1896.
Ritchie, D. G.: *Principles of State Interference.* 1902.
Salmond, J. W.: *Jurisprudence, or the Theory of Law.* 1902.
Sidgwick, H.: *Elements of Politics.* 1919.

IX

THOMAS HODGSKIN AND THE INDIVIDUALISTS

INDIVIDUALISM is the offspring of change. In one sense, of course, it is only an outgrowth of the nature of man, the simple functioning of an instinct. But it becomes rationalised into a political theory only during those epochs when the crust of established custom gets broken; when well-nigh limitless vistas of possibility seem to open themselves as inducements to individual initiative. Such an epoch was the period of the early Industrial and Agrarian Revolutions in England. The social and economic changes of those movements resulted in one of these rebirths of individualism. It began as an argument of criticism; it ended as an accepted dogma. But one feature of the new individualism was unique: it concerned not merely political life and the desire for political power; it was bound up with the new industrial life and the desire for increased wealth; and it affected not merely a select few in the community, but increasingly spread among all classes. The productivity of human labour was now vaster than ever before, and the producers sought a creed which should justify them in claiming a proportionate share of that increased wealth. One line of thought along which this was attempted was the collectivist: the work of Owen and Thompson and their followers. The other line of thought was that sketched in this essay: the assertion of individual rights—both political and economic—and of the equality of worth among human beings, culminating in the optimistic belief that the progressive emancipation from all restraint would produce an harmonious and automatic equilibrium of forces.

There were, of course, many different varieties of individualism, and this essay concerns only one of them. Until

1820 old Major Cartwright was still preaching his apocalyptic rationalism. Richard Carlile, in *The Republican* (1820–26), was continuing the work of Tom Paine, and (at one time) advocating the general strike as well as manhood suffrage. William Lovett was preaching a creed half Owenite and half Hodgskinite, stressing the need for both complete democracy and national education to give men equality of opportunity. The Benthamite School claimed to be individualistic through and through. And even the devil cited individualism for his purpose, as Richard Oastler learned when he began his campaign for factory legislation in the *Leeds Mercury* (October 1830): for the factory owners at once raised the cry, " May we not do what we like with our own? " A score other examples might be cited of the manifestations of the individualistic spirit. Here, however, we shall concentrate our attention only on Thomas Hodgskin's remarkable attempt to establish a creed of industrial individualism in the interest of the workers.

I

Less is known of the details of Thomas Hodgskin's life than of any other thinker dealt with in this volume. Unlike Owen, Hunt, Lovett, Bamford, Knight, and a score or more of his Radical contemporaries, he neither wrote nor contemplated writing an autobiography; and since he was apparently of a more retiring temperament, and less enamoured of the platform, than the other leaders of the reform movement, the significance of his work and the strength of his influence have been overlooked until recent years.

Yet to overlook that work will only lead to a false perspective of the ideological forces in England in the thirty years following Waterloo. For his position, and that of the men whom he influenced, is distinctive, and markedly different from the two schools of reformist thought with which the period is most frequently associated. Benthamism and Owenism both came in for his caustic criticisms, as the sequel shows; and the adherents of both

192

schools agreed in regarding his teaching as dangerous and pernicious. Yet he never succeeded in attaching a label to his doctrine; nor did he secure a compact body of followers. Therein may be found one of the causes of the oblivion into which his name has since fallen, though others may appear in the course of the discussion.

Thomas Hodgskin was born at Chatham on December 12, 1787. His father, it seems, was storekeeper in the commissary department of the Admiralty docks. His childhood appears to have been far from happy. According to the son's description, his father was selfish and recklessly extravagant, and reduced the family to misery, in spite of the mother's efforts to keep up appearances. At twelve years old Thomas was entered as a naval cadet. For about twelve years he remained with the fleet and saw extensive service in many parts. But he resented the strictness of naval discipline and the capriciousness of those exercising it, and, although for a time he endured it, eventually, in about 1812, his resentment blazed out. "I complained of the injury done me by a commander-in-chief," he writes, "to himself, in the language I thought it merited." The result was obvious. He was forthwith put on the retired list on half-pay with lieutenant's rank, and at the age of twenty-five had to set about making a new career for himself.

This dismissal, and the necessity of starting life over again, naturally embittered him. But he was so convinced of the justice of his defiance, and of his resentment against naval laws and customs, that (as he tells us) he considered it incumbent upon him to rouse public opinion in order to get such conditions altered. He accordingly wrote and published his first work in 1813. Its full title is *An Essay on Naval Discipline, showing Part of its Evil Effects on the Minds of the Officers and the Minds of the Men and on the Community, with an Amended System by which Pressing may be immediately abolished*, by Lieutenant Thomas Hodgskin, R.N. Though the work calls for no close examination here, it is an interesting essay, urging the reform of obvious abuses and advocating voluntary enlistment for short-time terms, with better pay as one of the attractions to recruits. The germs of a number of Hodgskin's later ideas can, moreover, be found in the *Essay* : his theism, his Utilitarian individualism, his cosmopolitanism, and his hatred of man-made laws. But all these doctrines were to be developed at much greater length in the next twenty years.

About the time that this work was published Hodgskin first came into contact with Francis Place. We have few details of his movements, and are dependent upon his correspondence with Place, and upon Place's correspondence with Mill, for our information. In one of these letters Place describes him as modest, gloomy, unobtrusive, and easily excited. He also adds that Hodgskin is of a speculative turn of mind, and " entertains some very curious metaphysical opinions." [1] It was these same " curious metaphysical opinions " which were to lead Hodgskin to fall out with Benthamite individualists on the one hand and Owenite collectivists on the other. It was these opinions which formed the core of his social philosophy and gave him his distinctive place in his generation.

In 1815 we find Hodgskin is at Edinburgh, and is proposing to embody his philosophy in a work *On Mind*. The manuscript of the work was apparently sent to Place, who tried to find a publisher for it and failed. With what else he was occupied, or whence he derived an income (other than his naval pension), we do not know. But when the war was ended he projected a journey across Europe, in the fashion of Arthur Young, to study the working of Governments and the influence they have on national character. The journey began in July 1815, and lasted three years. While abroad he corresponded constantly with Place, and the correspondence not only gives us sidelights on Hodgskin's own character—his shyness, his pessimism, and the introspective twist of his mind—but also shows us that he was clarifying, and defining more precisely, his social and political ideas. He passes through France, Italy, Switzerland, Austria, and Germany. But it is not until he gets into North Germany that he decides to act on Place's advice

[1] British Museum Add. MSS. 27791, f. 269.

and to write a work describing his travels in those parts. Place thereupon forwards a questionnaire which Bentham had dictated to James Mill for him; and Hodgskin's letters to England now become extensive drafts of the proposed book. He returns to England in November 1818, but refuses an invitation to stay with Bentham at Ford Abbey, and goes north to Edinburgh once more. There he was rejoined by a German lady he had met in Hanover, and married her in the early part of 1819. He then began upon his book of travels. The work was published in two volumes in January 1820, under the title *Travels in the North of Germany*. It is in many respects the most interesting and readable of all his writings. Its criticisms and comments show clearly the development of his ideas since the *Essay on Naval Discipline*; they show, moreover, that Hodgskin's ideas were diverging markedly from the orthodoxy of the Benthamites in the direction of anarchism; for not only is the control of economic life by State and corporation denounced, but the creation of democratically elected representative assemblies is also severely criticised.

Since Hodgskin had first come into contact with Place and his friends two events of outstanding importance in the development and promulgation of Philosophical Radicalism had taken place. One was the publication of Ricardo's *Principles of Political Economy* in 1817, and the other was James Mill's writing of his famous article on "Government" for the new supplement to the *Encyclopædia Britannica*. (This article was published shortly after the appearance of Hodgskin's *Travels*.) The one represents the defining of Utilitarian Radicalism on its economic side, the other presents an unmistakably clear summary of the doctrine and implications of Benthamism on its purely political side. Bain has said of the latter [1] (not without exaggeration) that "in the train of events culminating in the Reform Bill of 1832, this article counted as a principal factor." Certainly both events had important consequences. It was just at the time, then, when middle-class Utilitarianism was being defined in popular form that Hodgskin was himself

---

[1] *Life of James Mill*, p. 215.

developing a rival political theory, more purely proletarian in appeal and more revolutionary in its implications. But this divergence in doctrine does not result in any break with Place. Hodgskin's relations with that group do not seem to have become strained until some years later—especially when the imminence of reform in 1830 produced the cleavage between the 'moderate' and 'extreme' sections of the democratic party. But for the moment there is much on which Hodgskin and the Benthamites are at one, and the letters are cordial. Place, indeed, even succeeds in persuading Hodgskin (in June 1819) to drop a projected scheme for writing a book in criticism of Ricardo's teaching.

We do not know much of Hodgskin's life in Edinburgh. We find him in close touch with MacCulloch, editor of *The Scotsman*, especially when the campaign for the abolition of the Combination Acts is begun in that paper. He acts as a kind of intermediary between Place and MacCulloch. But this friendship with the editor did not prevent *The Scotsman* rejecting an article which Hodgskin had written in January 1820 attacking the very basis of positive law in terms of his own doctrine of natural law. Other articles were refused by other papers, and Hodgskin's position became serious. In January 1822 he is writing in a depressed strain to Place. The *Travels* has produced no royalties; his wife can find no pupils; then she becomes ill and is sent to Hodgskin's father at Deptford. Hodgskin becomes more distraught and miserable. Finally, Place rescues him from these depressing circumstances by securing for him a post as Parliamentary reporter on the *Morning Chronicle* through the good graces of James Mill, who is a friend of Black, the editor. At the end of 1822, therefore, Hodgskin returns to London.

Soon after he had taken up this post Hodgskin is undertaking a new and unique project. In co-operation with a man named Robertson, he plans a weekly journal of popular science addressed mainly to artisans. It is of the type that has since become common, but it was the first of its kind in England. The first number was issued in August 1823, with the title of *The Mechanics' Magazine*. Hodgskin writes

196

two articles for the early numbers to dissuade the Spital-fields silk-weavers from protesting against the repeal of the statutes which provided for the fixing of their wages by the magistrates, and to warn them generally against " the legislative illusion." Then Hodgskin and Robertson, having successfully launched their first project, embark upon a second. They propose to establish in London a " mechanics' institute " such as Glasgow, Edinburgh, and Liverpool already possess. The project is first set forth in the *Magazine* for October 11, 1823, where Hodgskin writes on the necessity for working men's education. The originators of the scheme intend to carry it out by means of subscriptions from the workers themselves. But Place persuades them that this is impossible, and gets them to agree to a public appeal backed by the chief Radical reformers. This is done ; but another struggle ensues over the question of Dr Birkbeck's loan—at interest—of a large proportion of the necessary money. Hodgskin strongly disapproves of such a transaction, but is over-persuaded by Place. When the scheme was first mooted Hodgskin and Robertson had been made temporary honorary secretaries. But subsequently they were replaced by a paid secretary ; nor were they elected to the governing body when that was established in December. The details of the episode are rather obscure ; but they sufficiently illustrate the inevitable cleavage that was to come between Place and the middle-class reformers on the one hand, and the proletarian group who distrusted middle-class interference on the other. Yet it does not appear that Hodgskin broke with the Benthamites at this jucture. Indeed, M. Halévy suggests that Hodgskin accompanied Bentham to Paris in September 1825. Certainly Hodgskin did not sever his connections with the institute where he was hoping to lecture on political economy.

The year 1824 witnessed the climax of the movement for the repeal of the Combination Acts. Hodgskin was dissatisfied with both the statement of their case made by the workers themselves, and the Ricardian case that combinations would do no harm. He therefore put together for the occasion his own case for repeal, based upon the claim of the worker to the " right to the whole produce of labour," and hoped that its doctrines might be spread through the mechanics' institutes. The publishers of *The Mechanics' Magazine* published the pamphlet in 1825, with the title, *Labour Defended against the Claims of Capital, or the Unproductiveness of Capital proved with reference to the Present Combinations amongst Journeymen, by a Labourer.* The same year he apparently quarrelled with Robertson, and gave up the editorship of the *Magazine*; but he also became friendly with Dr Birkbeck. It was in all probability through the latter's influence that Hodgskin—in spite of the protests of Place—was allowed to give a short course of lectures on economics at the institute in 1825. Two other courses were subsequently given, on grammar and on social progress, but only the first of the three was published. Hodgskin developed his economic lectures during 1826, and in the following year they were published as *Popular Political Economy*. The word ' popular,' the author is careful to explain, is used not to denote the nature of the appeal; it is meant rather to indicate the scope of the philosophy. In other words, the book is intended to provide a working-class political economy in opposition to the prevailing middle-class social philosophy now establishing itself as an orthodox dogma. The basic ideas of the book are not dissimilar from those of *Labour Defended*, though they are more fully worked out.

Political economy, however, was not, strictly speaking, Hodgskin's main interest. It was only a development of, and deduction from, that main interest; " an episode," he calls it. What had occupied Hodgskin's mind ever since the *Essay on Naval Discipline* was the problem of law and the nature of political obligation. He had long been considering writing a book on the subject. What he had so far written was merely a particular application to special circumstances of his own philosophy of law. As things turned out, he was destined never to write that long-projected work. But between 1829 and 1832 he wrote what was, in substance, an epitome of his doctrine, and what was,

198

in fact, his last completed book. In 1829 Brougham made his famous speech in the House advocating law reform and adumbrating his legal philosophy along Benthamite lines. Hodgskin wrote " open letters " in reply, though they were not published at the time. In 1831, however, the Society for the Diffusion of Useful Information (of which Brougham was president) published anonymously an essay on economic matters entitled *The Rights of Industry*. This interesting pamphlet is a vigorous statement of the middle-class attitude warning the workers against " dangerous " doctrines. It was obviously meant as an attack on Hodgskin's theories, and on " the pretended teachers of political economy who were ranting in popular assemblies about the unequal allotment of riches."[1] Hodgskin thought that Brougham had written it (indeed, the lurid phraseology and purple passages might not unjustifiably lead to that conclusion), and Hodgskin hated Brougham as both man and thinker. In actual fact, the book had been written by Charles Knight, the journalist, publisher to the society. Believing, then, that this attack on him came from the hand of Brougham, Hodgskin supplemented what he had already written in the " open letters " and published his reply in 1832 as *The Natural and Artificial Right of Property Contrasted*. It was a full defence of his doctrine of the worker's right to the whole produce of his labour, and a clear presentation of the doctrine of a natural law superseding and overcoming positive law and leading eventually to anarchism. Hodgskin bases himself on Locke, as against Bentham, and presses Locke's doctrine of a natural law to its extreme conclusions ; at the same time attacking Owen, Saint-Simon, and the Moravians as vigorously as he criticises the Philosophical Radicals.

Hodgskin's influence at this time was perceptibly growing. He had given the workers an alternative creed to Benthamism and Owenism, and to those who were disappointed and resentful at the nature of the Reform Bill he offered a rallying cry. The extent to which the later Chartists were indebted to his teaching can never be

[1] Charles Knight, *Passages in a Working Life*, vol. ii, p. 169.

precisely judged. Certainly it was great. Place and Mill were equally annoyed at his increasing influence over the London working men, as well as at the influence they believed he exercised over Black, the editor of the *Morning Chronicle*. Place's estimate of Hodgskin's work is important not only as coming from a man avowedly critical of that work, but from the man above all others capable of judging London working-class sentiment. Writing of the teaching of Owen and Hodgskin, Place says :

> The mischief these two men have in some respects done is incalculable. They have, however, set thousands thinking; and difficult as it is, and will be, to eradicate the false notions they have inculcated, yet the thinking portion of the working people having been led by them to believe themselves of some importance in the State, will never cease to think so; and the time will come when they will think correctly on all which concerns their real condition in society.[1]

Elsewhere he says that the workers passed on, in their thinking, from the teaching of Owen to that of Thomas Hodgskin. The doctrines of the latter

> were carefully and continually propagated among them as well orally as by small publications. Many of them were sold for two-pence a dozen. They were carefully and cleverly written for the purpose intended, and were very widely circulated.

Moreover, small societies, " unknown to all but themselves," were formed by Hodgskin's followers, especially in London. And the well-known verses used by the National Union of the Working Classes were, after all, but a statement of what Hodgskin had taught in *Labour Defended* and *Popular Political Economy*.

> Wages should form the price of goods,
> Yes, wages should be all.
> Then we who work to make the goods
> Should *justly have them all.*
> But if their price be made of rent,
> Tithes, taxes, profits, all,
> Then we who work to make the goods
> Shall have—just none at all.[2]

[1] Add. MSS. 27791, f. 270.   [2] Add. MSS. 27791, f. 240.

THOMAS HODGSKIN

At the height of the Reform Bill excitement James Mill was definitely alarmed at the spread of these ideas, though he seemed singularly confused as to their nature. He wrote to Place on October 25, 1831, about a deputation of workers that had been sent to Black, of the *Morning Chronicle*.

> Their notions about property look ugly; they not only desire that it should have nothing to do with representation, which is true, though not a truth for the present time, as they ought to see, but they seem to think that it should not exist, and that the existence of it is an evil to them. Rascals, I have no doubt, are at work among them.[1]

This comment shows how completely Mill was out of touch with the new ideas among the workers, and Place's reply corrects the misconceptions, and illustrates further Hodgskin's influence. " The men who called on Black," he says,

> were not a deputation from the working people, but two out of half a dozen who manage, or mismanage, the meetings of the Rotunda in Blackfriars Road, and at the Philadelphian Chapel in Finsbury. The doctrine they are now preaching is that promulgated by Hodgskin in a tract in 1825 entitled *Labour Defended against the Claims of Capital*.

The Rotundanists ran weekly meetings for the further dissemination of these ideas, and for a while produced a magazine expounding not only their demand for manhood suffrage, but also Hodgskin's economic teaching. Apparently in the ensuing twelve months Mill had been made more familiar with the new ideas and the strength of the proletarian organisation, for he wrote a long letter to Brougham [2] giving the Lord Chancellor his attitude to the extreme democrats. " Nothing can be conceived more mischievous than the doctrines which have been preached to the common people," he writes.

> The nonsense to which your Lordship alludes about the rights of the labourer to the whole produce of the country [*sic*], wages,

---

[1] Add. MSS. 27790, f. 23.   [2] Bain, *Life of James Mill*, p. 363 ff.

profits, and rent all included, is the mad nonsense of our friend Hodgkin [*i.e.*, Hodgskin] which he has published as a system and propagates with the zeal of perfect fanaticism. Whatever of it appears in the *Chronicle*, steals in through his means, he being a sort of sub-editor, and Black not very sharp in detecting.

These opinions, he thinks, if they were to spread, " would be the subversion of civilised society; worse than the overwhelming deluge of Huns and Tartars." Later he goes on to say that one of the most disquieting features of the situation is

the illicit cheap publications, in which the doctrine of the right of the labouring people, who, they say, are the only producers, to all that is produced, is very generally preached. The alarming nature of this evil you will understand when I inform you that these publications are superseding the Sunday newspapers, and every other channel through which the people might get better information.

Meanwhile, when Place and Mill were growing steadily more suspicious of the tendency of Hodgskin's teaching, the latter was attaining still more publicity by the attacks levelled at him by Thomas Cooper, author of the American *Lectures on the Elements of Political Economy*, in the second edition of that work, 1829, and by Charles Knight in *The Rights of Industry*.

Strangely enough, it was just when Hodgskin was becoming known to a wider circle that his active political career came to an end, and that the hack journalist submerged the political thinker. He still proposed to write his *magnum opus* on law; but his immediate personal needs, for some reason that we know nothing of, became pressing again. He was already the father of seven children, and his wife was frequently ailing. From now until the end of his life—with a single exception—he disappears from the public sight, and all his time is taken up with ephemeral journalism. He writes for the *Chronicle, Daily News, Courier, Brighton Guardian*, and *Illustrated London News*. He also worked with Hansard at his *Parliamentary Debates*. What part he took in the Chartist movement we do not know. Certainly

THOMAS HODGSKIN

he supported the Anti-Corn Law agitation by his articles. Then in 1846 he joined the staff of *The Economist*, which James Wilson started in 1843. For the next twelve years he was writing articles and reviews for that magazine every few weeks, and dealing with every kind of social and economic theme; and, although in some details his opinions may have changed slightly, yet in essentials his philosophy remained what it had been in the twenties. Indeed, the surprising fact is that, with such uncompromising doctrines as he held, he should have kept his post so long. He eventually broke with Wilson in May 1857—apparently on the question of prison reform and capital punishment. One interesting and important fact, however, has to be noticed in connection with his association with *The Economist*, and that is the close contact he had with Herbert Spencer, who was sub-editor of the paper from 1848 to 1853, and who published his *Social Statics* during that period (1851). We do not know the details of that association, and Spencer mentions Hodgskin only once in the *Autobiography*. But Spencer's doctrines are, in many respects, so strikingly similar to Hodgskin's that it is not fanciful to assume that the older man to no small degree helped to confirm the younger in the quasi-anarchistic philosophy to which his temperament and upbringing had inclined him and which Hodgskin had spent so many years in developing.

In the summer of 1857 Hodgskin made what was apparently his last public appearance. He delivered two lectures in St Martin's Hall, and published them the same year under the title *What shall we do with our Criminals?* But the lectures were poorly attended, and he did not repeat the experiment. He was still announcing, however, in this (his last) publication his intention to write a fuller work on law " which will be called *Demonstration of the Absurdity of Legislation*." But it was never written. The last years were spent uneventfully, his children helping to keep their parents; and he died on August 21, 1869. Not a single London journal noted his death.

II

There are certain general characteristics which are to be found in all Hodgskin's thinking. Undoubtedly the most important of these is his firm belief in the conception of the universe as an organised *system*, and the " materialism " of his conception of history has to be qualified by this fact. For him—and he states the fact in terms as uncompromising as any to be found in the pages of Godwin, by whom he was obviously much influenced—the world is a system determined by fixed, immutable laws, which, if allowed to work without the interference and tampering of man, would produce perfection. These laws are not made by man, but by " the power which sustains, informs, and regulates the moral as well as the material world." [1] It is man's duty simply to discover those laws, and, having discovered them, to live by them. Legislation in any sense of the word is unnecessary. Hodgskin takes as his motto some words from J. B. Say : " The laws which determine the prosperity of nations are not the work of man ; they are derived from the nature of things. We do not establish, we discover them." Almost every page of his writing emphasises this conception. He was always thinking of the " wisdom and spirit of the universe," immanent in all things, working according to fixed laws. Consequently, morality and science are but two aspects of the same thing, since they are both expressions of omnipresent reason. " Moral feeling and scientific truth must always be in harmony with each other." [2] In one place this rationalism becomes almost lyrical. " Thus we see," he says,

> that the world, every part of which is regulated by unalterable laws, is adapted to man, and not man to the world. This reciprocity, or rather uniformity, of the laws regulating the conduct of man and the material world connects him at all times, however high may be his bearing and exalted his hopes, with the clod from which he sprang and with the vast universe which he has the intelligence to

[1] *Popular Political Economy*, p. xix. [2] *Ibid.*, p. xxii.

scan and a soul to reverence. He is a part of the wisely regulated creation.[1]

In another place he says that man " is regulated by permanent and invariable laws." This scheme of the universe Hodgskin calls by different names, but it is most often designated as nature. For him nature is the supreme value which man must learn to apprehend.

The second characteristic of his thinking is but a corollary of the first: thorough and uncompromising individualism. Hodgskin, who began his public career by a revolt against a discipline which crushed individuality, never lost the intensity of that individualism throughout life. Believing as he did that universal nature was working through every single man, he quite logically denied the necessity for any governmental authority at all. The rational urge within is sufficient. This dogmatic individualism, also, is as definite as Godwin's. One might almost be justified in saying that Hodgskin was a mystic; for he believed in an omnipresent Spirit working through the whole of the material universe, and he believed that this Spirit could be directly apprehended by the individual, who would then order his life in the light of that experience. Ardent individualism is often the offspring of mysticism, and Hodgskin was no exception to that dictum. He thoroughly disapproves of government, and even as early as his book on Germany declares that the State-built roads of the Continent are inferior to the private ones of England.[2] Similarly he condemns the guild and the trade regulations and the Government monopolies which he finds on the Continent; yet, strangely though consistently enough, he declares that even here Government is not to interfere to abolish them, but must leave them to be abolished by the rest of society.[3] Thus he naturally objects to a census, because it is treating men " something like beasts." It calls for no comment, therefore, that he opposes any form of interference in the relations between capital and labour, and condemns the activities of " meddling philanthropists and factitious demagogues."

[1] *Popular Political Economy*, p. xxviii.
[2] *Travels in the North of Germany*, vol. i, p. 140.   [3] *Ibid.*, vol. i, p. 185.

His third characteristic has already been touched upon, since it is closely bound up with the others : his fierce assertion of *laissez-faire*. If the finite intellect of man did not tamper with the infinite laws of the universe everything would work together for good. Unrestrained competition should exist within the community, for that alone will produce social perfection. Every problem on which Hodgskin gives an opinion brings out again and again this unshakable belief that he has at the back of his mind in pre-established harmony. That is why competition should be utterly unimpeded, and that again is why " the author has satisfied himself that all law-making, except gradually and quietly to repeal all existing laws, is arrant humbug."[1] Moreover, " society can exist and prosper without the lawmaker, and consequently without the tax-gatherer."[2]

Such, then, are the three chief characteristics of his thinking—mechanical philosophy, uncompromising individualism, and a political and economic policy of *laissez-faire*. How it can possibly have occurred that Hodgskin should have been mistaken by contemporaries for a collectivist one is unable to explain, because he himself had provided a warning in the preface to one of his books. He says of his theory:

> It is not likely, indeed, to be popular with any class. It flatters no passions, it neither proves that the wealth of the rich is in the order of nature, nor justifies the desire of spoliation in the poor. It encourages no hope of finding a speedy remedy for present evils and seems destined to find no favour with any one class, because all look only to the law for protection or improvement. It appeals to reason, and the author knows that the judges in that court are few.[3]

This passage is typical of Hodgskin's pessimism.

What is the nature of political economy? Obviously, given the presuppositions just mentioned, political economy is for Hodgskin a science, since " the laws which regulate the production of wealth form part of the system of the universe."[4] He protests against the prevailing idea of the

---

[1] *Natural and Artificial Right of Property Contrasted*, p. i.   [2] *Ibid.*, p. ii.
[3] *Ibid.*, p. iii.   [4] *Popular Political Economy*, p. viii.

subject as a mere abstract science of the measure of values. He even objects to the name ' political economy,' since that gives a false idea of the subject and implies that wealth can be increased by political action. Adam Smith had not used that title to describe his work, but had, on the contrary, criticised the notion implied by these very words.[1] The true science of wealth

> looks on man as part of the great system of the universe, and supposes that his conduct is influenced, regulated, and controlled or punished in every minute particular by permanent and invariable laws, in the same manner as the growth of plants and the motion of the heavenly bodies.[2]

That is why Hodgskin takes as his motto the quotation from Say noted above. It is a natural science, and its scope should be limited to the study of those factors alone which influence " the productive power of labour." It has nothing to do with the study of consumption or the problem of the land. Land is productive only when labour is applied to it. Labour alone creates wealth, and without labour capital and land are alike useless. All Hodgskin's writing is devoted to driving home this idea, and pressing it to its logical conclusion. He wants to destroy the element of sanctity which he thinks is growing up round the word ' capital,' as though it were " a sort of cabalistic word like the words Church and State." For labour alone can render capital useful. So political economy must examine the two sets of circumstances which influence production and distribution of wealth—viz., (a) natural (i.e., the laws of man's being, his nature and faculties) and (b) social (i.e., rules derived from Governments). Economists since Adam Smith have forgotten that natural laws govern distribution as well as production, and have confused the *natural* social order with the *artificial* social order of civilisation. From this all its errors flow; and from its application all the existing social misery develops.

So the question arises whether the product of labour is being distributed in the right way, and whether the basis of

[1] *Popular Political Economy*, p. 36.   [2] *Ibid.*, p. 42.

the existing capitalist's property is to be found in natural right. This is the subject of *Labour Defended*, which is devoted to showing "not so much what labour ought," as "what capital ought not, to have." Most of that work, as Professor Graham Wallas has well said, is accordingly a

> temperate and searching criticism of what are now acknowledged to be two of the main defects of the ' classical ' economics—the clumsy assumption that all commodities were sold exactly a year after the commencement of their production (and that in consequence all labourers were supported for each succeeding twelve months by the accumulated capital of their employers), and the unpardonable *ignoratio elenchi* by which an analysis of the differential advantage of land and capital in production was treated as an ethical and political justification of the landlord and the capitalist.[1]

" Labour is the source of all wealth." From this theorem all Hodgskin's economic theory starts, and to it he is always returning. He was the first populariser of the doctrine of the labour theory of value among the workers, and the first to show how a theorem which looked innocent in Lockian or Ricardian setting could be turned into a militant doctrine of revolt. It was the promulgation of this theory which alarmed the Benthamites ; it was this same fact which led his contemporaries, as well as subsequent writers, wrongly to assume that Hodgskin was a Socialist. Hodgskin drew only an individualistic conclusion from the dogma. It was William Thompson who incorporated it into the case for Socialism. But, as the sequel shows, Hodgskin soon came to stress other sides of his doctrine even more than this one. That fact, coupled with the fact that to the very end he was opposed to any kind of State interference, helped to prevent his becoming the intellectual leader of proletarian revolt which a reader of *Labour Defended* might consider his natural destiny. Moreover, it must always be remembered that he nowhere glorifies manual labour at the expense of other forms of work. He shares the respect of his age for the inventor, and is at great care to distinguish " mental " and " bodily " labour. Both are necessary : the one consists in " observing the laws of the material world," the other in

[1] G. Wallas, *Life of Place*, p. 268.

carrying out the suggestions made by the observer. The preservation of existence itself, says Hodgskin in the second chapter of *Popular Political Economy*, depends in the last resort upon knowledge; and the history of the world's increased productivity is the history of man's improved observation of natural laws.

When Hodgskin comes to consider the question of wages and capital he is very interesting. If this part of his work were considered apart from the rest some colour might be lent to the suggestion that he was a subversive Radical. But it must be remembered that these theories are painted on a background of a hue already described. He says that the social curse of his day is the fact that the standard of wages among the labourers is always treated in a relative way; that is to say, capitalists plead that the wages of a labourer of the time are considerably superior to the remuneration which a feudal serf obtained. The capitalist, having at the back of his mind the standard of the serf, consequently judges more favourably the standard of his own workers. This, says Hodgskin, distorts the issue. Labour is now ten times more productive than it ever was before, but does not secure the increased wealth. It pays the enormous surplus of production " for the privilege of eating the food we have ourselves produced." The wages of labourers ought not to be computed on any relative basis, but are to be worked out from the first principles.[1] Hodgskin, unfortunately, does not develop the vast implications of this idea of ' surplus.'

He next goes on to analyse capital, and makes the current distinction between circulating and fixed capital. The function and advantage of circulating capital, he tells us, is that by it the labourer is enabled, when he is assured of his present subsistence, to direct his power to the greatest advantage.[2] But he emphasises the point that labour must be based on the evidence and assurance of subsistence. It is in this connection that he makes the most interesting, and certainly the most original, of all his contributions to the problem. He vehemently attacks the ' wages fund ' doctrine and

[1] *Labour Defended* (1922 edition), p. 26. [2] *Ibid.*, p. 36.

opposes to it the idea that circulating capital is not a fixed fund at all, but a *stream*. By changing the metaphor he quite alters the tone of political economy, and hits on what is probably the only theory of the time which could seriously rival the classic one of Ricardo. " The effects attributed to a stock of commodities in the name of circulating capital are caused by co-existing labour." [1] There is no such thing as " a stock of stored-up commodities." [2] The only thing stored up is skill, and that is inherent in the labourer himself. The conception of a stream of co-existing labour is one which Hodgskin does not work out to the full, because his chief interest, as we noted above, seems to have been rather in law than in pure economics. Nevertheless this stream theory is of profound significance. It challenges the classical theory of wages, and gives the lie to those supporters of the Combination Acts who assert that more wages mean less profits, and less profits mean the migration of capital. As for fixed capital, that too is dependent on labour. It is produced by labour. It is effective only when used by labour ; and consequently " does not derive its utility from previous but from present labour." It is *à propos* the subject of fixed capital that Hodgskin has a very eloquent passage about the new machine age. In the minds of the classical political economists, he says, tools have come to dominate the user, shutting out of view man himself. " The skill and the art of the labourer have been overlooked and he has been vilified, while the work of his hands has been worshipped." [3] This section is perhaps the finest emphasis on human value anywhere in Hodgskin's works. It is to be noted that this is his earliest work, and that as time went on his writing became steadily more abstract.

The capitalist insinuates himself between the workers. " He is the middle-man of all labourers," [4] and his savings increase at compound interest. But by what principles should wages be determined? We have already seen that Hodgskin repeatedly puts forward the theory that labour is entitled to the whole produce of industry. He bases his

[1] *Labour Defended*, p. 38.   [2] *Ibid.*, p. 46.
[3] *Ibid.*, pp. 65, 66.   [4] *Ibid.*, p. 72.

reasoning explicitly on Ricardo, and points out the logical and ethical inconsistency between the labour theory of value implicit in Ricardo, and the subsistence wage theory which the classical economists (and from them the Whigs also) maintained. But when it comes to a question of procedure for deciding the wages he confesses, " I know of no way of deciding this but by leaving it to be settled by the unfettered judgment of the labourers themselves." [1] When discussing in this connection the legitimate earnings of the capitalist he distinguishes between the two functions of the employer. The masters are middle-men from one point of view—that is to say, unproductive capitalists merely usurping surplus value ; and from another point of view they are what he calls " contrivers," who ought thus to receive a wage proportionate to their usefulness. For the rest, he thinks that labourers know their own interest best, and should be left unfettered ; but education can illuminate their path. " No Holy Alliance can put down the quiet insurrection by which knowledge will subvert whatever is not founded in justice and truth." [2] But even education is not to be fostered or controlled by the State. Before passing on to a consideration of his theory of property it may be remarked that he calls merchants mental labourers.[3] They are productive because they take goods from where they have no value to where they have most, and so they create wealth.[4] (The inconsistency of this conception with some of the ideas put forward earlier need not be pointed out.) Their motives are selfish, but the consequences of their proceedings are no less beneficial to society.

The last aspect of his social economics to be considered is his theory of property. Hodgskin *does* believe in a right to property, but he says there are two rights, one natural and the other artificial. So he wrote his book of 1832 [5] to distinguish between them. But he dissociated himself completely from the collectivists, and, lest he should be misunderstood, wrote an emphatic paragraph of warning :

[1] *Labour Defended*, p. 85. [2] *Ibid.*, p. 101.
[3] *Popular Political Economy*, p. 172. [4] *Ibid.*, p. 173.
[5] *The Natural and Artificial Right of Property Contrasted.*

Allow me at once to declare (as there have been in almost every age individuals such as Beccaria and Rousseau—and sects, some existing at present, such as Mr Owen's co-operative societies, the Saint-Simonians in France, and the Moravians, who have asserted that all the evils of society arise from *a* right of property, the utility of which they have accordingly and utterly denied), allow me to separate myself entirely from them by declaring that I look on a right of property—on the right of individuals to have and to own for their own support and selfish use and enjoyment the produce of their own industry, with power freely to dispose of the whole of that in the manner most agreeable to themselves—as essential to the welfare and even to the continued existence of society.[1]

We have seen that his work on property arose out of Brougham's speech on the necessity for law reform. Hodgskin says in his "Advertisement" that legislators are completely ignorant of the nature of law, and he therefore writes to illuminate them, and to show them how fatuous all legislation really is. He goes on to say that Brougham's speech implies that there was once a time when administration was perfect. But this is not so, for positive law is more perfect under George IV than ever before. The trouble arises from the fact that society has grown more rapidly than law itself. Consequently it is cramped by the effete. The argument begins from the confession which Brougham himself had made and which Dugald Stewart also had adumbrated, that "society has a course of its own." Has any law-giver, even Brougham himself, tried to find out what is that course of society? Until that is done legislation will remain a mere patchwork and utterly useless. There is a fundamental need for an inquiry into first principles. Hodgskin then contrasts Locke and Bentham on this question. Locke, he says, believes in natural rights prior to law. Bentham believes that property is a legal creation, and that there are no such things as rights. Here he makes a bitter Carlylian attack on Bentham, and asks ironically if there is not a natural right which prevents a mother from devouring her child? Having said that, he refutes the "greatest happiness" principle along the following lines : There can be no doubt

[1] *The Natural and Artificial Right of Property Contrasted*, p. 24.

212

that the Deity wills the greatest happiness. The legislator
pretends to will it too; but the faculties of individuals,
although capable of measuring their own preservation,
" are not competent to measure the happiness of nations."
Since, however, nobody knows what *will* produce the
greatest happiness, therefore there ought to be no laws, for
the Utilitarian principle " is suitable only to omniscience."
Therefore Bentham's edifice falls to the ground. The next
step in the argument is to recapitulate the labour theory
of value. Locke is again quoted [1] in support of it, and
Hodgskin goes on to show that property is an extension
of the idea of individuality which nature plants in all men,
covering the ownership of all those goods produced by
man's labour. General security for these products of one's
labour is obtained through an innate reverence for property
in mankind arising from the fact that " the great mass of
mankind seem to have been created nearly equal to each
other." [2] So it is easier to appropriate afresh from nature
by means of one's own labour than to appropriate from a
labourer essentially equal to oneself. He completes this
line of argument by enunciating Locke's famous theorem. [3]
Property in land should be limited by the extent of man's
labour, and his capacity to enjoy that which he legitimately
appropriates. This is the ideal " which in the long run
will guide the conduct of mankind." [4]

Having sketched the evolution of society, Hodgskin
shows that the present political and legal edifice of Europe
is based on the appropriations of the barbarians when they
came into the Roman Empire. [5] On conquest all the legislation of Europe is founded, and the conquerors and their
descendants have been the law-makers. Such being the case,
obedience to those laws is the master folly of mankind, and

this folly is inculcated with as much pertinacity by those who have
apparently no interest in making men fools as if their own bread
and their own breath hung on the doctrine. [6]

[1] *Two Treatises of Government*, Book II, chapter v, sections 28 and 30.
[2] *Right of Property*, p. 30.
[3] *Two Treatises of Government*, Book II, section 36.
[4] *Right of Property*, p. 62.
[5] *Ibid.*, p. 73.   [6] *Ibid.*, p. 74.

We are presented then with a contrast; the *natural* right to property depends on productive labour and capacity for enjoyment, as shown by Locke. *Artificial* right to property arose through conquest and force, which interfered with universal laws; and it is because these universal laws have been so defied that misery is the lot of the majority of mankind. But immutable law will eventually wreak destruction upon those who tamper with it. This retributive process has been at work through the ages. "The power of kings and nobles and priests has gradually decayed," [1] because society has such a course of its own. Brougham's motion itself is a sort of dim and unconscious recognition of the movement. The repeal of the Test Act is also part of the same movement. So is the failure of the gentry to preserve intact their large feudal estates by means of the law of primogeniture; likewise, too, the abolition of slavery. Society is like the hour hand of a watch; it moves, but we do not see it.

Here Hodgskin lets us see his hope for the future.

> We find, in consequence of the respect for the natural right of property, that a large middle class, completely emancipated from the bondage and destitution which the law sought to perpetuate, has grown up in every part of Europe, uniting in their own persons the character both of labourers and capitalists. They are fast increasing in numbers, and we hope, as the beautiful inventions of art gradually supersede unskilled labour, that they, reducing the whole society to equal and free men, will gradually extinguish all that yet remains of slavery and oppression. [2]

And if he had been critical of the capitalist in his pamphlet of 1825 his tone seems more moderate now; the capitalist's power, he tells us in this passage, has grown up as

> the moral result of the homage men pay to that great natural principle, the foundation of all property, that each individual has a right to the free use of his own limbs and to the produce of his own labour.

Out of the respect for this natural right to property implanted in the hearts of all has sprung that new order of

[1] *Right of Property*, p. 78. [2] *Ibid.*, p. 101.

society. The best the law-maker can do is to copy from " rights existing in practice"; he cannot create rights by his own laws.[1] All the changes that have taken place have been effected in spite of positive law, because they have been brought about " by the moral law implanted in our hearts."[2] Population as it expanded necessitated invention to supply food, so that economic forces have entered into the question; but

> the events to which historians, each of them partially selecting one, ascribe these alterations [*i.e.*, social reforms] are undoubtedly links in the great chain of causation; but only the materialist overlooking the moral laws of man's being will ascribe to those events the merit of social improvement.[3]

The evils of the artificial right of property are well known. It is " half-starved, toil-worn, and degraded labourers " who foot the bill,[4] and the great mass of mankind is in this state of destitution. So long as the inefficient control affairs improvement is prevented; industry and commerce are checked; suffering and unhappiness are rife; and even among the opulent there is " weariness and loathing of life." He concludes his political theory as he began it, by an uncompromising assertion of the divine law which governs the universe. All circumstances of ordinary life, he says, " are the immediate creation of the Deity," if not " emanations from, or revelations of, the Deity himself." In any case, the government of the whole material world, even to its minutest particular, is carefully regulated by divine providence.[5]

To sum up: with the universe arranged in such a way, and so inscrutably, man has one aim only—to follow his own selfish interest. " Narrow as the principle of self-love has been called, it is the sole motive for the actions of human beings." Man has wants and the power to supply them. To use Professor Sir Arthur Thomson's expressive phrase, which is particularly appropriate here, man's wants and powers are " organic to nature." The way in which he

---

[1] *Right of Property*, pp. 123, 124. [2] *Ibid.*, p. 102.
[3] *Ibid.*, p. 103. [4] *Ibid.*, p. 148.
[5] *Ibid.*, pp. 147–148.

learns that he has violated a command of nature is through the suffering which ensues.[1] So there is abundant proof in society that fundamental laws have been violated. But we are told emphatically, " I have no wish by expatiating on the privations and sufferings of the poor to rouse in them the slumbering feelings of hatred and revenge." [2]

It remains for us to note Hodgskin's theory of progress. He has a very definite and firm belief in the inevitability of progress. This has already been implied when considering his idea of natural law. He seems to regard nature as a sort of Demiurge. Nature, he says,

> suffers us not to abrogate her decrees in the moral world. She only permits us, at our own cause, to inflict pain on ourselves or do wrong for a season, which we can do as well by violating physical as by violating moral laws. Protesting continually against our rebellion, and warning us continually against its evil consequences, she ultimately, in her own good time, reasserts her authority. She is absolute in the moral as in the physical world, governing and regulating every part with the most thorough mastery. But kindly compassionate to the infancy of her children, she allows them a long probation to learn her commands.[3]

In the *Right of Property* Hodgskin puts forward his idea of the evolution of society. There have been certain well-defined stages. First came the hunting stage, when man wandered over the face of the earth to secure subsistence wherever he could. Next there came the pastoral stage, when man's search for food was facilitated by the domestication of animals; but man was still nomadic. In the course of ages came the discovery of agriculture, and a new stage began. Man then ceased to be a wanderer, and settled down in one locality. The fourth and last stage is the scientific one, when agriculture is further improved, and the means of obtaining the necessities of life are enormously increased. These stages in the evolution of humanity are important, because they show that at each new stage the amount of land necessary to obtain a livelihood grew less and less, and will continue to do so.[4] Thus,

[1] *Right of Property*, p. 151.   [2] *Ibid.*, p. 148.
[3] *Ibid.*, p. 59.   [4] *Ibid.*, p. 65.

in the hunting stage man had the whole of earth for his field. In the pastoral stage man's activities were limited by the grasslands to be found for the sheep. In the agricultural stage the consequent limitation was obvious; and so, too, when agriculture had improved through scientific farming and intensive cultivation. Meantime the population had been increasing steadily. Therefore Hodgskin draws the conclusion, partly from the historical evidence and partly from Locke's principles previously enunciated, that the individual holdings of land ought to grow smaller and smaller. As has been shown before, this normal evolution of society has been complicated by the incursion of the barbarians into the Roman Empire. They superimposed on it a political and legal system based entirely on force.[1] It is this system that Hodgskin is so anxious to get rid of. Nevertheless, throughout the course of social evolution natural laws have been regulating the progress of society in knowledge—natural laws working through the material world. The first cause of such a progress is animal necessity due to increasing population. Hodgskin lays great store by this increase in population as a factor in social development. With the increase in the number of mouths to be filled has come an acute need for food. This has given rise to new inventions with which increased wealth has come into being.

> I look upon the increase of people as the great physical cause of all the moral changes in society. Everything else is subordinate to, and depends upon, the increase in population.[2]

He even goes so far as to say [3] that inventions occur mostly in crowded cities. He flatly opposes the pessimism of Malthus' theory, declaring that that clergyman looks upon the problem " only in its operation under the perverting control of human institutions, and an unjust distribution of the production of labour." Increase in the

---

[1] *Right of Property*, p. 73.
[2] *Ibid.*, p. 92. These theories, it must be pointed out, appear to be taken *en bloc* from Ravenstone's book on *Population* (1821).
[3] *Ibid.*, p. 95.

world's numbers, then, is the first cause of the progress of society in knowledge. The diversity of organisation among tribes and races, and the differences due to geographical position and language, are other factors which he enumerates. The progress of civilisation is world-wide and uniform, and this truth serves but to emphasise further the fact of the reign of law.[1] Other influences besides natural law which determine progress are the adopted religions of the world, the variety of constitutions and laws, and the artificial regulations of each country. " The conclusion I come to," he says,

> and I wish to state it plainly, is that independent of all government and of all other regulations, there is in the universal necessity of labour, a universal stimulus of all men to exert those natural faculties with which all are endowed; that this stimulus is at all times the cause of observation; and that observation brings knowledge; and that there is a natural and necessary tendency independent of all and every sort of social regulation to a gradual increase of knowledge as the world grows older, as generation follows generation, and as mankind are multiplied on the face of the earth.[2]

What is the ideal, then, which lies at the back of Hodgskin's mind? It is not easy to delineate with any precision his social ideal, because of his gigantic act of faith regarding the beneficence of the world-process. He says in one place that his work is merely to point out that society is a natural phenomenon and to inquire into the laws which regulate it, but in no wise to put forward a political programme or to suggest lines of improvement. He confesses that he has not the "unholy craving to regulate what no individual does or can comprehend, viz., ' society,' " for the progress of society is not complete, and all its phenomena are " not yet unfolded to our understanding." [3] Nevertheless it is possible to get an occasional glimpse of his economic ideal. In it governmental interference will be reduced to the absolute minimum. The sole function of government, he said in later life, will be

---

[1] *Right of Property*, p. 84.   [2] *Ibid.*, pp. 96–97.
[3] *Ibid.*, p. 160.

to " preserve peace, see justice done between man and man, enforce obedience to the laws, and give security to property and life." [1]   To what extent even this amount of interference is compatible with the foregoing theories we need not now consider.   The land of *laissez-faire* is his land of heart's desire.

> Final success, I would fain hope, must be on the side of justice. I am certain, however, that till the triumph of labour be complete, till productive industry alone be opulent, and till idleness alone be poor; till the admirable maxim that he who sows shall reap be solidly established; till the right of property be founded on principles of justice, and not on those of slavery, till *man* shall be held more in honour than the clod he treads on, or the machine he guides —there cannot, and ought not to be, peace on earth, and good will amongst men. [2]

When man is thus completely unrestrained and can follow the divine urge of self-interest within him, and when the middle class has grown in prosperity and in size, so as to incorporate within itself all the other classes, then Hodgskin's Utopia will be realised. [3]   That is the dawn for which his eyes scan the horizon.   It is really, after all, a *bourgeois* Utopia based upon the belief in the pre-established harmony of self-interest, wherein social responsibility will be synonymous with responsibility to oneself.

C. H. Driver

[1] *Economist*, October 20, 1848, p. 1191.   [2] *Labour Defended*, p. 105.
[3] *Right of Property*, Epilogue.

BOOK LIST

A. Primary Sources

(i) Works by Hodgskin:
> *An Essay on Naval Discipline.* 1813.
> *Travels in the North of Germany.* 1820.
> *Labour Defended against the Claims of Capital.* 1825.
> *Popular Political Economy.* 1827.
> *The Natural and Artificial Right of Property Contrasted.* 1832.

Articles in *The Mechanics' Magazine*, 1823.
Articles in *The Economist*, 1844–57. (For a full list of these see Halévy, pp. 214 *et seq.*)

(ii) Correspondence:
Place MSS., British Museum; references quoted in text.
Letters in Halévy (see below).

B. Secondary Sources

The only monograph on Hodgskin is by Elie Halévy, *Thomas Hodgskin* (1903). This contains a full bibliography.
See also the same author's *Growth of Philosophic Radicalism* (1928).

Hodgskin's economic theories are also discussed in the following works :

Lowenthal: *Ricardian Socialists.* 1911.
Menger, A.: *The Right to the Whole Produce of Labour*, with an introduction by H. S. Foxwell. 1899.
Beer, M.: *History of British Socialism.* 1919.
Cole, G. D. H.: Introduction to *Labour Defended.* Edition published by the Labour Publishing Company. 1922.

DATE DUE

GAYLORD			PRINTED IN U.S.A.